THE LOTUS UNLEASHED

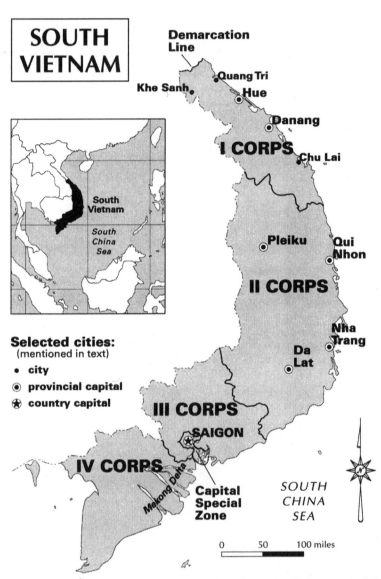

Map prepared by Dick Gilbreath, UK Cartography Lab

THE
LOTUS
UNLEASHED

The Buddhist Peace Movement
in South Vietnam, 1964–1966

Robert J. Topmiller

THE UNIVERSITY PRESS OF KENTUCKY

Publication of this volume was made possible in part
by a grant from the National Endowment for the Humanities.

Scholarly publisher for the Commonwealth,
serving Bellarmine University, Berea College, Centre
College of Kentucky, Eastern Kentucky University,
The Filson Historical Society, Georgetown College,
Kentucky Historical Society, Kentucky State University,
Morehead State University, Murray State University,
Northern Kentucky University, Transylvania University,
University of Kentucky, University of Louisville,
and Western Kentucky University.

Editorial and Sales Offices: The University Press of Kentucky
663 South Limestone Street, Lexington, Kentucky 40508–4008

06 05 04 03 02   5 4 3 2 1

Library of Congress Cataloging-in-Publication Data

Topmiller, Robert J., 1948–
  The lotus unleashed: the Buddhist peace movement in South Vietnam / Robert J.
Topmiller.
     p. cm.
  Includes bibliographical references and index.
  ISBN 0-8131-2260-0 (cloth : alk. paper)
  1. Vietnamese Conflict, 1961–1975—Protest movements—Vietnam (Republic)
2. Vietnamese Conflict, 1961–1975—Religious aspects—Buddhism. 3. Buddhism
and politics—Vietnam (Republic). 4. Vietnam (Republic)—Politics and government.
5. Vietnamese Conflict, 1961–1975—United States. I. Title.
DS557.62.T66 2002
959.704'31—dc21   2002014609

Contents

For the South Vietnamese Buddhists
who sacrificed everything
to bring peace to their country

Preface

> But for those still living to know that the kindest, most worthy
> people have fallen away, or even been tortured, humiliated
> before being killed, or buried and wiped away by the machinery
> of war . . . is an appalling paradox. Justice may have won, but
> cruelty, death and inhuman violence have also won.
> —Bao Ninh, *The Sorrow of War*

 How could the United States have possibly lost the war in Vietnam? It had the best trained and equipped army in the world, able to move and strike with astonishing and unprecedented speed, combined with a well-trained, highly motivated officer corps inculcated with the latest military thinking and more experience combating insurgency than any military force in modern history. Yet the United States failed to gain the strategic initiative in Vietnam and never placed the Vietnamese insurgency in real danger. Numerous historians have attempted to resolve this conundrum with varying results and myriad answers. Some have argued that the United States did not appreciate the strength of Vietnamese nationalism, while others have claimed that the United States failed to develop an adequate strategy to carry its forces to victory. Others criticize American tactics for an overdependence on firepower that created massive civilian casualties, while some contend that the United States failed to utilize sufficient firepower. Many of the arguments seem as unresolvable as the discussions that polarized American political discourse during the war.

Yet these spirited disagreements mostly miss the mark, because they focus on America rather than Vietnam. The answer to the elusive question of why America suffered defeat in Vietnam lies in the widespread opposition of Vietnamese citizens to the government of South Vietnam (GVN). At the most basic level, the United States never really understood what issues remained important to the people of Vietnam and manifested a persistent inability to comprehend and confront the political dimensions of the war in the South.[1]

On June 13, 1965, the *New York Times* reported that twenty major government upheavals had occurred in South Vietnam since the fall of Ngo Dinh Diem in November 1963.[2] This short piece listing the various regimes that held power during this brief period illustrates one of the most troubling problems for American policy-makers during the Vietnam War. How could the United States establish a government in Saigon that displayed a sense of legitimacy, viability and sensitivity to the populace, a government, in other words, that commanded the loyalty of the citizens of South Vietnam?

The lack of GVN legitimacy called forth the Buddhist Movement, since most South Vietnamese had no legal way to confront their government. Indeed, only two groups challenged the GVN internally: the National Liberation Front (NLF, commonly referred to as the Viet Cong) and the Buddhist Movement. By emphasizing Buddhism, opponents of the regime highlighted its association with foreign elements and its alienation from the people. Thus, when Buddhists demonstrated against the government while claiming to represent the will of the people, they emphasized their dedication to Vietnamese history and tradition. This stood in stark contrast to the GVN, which had allowed the introduction of American forces into the country, turning South Vietnam into a battleground between the United States and Asian Communism.

A succession of South Vietnamese governments tried to bring peace to the country from 1963 to 1965. Every effort to negotiate with the NLF and create a neutral government, however, brought a violent reaction and ejection from office by the American–created/financed/backed South Vietnamese military. More importantly, from 1963 to 1966, Buddhists led a mass movement aimed at installing a civilian government through free elections with the intention of inviting the NLF to join a government dedicated to neutralism. Buddhist leaders believed that a large segment of the NLF consisted of non-Communist elements and saw negotiations and a coalition government as a way to separate moderates from diehard Communists.[3]

Preface

Although the Buddhist Crisis of 1963 has been examined extensively, the Buddhist Crisis of 1966, the culmination of Buddhist peace efforts and the focus of this study, holds the key to understanding the issues that drove Buddhist objections to the United States and the GVN. In fact, no other event in the long U.S. involvement in South Vietnam better typified America's frustration over its inability to influence events in South Vietnam and the ambiguity felt by many Vietnamese over the American crusade to defend them from their countrymen. As a result of Buddhist-inspired upheaval in 1966, the critical northern provinces of South Vietnam (known as I Corps for their designation as the First Corps area; South Vietnam was divided into four military regions or Corps areas, starting with I Corps in the north down to IV Corps in the Mekong Delta) plunged into what historian George C. Herring refers to as a "civil war within an insurrection."[4] This internal ferment witnessed an alliance between rebellious ARVN (Army of the Republic of Vietnam, the South Vietnamese Army) troops and the Buddhist-dominated Struggle Movement on one hand and the GVN and the United States on the other, in the most serious non-Communist threat to the GVN in its short but tumultuous history. In the middle of the conflict stood the first American combat forces in South Vietnam. At the same time, the Buddhist rebellion caused the U.S. government to question its commitment to the GVN, raised doubts in the U.S. Congress over America's role in South Vietnam, and triggered a decline in U.S. public support for the war.

No one can say for sure how the majority of the Vietnamese people felt about the war. Certainly, the United States never tried to find out. The ability of the Buddhist hierarchy, however, to call thousands of protesters into the streets and topple a number of American-backed regimes indicates their ability to articulate a message that resonated deeply with the Vietnamese people. In fact, even though the Unified Buddhist Church (UBC) constituted only about one million of the estimated sixteen million Buddhists in South Vietnam, the *New York Times* acknowledged in 1966 that it was the foremost interest group in the country.[5] Thus, the largest non-Communist group in the nation opposed the war and the American-controlled government prosecuting it. By combining the NLF, which assuredly opposed U.S. intervention in the country, with the UBC and the other religious sects that silently supported the Buddhists, it seems possible that a majority of South Vietnamese objected to American interference in the affairs of their country.[6] After conducting over eighty interviews with Vietnamese associated with the Buddhist Movement, I am convinced that most South Vietnamese did not want to fight the war. Almost every person interviewed made it clear that the Buddhists believed it also and were deeply concerned with the impact of the war on their people and took extraordinary risks to end the conflict. I received further confirmation of this in my interviews with General Nguyen Khanh and General Nguyen Chanh Thi, both of whom concluded that the war had to end while they held power, and George Kahin, who heard the same thing from Buddhist activists during his trip to South Vietnam in 1966.

By studying the Buddhist challenge to the South Vietnamese government, I intend to demonstrate the importance of Buddhist efforts to end the war and to create a neutralist government, and expand our knowledge of the impact of internal Vietnamese politics on U.S. decision-making and the missed opportunities for peace caused by Washington's indifference towards Vietnamese opinions on the war. Finally, I want to examine the ability of Buddhist leaders to tap the immense reservoir of Vietnamese nationalism to confront the GVN and the United States, while explaining their ultimate inability to carry out their program despite the widespread support they enjoyed in the beginning.

Interestingly, although the war took place mainly in South Vietnam, historians have written little about the South Vietnamese. But to achieve an accurate and balanced analysis of the war, historians must move the Vietnamese from the periphery to the center of the story.[7] This work attempts to do that by telling the story of one group of South Vietnamese who tried to stop the war and bring peace to their country. Readers will likely note that this account contains few American heroes but focuses instead on the enormous sacrifices of Vietnamese Buddhists to halt the conflict. Indeed, I find it hard to ignore the moral quality of a movement whose members were willing to immolate themselves for their religious principles. Thus, the heroes in this book are the South Vietnamese who risked everything for peace.

The United States paid a heavy price for its determination to continue the war despite evidence that many Vietnamese wanted the fighting to end. Yet, compared to the cost paid by the Vietnamese, American losses seem inconsequential. This was the Buddhist point all along. Their people and country bore the burden of America's dedication to stop the spread of Communism. Ironically, Buddhist leaders, in trying to rescue their country, almost saved the United States from pursuing its self-destructive course in Vietnam.

When I refer to Buddhists in this study, I mean the group who followed the lead of Thich Tri Quang and the Vien Hoa Dao (Institute for the Execution of the Dharma). Buddhists in South Vietnam split into a number of major groupings, of which the Buddhist Movement represented about one million Buddhists in the country. Internal divisions between moderates, led by Thich Tam Chau, and radicals, who followed Thich Tri Quang, also weakened it. The movement had a regional component as well; Thich Tri Quang remained most powerful in central Vietnam, while Thich Tam Chau retained an edge in Saigon. Neither side had much influence with the Hoa Hao or the large number of Buddhists who lived in the Mekong Delta.

One of the great challenges in studying the Buddhist movement lies in estimating the exact number of Buddhists in South Vietnam. According to an Asia Foundation study, a 1961 survey conducted in Saigon concluded that over 80 percent of the population considered themselves to be Buddhists, while Catholics constituted 13 percent of the count and 3 percent labeled themselves as Confucians. The Asia Foundation estimated that the same number would apply to South Vietnam, in general, although probably only about 40 percent of the populace actively practiced Buddhism.[8]

While it remains difficult to acknowledge adequately the many contributions made by friends and colleagues during the assembly of this work, a few stand out and deserve special recognition. Many thanks to *Peace and Change, Cross Currents, The Journal of American East Asian Relations* and the *Western Association of Asian Studies* for allowing me to reprint sections that originally appeared in their journals. I would also like to recognize Eastern Kentucky University, the University of Kentucky, the Lyndon Baines Johnson Foundation and the Marine Corps Historical Foundation for their generous grants that allowed me to make four research trips to Vietnam. In addition, a Foreign Language and Area Studies Fellowship enabled me to study Vietnamese language at the

Preface

University of Wisconsin-Madison. Douglas Pike and Stephen Denny at the Indochina Archive proved particularly helpful in assisting my research, as did the archivists at the LBJ presidential library. Douglas Pike also consented to two very illuminating interviews. I also want to thank the many Vietnamese in the United States and Vietnam who consented to be interviewed for this work, especially Professor Minh Chi, Vo Van Ai, General Nguyen Chanh Thi, General Nguyen Khanh, Father Josephus Le Van Phuc, Tran Huu Duyen, Thich Minh Chau, Thich Quang Lien and Thich Quang Do. I would also like to express gratitude to Vietnamese who assisted me in my research, especially Ho Thi Long An, Thich Nguyen Tang, Nguyen Huynh Mai and Tam Bang Tran. Particular thanks must be extended to the recently deceased George McT. Kahin, who aided me in collecting the materials for this work, agreed to a lengthy interview and turned over his files on the Buddhist Movement to me.

I want to express gratitude to my colleagues at the University of Kentucky and Eastern Kentucky University who graciously reviewed parts of this work, including Tom Appleton, Jeff Mathews and David Hamilton. William Duiker also looked over an earlier version of this work and offered valuable input. The chair of the Eastern Kentucky University History Department, Ron Huch, has been very supportive of my work as well. I wish to offer special thanks to Eric Christianson, who assisted me during my graduate program as director of graduate studies at UK and has since remained my close friend and drinking buddy. Finally, George Herring supervised my dissertation and patiently guided me all the way through this whole process with the good humor, steady hand, and gentlemanly demeanor that numerous Vietnam War scholars have noted in him and, like myself, have greatly appreciated.

Introduction

Vietnamese Buddhism as a Political Force, 1963–1965

Whoever is listening, be my witness: I cannot accept this war,
I never could, I never shall.

—Thich Nhat Hanh

 In May 1963, a group of students in Hue, South Vietnam, marched through the city carrying Buddhist flags in defiance of a recent order by President Ngo Dinh Diem. South Vietnamese security forces soon confronted and fired on the demonstrators, killing eight young people. Buddhists throughout South Vietnam reacted with indignation to these killings, leading to a series of protests against the government.

Led by their charismatic leader, Thich Tri Quang, Buddhist leaders in central Vietnam dreamed of bringing a social revolution to Vietnam. They wanted to eradicate poverty and injustice while bringing compassion and succor to the masses of Vietnamese whose lives of extreme poverty rendered them susceptible to NLF promises of a future egalitarian society under its tutelage. The growing war in the countryside particularly concerned Buddhist leaders because of the suffering involved and its potential to derail their social transformation. While Diem's Catholicism and favoritism toward Catholics irritated Buddhist leaders who perceived that their religion was not taken seriously by the regime, the introduction of American advisors inflamed the nationalism and urge for peace that always stood behind the Buddhist movement. Thus, they felt compelled to challenge Diem and his growing dependence on the United States.

Especially infuriating to Buddhists, Diem had retained the French-imposed Decree #10, which labeled Buddhism as an association rather than a religion. While the French had used this law to limit the authority of Buddhists and increase the power of their Catholic supporters, Diem's refusal to throw out the onerous law served as a constant reminder to Buddhists of their inferior status in South Vietnam despite their claim to represent over 80 percent of the populace. No longer willing to suffer humiliation from Diem and his Catholic-dominated government, Buddhist leaders resolved to have a showdown with Diem when the opportunity arrived.[1]

The simmering anger in the country finally found its expression in Hue on May 8, 1963, when Buddhists marched to protest Diem's recent order that banned the flying of any flag but the national colors of South Vietnam. Buddhists objected that they could not display their ensigns to commemorate the Buddha's birthday, though Catholics had recently carried papal flags while celebrating the Silver Anniversary of Archbishop Ngo Dinh Thuc, Diem's brother. The peaceful demonstration soon turned violent when riot police opened fire, killing eight and wounding four.[2]

EARLY MANIFESTATIONS OF BUDDHIST POLITICAL POWER

As a result of the bloodshed, Buddhist demands for equal treatment quickly resonated throughout the nation as the movement gained strength and adherents with each new act of defiance. The GVN, on the other hand, used force to put down the agitation, creating even more support for the Buddhists. By the end of May, the Buddhist Crisis had evolved into something far more serious than an argument over flags. Many observers in the American press and the U.S. mission recognized that the Buddhist rebellion had exposed wide divisions in South Vietnamese society and close to universal opposition to Diem's dictatorial rule. As the size and intensity of the Buddhist rebellion grew, moreover, many commentators realized that the Buddhists had energized a large segment of the population who wanted an end to the police state in South Vietnam.[3]

The defining moment of the Buddhist Crisis occurred on June 11, 1963, when an elderly monk, Thich Quang Duc, sat in a lotus position on a busy Saigon street and set himself on fire. This first and most spectacular self-immolation during the 1963 Buddhist Crisis stamped an image on the Vietnam War that has never faded away. While Thich Quang Duc died in the belief that he would become a bodhisattva in calling attention to the desperate condition of Buddhists in South Vietnam, his act also galvanized world opinion and became, throughout the world, a poignant example of South Vietnamese resistance to Diem.[4] More ominously for Diem, American public opinion increasingly swung toward the Buddhists, who seemed to be battling for the most cherished American value: freedom of religion.[5]

Diem eventually forced the issue by attacking the Buddhists. On August 21, 1963, GVN forces carried out a swift, brutal subjugation of the Buddhists during the transition period between U.S. ambassador Fredrick Nolting's departure and the arrival of the new American envoy, Henry Cabot Lodge Jr. Declaring martial law, Diem implemented a curfew and imposed press censorship as security forces carried out raids on Buddhist pagodas with great violence and repression throughout the country.[6]

The day after Diem's security forces attacked the pagodas, Lodge arrived in Saigon to take over the American embassy. The appointment of Lodge, a well-known Republican and former political rival of President John F. Kennedy, indicated a tough new American attitude towards Diem. His reputation as a no-nonsense diplomat seemed perfect for the difficult task of convincing Diem that his government must change its relationship with its citizens to retain American support. The selection of a prominent Republican also gave a bipartisan slant to American policy in Vietnam and provided Kennedy with a potential GOP scapegoat if the American position in Vietnam collapsed.[7]

Further aggravating relations with the GVN, Lodge granted asylum to dissidents sought by GVN security forces. On September 1, three Buddhist monks rushed toward the American embassy in Saigon, opening a bizarre chapter in American diplomatic history. One of them, Thich Tri Quang, had been the only high Buddhist official to escape the GVN on August 21. Thich Tri Quang's militant, politicized brand of Buddhism later caused the United States incredible grief, but in 1963, Americans viewed him as a heroic figure and a symbol of American resolve to force concessions from Diem. Lodge granted the monks asylum and had special vegetarian meals brought in for his guests, while resisting GVN demands that they be turned over to security forces.[8]

U.S. leaders soon curtailed aid to the GVN to gain leverage over Diem. The reduction in nonmilitary aid had little impact on South Vietnam, but the cuts provided ARVN generals with the clear signal they had sought from the Americans that they would not oppose a coup, which then occurred on November 1. The next day, after spurning Lodge's offer of safe conduct out of the country, Diem and his brother Ngo Dinh Nhu were executed by rebellious troops. Eventually, the clash between Diem and the Buddhists would have world-shaking implications far out of proportion to a religious struggle in a remote corner of Asia that, ultimately, created a U.S. commitment leading to 58,000 American and 3 million Vietnamese deaths.[9]

Thich Tri Quang walked out of the American embassy on November 4, 1963. His quiet departure and the deference accorded him by both the new rulers of South Vietnam and American officials gave no indication that in the coming years he would lead numerous attempts to topple the South Vietnamese regimes that emerged in the wake of the Diem coup. As a result of their impressive victory over Diem, Buddhists emerged as a potent political force and the only significant non-Communist opposition group in South Vietnam from 1963 to 1966. Their message of nationalism, peace and neutralism, moreover, carried so much weight that for a short time they gained the ability to bring down governments, veto appointments to high office and call thousands of followers into the streets.[10]

A great irony, however, lies within the Vietnamese Buddhist movement during these years. Buddhists opposed Diem because of his association with the Americans and his efforts to find a military solution to South Vietnam's problems. Little did they realize that he had exerted a major effort to restrain the Americans and that Washington had supported the November 1963 coup to gain a regime more amenable to its will. The demise of the Diem regime created the situation that the Buddhists fought to avoid at all costs: increased American involvement in South Vietnam's affairs and expansion of the war.

By destroying the Diem regime, Buddhists produced a political vacuum filled by the United States. Later Buddhist-inspired agitation created even more instability, again strengthening the U.S. position in South Vietnam. This situation perpetuated itself throughout the years of the Buddhist struggle: Every effort to find a government not under U.S. domination led to increased American influence. South Vietnamese, therefore, exerted less influence and control over their affairs as the war expanded and became more violent. Just as U.S. tactics sparked an increased insurgency, Buddhist campaigns led to greater American hegemony over South Vietnamese politics.

Vital differences highlighted the 1963 and later struggles between Buddhists and the GVN. Most Buddhist monks, nuns and laypeople viewed the events of 1963 as a struggle to preserve their way of life and as a response to the suppression of their religious freedom. From 1964 on, however, the conflict between Buddhists and the GVN became more politically and emotionally charged. To Buddhist leaders, nothing less than the fate of Vietnam and their centuries-old relationship with the people remained at stake.[11] They believed they had to save their country from a war driven by foreign ideologies that had swept aside traditional Buddhist attitudes of love and brotherhood. Political action evolved from their commitment to two of the fundamental tenets of Buddhism. compassion and nonviolence.

Buddhists, however, never successfully resolved the problem of confronting a violent government with nonviolence. Often, the emotions unleashed by the Buddhist challenge to the GVN led to dreadful savagery and destruction as the leadership lost control of its followers, particularly students who had much to lose in a country constantly expanding draft calls to fight an increasingly futile and senseless war. Buddhists responded to the challenge of violence by "finding means to avoid violence as much as possible" while confronting adversaries with various forms of nonviolent action, including efforts to address social problems caused by the war, publication of antiwar literature, alliances with peace organizations outside of Vietnam, hunger protests and general acts of non-cooperation with the GVN.[12]

Attempts by Buddhists to end the war remained consistent with the most basic precepts of Buddhism wherein they felt compelled to bring their organizational talents and moral leadership positions to the forefront to end the killing in South Vietnam. Regardless of their stand on the war, many Buddhists expressed contempt for Communism, which they viewed as a retarded form of Buddhism and a Western concept unsuited to Vietnam. Realizing that many non-Communists had joined the NLF, some Buddhists saw their movement as a way to lure non-Communist elements away from the NLF into a coalition government designed to end the war.[13] Buddhists believed that hastening an American exit and creating a coalition government in South Vietnam remained the only ways to deny the NLF victory, because GVN and U.S. actions served as the most potent recruiting tool for the NLF. Thus, the Buddhist movement could be viewed as a last, desperate effort to prevent a complete Communist victory in Vietnam.

FORMATION OF THE UNIFIED BUDDHIST CHURCH

Despite their success in toppling Diem, Buddhists did not have an effective national organization at the end of 1963. The multiplicity of sects in the country, including significant numbers of both major streams of Buddhism, and the historic autonomy of the pagoda frustrated efforts to create an effective political vehicle to transform the victory over Diem into an association that could challenge the GVN and end the war. The decentralized nature of Vietnamese Buddhism, likewise, worked against a nationwide establishment, while the liberal doctrinal basis of Buddhism invited the factionalism that plagued the movement. Buddhist leaders retained the ability to call thousands of followers into the streets when they articulated a popular message, but they seldom had the means to hold the separate factions together for an extended period of time. In the end, they temporarily overcame the severe regional, political and ideological divisions in the movement to challenge the GVN. Nevertheless, although politically powerful, the organized Buddhist movement never represented a majority of Vietnamese Buddhists.[14]

Buddhists spent the first part of 1964 attempting to fashion an adequate organization. Recognizing the need to project a united voice in opposing the war and carrying out political and religious activities, they announced in January the formation of a national association, the Unified Buddhist Church (UBC), which combined elements of eleven different sects and the Theravada and Mahayana streams of Buddhism.[15] Despite the creation of the UBC, seven major groupings of Buddhism still existed in South Vietnam: the UBC, Chinese Buddhists, Vietnamese Theravada Buddhists, Khmer Theravada Buddhists, Hinayana Buddhists, Hoa Hao Buddhists, and non-UBC Southern Buddhists.[16]

Much of the conflict within the UBC arose over the issue of neutralism. While Thich Tam Chau, the nominal leader of the Buddhists, advocated a progovernment, antineutral stance, Thich Tri Quang, leader of the Vien Hoa Dao (Institute for the Propagation of the Faith, the political arm of the UBC), and his followers wanted the GVN and the NLF to work out their problems and implement a Vietnamese solution, such as a coalition government, to end the war. Increasing levels of American interference in South Vietnamese affairs and growing violence in the country, moreover, strengthened the faction calling for neutralism.

The struggle over the proper role of Buddhism had deep roots. Vietnamese Buddhists argued with increasing ferocity throughout the century about the suitable character of Buddhism in a society permeated with violence and injustice. The disagreement raged between those who saw work for social justice and peace as proper for Buddhist clergy and those who emphasized religious values and removal from the world.[17] These conflicts often operated on different levels influenced by age, education, region, family background, rank in the religious hierarchy and attitudes toward authority, exacerbated by regional divisions, the bane of most attempts to achieve unity in modern Vietnam.[18] Buddhism, therefore, never spoke with one voice in Vietnam, particularly given the myriad attitudes within its organizations.

Some Buddhists perceived the deep distress in South Vietnamese society over the war and responded with calls for peace. Sensing significant war-weariness after a quarter-century of conflict, Thich Nhat Hanh introduced a resolution calling for an end to the fighting during a conference of monks early in 1964.[19] A diminutive, gentle-looking monk who radiated serenity and compassion, he eventually became an eloquent spokesman for peace in Vietnam by focusing on the moral malaise that had descended on the country as a result of the rapid changes brought on by the conflict. He also helped reintroduce the concept of Engaged Buddhism, a militant social activism that ignored both sides of the hostilities and concentrated on bringing succor to its victims.[20]

In contrast to the open, unassuming Thich Nhat Hanh stood Thich Tri Quang, leader of the radical antiwar faction in the UBC. An enigmatic figure who projected an aura of intensity with his stern bearing and obscure pronouncements, he remained the best-known Buddhist monk to Americans in Saigon.[21] American images of Thich Tri Quang, and Buddhists generally, changed dramatically in 1964. Often referred to as a provocateur and a schemer by Americans, Thich Tri Quang became the personification of evil to the U.S. embassy and much of the press. Numerous articles speculated on his motives, his possible Communist connections and his thirst for power. Yet his actions and words changed very little between 1963 and 1964. A hero for contributing to the demise of Diem, he appeared extremely dangerous when he challenged the GVN and questioned American involvement in South Vietnam. Nor was the bewilderment over Thich Tri Quang confined to the U.S. government and the American press; many Buddhists also found his tactics and message confusing.[22]

Another Buddhist monk, Thich Tam Chau, represented the conservative mainstream faction of Vietnamese Buddhism. A small, thin man with unremarkable features, he reveled in the publicity and prestige accorded him as the official head of South Vietnamese Buddhism, while opposing the political and social activism of the younger monks. An ardent anti-Communist and refugee from North Vietnam, he stressed moderation and opposition to the NLF, but he attempted, at the same time, to hold the fragile Buddhist movement together.[23]

Thich Tam Chau and Thich Tri Quang eventually engaged in a bitter battle for control of the organization. In fact, if unanimity is possible in any discussion of the Vietnam War, it comes closer over the impact of the struggle between the two leaders of the movement. Almost all Buddhists agree that their personal rivalry, which reached its climax during the Buddhist Crisis of 1966, hurt the movement badly, causing confusion among their followers and making it easier for the GVN to suppress the UBC.[24]

Despite their different approaches, all three men had a vital stake in democracy. The outburst of political activity that followed Diem's death ended official repression of Buddhists, gained them an equal voice in shaping government policy and enabled the hierarchy to counter the growing influence of ARVN generals. All three equated the survival of Buddhism with upholding the national character of Vietnam.[25]

U.S./BUDDHIST RELATIONS

The relationship between the U.S. government and Buddhists was one of escalating tension after 1963 because significant cultural and philosophical differences clouded their discourse and both held fundamentally different worldviews. Much of the difficulty in ascertaining the true nature of the Buddhist movement resulted from a changed relationship between Washington and the American press in 1964. As historian Clarence Wyatt points out, after the Buddhist Crisis of 1963, the United States embarked on a new program of "maximum candor" to bring the press over to its point of view. Given that they suffered from a critical shortage of personnel in South Vietnam, American reporters depended on U.S. sources for information on the war and the political situation in South Vietnam.[26] When Maxwell Taylor, a career military officer with little patience for an indigenous South Vietnamese peace movement, assumed control of the American embassy in 1964, his hostility towards the Buddhists soon found expression in U.S. press reports.

On the other hand, Vietnamese responses to American actions flowed mainly from their religious and cultural orientation. Although Buddhism has had a significant impact on the country's development, the most important religious influence in Vietnam and the rest of East Asia is ancestor worship. Every Vietnamese home has a family altar with pictures of earlier generations who receive homage for their wisdom and respect for the wrath that can descend on a household failing to give proper respect to its ancestors. By worshiping one's ancestors, a person becomes linked to the past and is made extremely conscious of the importance of tradition in society. A culture that venerates its ancestors naturally places the family at the center of society and shows great respect for elderly people because they speak with the wisdom of experience and history. It is not hard to imagine the impact someone like

Nguyen Cao Ky, South Vietnam's prime minister from 1965 to 1967, with his youthful impetuosity and playboy image, had on a society so closely in touch with its history. In the same fashion, scholars stand at the top of the social hierarchy and military people at the bottom, reflecting the Confucian emphasis on attaining social harmony through benevolent action by the ruled and the ruler.

Buddhism came to Vietnam in the early part of the Christian era by way of China and India. Vietnamese Buddhism, heavily influenced by China, absorbed elements of Taoism, Confucianism and ancestor worship along with the veneration of local deities. The emphasis in northern and central Vietnam came mainly from the Mahayana school of Buddhism, which predominated in Vietnam, China, Korea and Japan. Mahayana Buddhism, which developed several centuries after the death of the Buddha, focuses on achieving social justice and assisting others to reach enlightenment and worships a multiplicity of deities. Theravada Buddhism, which prevails in Sri Lanka, Thailand, Laos, Burma, and Cambodia and among ethnic Cambodians in the southern part of present-day Vietnam, is more fundamentalist and conservative, places greater emphasis on monasticism and focuses on the Buddha alone.

Buddhists, in general, subscribe to a number of beliefs drawn from Hinduism. One of the most important is the concept of karma, wherein Buddhists believe that an individual's station in life is determined by actions in a previous existence. Good actions confer higher status, while immorality can cause one to return as an insect or a snake or some other unfortunate creature. Most Vietnamese lay people belong to the Pure Land school of Buddhism and trust that their actions today can influence their fate tomorrow. Thus, they have faith in the importance of performing meritorious acts to ensure that their future will be easier. Many monks and nuns, on the other hand, subscribe to Thien (better known as Zen), a discipline that teaches that the key to liberation can be attained through meditation on a seemingly incongruous statement or question.

Despite the doctrinal differences between Theravada and Mahayana Buddhism, both streams place the concept of compassion and nonviolence at the center of their ideology. Nonviolence, however, constitutes more than a strategy to win expanded civil rights or other political goals. It is a way of life that respects the rights of every living creature.[27] Therefore, Buddhist attempts to end the war remained consistent with the most basic precepts of Buddhism.

Buddhists had traditionally participated in battles against foreign invaders. Pagodas had served as supply depots and centers of resistance during the struggle with the French, and Vietnamese monks had historically taken an active role in political affairs, particularly in the campaign to expel the Chinese.[28] Thus, they sensed no contradiction in upholding the rights of the people against an oppressive government and a foreign invader.[29]

Buddhist efforts to bring democracy to the country resulted from more than a political strategy to end the war. Buddhism is inherently egalitarian, and most monks and nuns had grown accustomed to working in a system where the majority ruled. Buddhists consider all people equally responsible for their actions and follow the Protestant principle wherein individuals and groups who disagree with the will of the body are encouraged to form their own assemblages. The Sangha (monks, nuns, and laypeople) conducts its business democratically, and Zen teaches its adherents to seek true freedom from the restraints of traditional thinking. Thus, Buddhists naturally believed in a democratic system as a vehicle to express the people's will and to voice objections to the misrule, rampant corruption and infighting of the GVN.[30] The absence of a legal system to redress grievances with the GVN, moreover, led Vietnamese to turn for leadership to Buddhist monks and nuns, the intellectual and moral guides of the nation. Buddhists, however, saw democracy more as an expression of the popular will to end the war than as the special-interest pluralism common to American political discourse.

Washington eventually directed enormous hostility toward the Buddhists, because neither side could part the cloud of misunderstanding that separated them. Each followed significantly different approaches to life and considered its system to be superior to the other. Buddhist logic particularly rejected U.S. involvement in South Vietnam, while Washington simply could not understand how groups like the Buddhists could even consider talking to the Communists, much less joining them in a coalition government. Buddhist efforts to seek an accommodation with the NLF seemed tantamount to treason to U.S. officials.

Further compounding tensions, it was simply incomprehensible to

U.S. officials steeped in Cold War thinking about the malevolence of Communism that the Buddhists would want to seek an accommodation with the NLF. Many members of the U.S. mission assumed that Buddhist leaders were naive in their assessment of the NLF. Yet Buddhists had formed what they believed to be a realistic appraisal of the dangers of a coalition government and decided that the risk of a Communist power grab outweighed the destruction wrought by the U.S. military in South Vietnam. They may have been naive in assuming they could join with the non-Communist elements to control the Communists in the NLF, but they had a far more realistic assessment of the possibility of a U.S. victory and the ability of the NLF to prolong the stalemate on the battlefield until the United States gave up and withdrew its forces.

Western and Asian cultures also have different approaches to conflict. The West, especially the United States, considers the direct approach the hallmark of business practice and discourse in general. Asians, however, value indirectness, and Asian philosophy enhances this approach. Confucianism stresses the importance of attaining social harmony, while Taoism emphasizes accord with the universe. Both philosophies denigrate violence and the use of force to gain power.[31] Zen particularly focuses on the use of obscure or indirect questions and statements to create puzzlement, which, it is hoped, will force the listener to look at the situation in a new and unexpected way. Thus, what Americans often considered deceitful or dishonest behavior on the part of Vietnamese actually reflected their cultural emphasis on avoiding the outward appearance of conflict.[32]

While some Americans remained sure of the excellence of their system, many Vietnamese Buddhists suspected differently. Considering American thinking to be one-dimensional and believing that the West remained in the midst of a spiritual quandary, they perceived that Buddhism had the ability to solve their problems.[33] Thus, both groups considered their philosophy superior to the other's, while dismissing the other side's belief system.

Finally, Buddhist philosophy had a major impact on Vietnamese views of the United States. Religious historian Trevor Ling has characterized the development of Buddhism as an explosion of rational thought over the problem of human suffering, an argument that would shock Americans who viewed Buddhist prelates as wandering ascetics uninterested in the cares of this world.[34] Siddhartha Gautama (the Buddha) and his followers, however, set out to discover why humans suffer. They concluded that people ail because they crave things like money, possessions, power, long life or fame. After considerable reflection, the Buddha realized that the major difficulty for humans resided in the fact that the things they yearn for are impermanent and in a state of decay. Thus, they never satisfy the people who covet them. In fact, the more people get, the more they want, so that many humans live a life of increasing demands and downward-spiraling unhappiness. The Buddha recognized that the key to enlightenment and escape from the endless cycle of birth, death and rebirth lay in the renunciation of craving. By destroying desire, he argued, humans could find true happiness. In addition, the Buddha taught that everything humans needed to complete this process existed within them. From this great insight, Buddhists developed the concept of nonattachment to all things, including ideology.

Many Buddhists found American capitalism repulsive and believed they understood what drove American actions in Vietnam more than the United States did. Some sensed that American problems had resulted from efforts to protect its wealth and power, which were in a state of decay. Therefore, even though the United States held more riches than any other country in the world, it hungered for more while going to fantastic lengths to protect what it had. Given that Communism threatened American treasure and power, the United States had to combat it to preserve U.S. affluence. Buddhists realized the futility of the American effort. They could see where the Americans' longing for security had led them, while Vietnamese appetites brought on by the adoption of American habits and mores seemed sure to destroy their society also.

Closely aligned with the idea of nonattachment is compassion. Even though most suffering is self-inflicted, the Buddha called on his followers always to practice nonviolence and compassion. Buddhist monk Thich Nhat Hanh has advanced the argument that full shelves in Western grocery stores while people starve in the Third World constitutes a form of violence. Yet he argues that the great wealth of the West has done nothing to cure the intense religious crisis that gripped it for most of the twentieth century. He claims that the vast riches of the West have created a situation in which the more the nations owned, the more they wanted to protect, leading to a ruinous arms race that further deprived the poor of their share of the world's resources.[35]

Another difficulty came from the bipolar attitude of American officials. In their Cold War view, one must support either the United States or the Communists. Those who stood in the middle and attempted to steer a course between the two ideologies appeared more dangerous than anyone else. The idea of rejecting both seemed incredible since American logic said one is either with us or against us. After all, what good is a superpower-dominated bipolar world if groups decline to sign up with either side? Thus, American leaders could not understand neutrality, while Buddhists opposed adherence to any ideology.

Zen logic also rejected the basis of the Cold War. Zen teaches that the key to enlightenment lies in understanding the true nature of the universe while specifically refuting duality and adherence to any belief system. Zen holds that that the normal dichotomous descriptions that split the world into two spheres cannot provide an accurate understanding of human existence. Zen practitioners only begin to sense the proper character of the world when they move to this more nuanced understanding of the universe. Thus, the philosophy that informed many Buddhist monks and nuns in Vietnam rebuffed Cold War ideology and the American argument that Communism had to be confronted in Vietnam. Adding to American confusion, Zen remains almost incomprehensible to a person unprepared for its unique qualities, vague statements, slaps in the face and weird humor. In fact, in Zen, enlightenment comes all at once, like a thunderclap, when the disciple finally senses the precise makeup of the universe.[36]

Buddhism had survived for two thousand years in Vietnam by understanding the transitory nature of power. Buddhist clerics have often opposed the government but always retained close ties to the people. Thus, they remained very shrewd in understanding their relationship with their fellow Vietnamese. Buddhist prelates depended on the Sangha for their daily necessities, while the laity looked to the clergy for leadership and moral guidance. Out of this symbiotic relationship grew the interdependence that represents the essence of Vietnamese Buddhism. After all, what is more rational than wanting to survive? Equating their future with the people meant Buddhist monks and nuns had to attempt to stop the war while adhering to traditional Buddhist concepts of compassion and nonviolence.[37] Significantly different philosophies and worldviews ensured that Americans and Buddhists would clash over the issue of war or peace in Vietnam. Neither side particularly tried to understand the other, while each considered its system superior.

One great exception to the Buddhist approach toward the war occurred in the Mekong Delta among Hoa Hao Buddhists. Founded in 1939 by a charismatic young healer named Huynh Phu So, Hoa Hao Buddhism matched the conditions and lifestyle of the peasantry of the area well. Realizing that extreme poverty and ties to the land prevented many peasants from participating in Buddhist rites, Huynh Phu So called for a Buddhism bereft of clergy and temples. Instead, he combined ancestor worship with Buddhist ritual and invited his followers to practice their religion at home. At the same time, stories of miraculous healings on his part greatly enhanced his reputation with the people of the region.

In 1947, the Communists captured, tried, and secretly executed the founder of Hoa Hao Buddhism because they feared his growing influence in the anti-French resistance. Then they dismembered his body and dumped it into a river so that his followers would not expect him to be reincarnated. However, because no one ever recovered the corpse, many Hoa Hao expect him to return someday as a Buddha who will bring them peace and happiness. Not surprisingly, Hoa Hao people never forgave the Communists for assassinating their founder and became fervently anti-Communist, joining the French against them, and later, the South Vietnamese government against the NLF. As a result, the Hoa Hao opposed efforts by Buddhists to negotiate with the NLF, instead choosing to fight the Communists until the collapse of South Vietnam in 1975.[38]

THE IMPULSE TOWARD NEUTRALISM

With Diem's removal in 1963, the Buddhist movement appeared triumphant. Their fervent desire to end an increasingly violent war in the countryside and to create a situation where Vietnamese could decide their fate irrespective of Cold War rivalries seemed to Buddhists to be realized with the installation of the new government of General Duong Van

Minh. After Diem's fall, moreover, South Vietnam's future looked bright. Newspapers sprang up, political parties proliferated, and for the first time in its brief history, open discussion began on the direction of the country.

Severe tensions soon arose, however, over the extent of freedom allowable in a country at war. A widespread feeling that the United States had engineered the Diem coup to bring a more representative government to South Vietnam contributed to a rising tide of democracy and, later, extreme disillusionment when it failed.[39] Unfortunately, the United States squandered the immense political capital it had gained with the Diem coup by moving away from its often-stated commitment to democracy in favor of stability, because it remained chiefly concerned with defeating the insurgency.[40]

NLF activity increased dramatically in the weeks after the coup, leading to an agonizing U.S. reappraisal on the progress of the war. Within a short time, Washington discovered that the uprising in the countryside ranged far wider than U.S. officials had realized and that the war would soon be lost without an extraordinary reversal in the field. The contradictions inherent in the creation of South Vietnam and the intense power of Vietnamese nationalism, combined with Diem's inept rule, foreclosed any possibility of a speedy victory.[41]

At the same time, Minh assessed the war-weariness among the people and began to hesitate in prosecuting the war. A popular Buddhist general commonly referred to as Big Minh, due to his unusual height for a Vietnamese, he formed a government of prominent civilians and like-minded military leaders with the goal of seeking a neutral solution to the war through a negotiated settlement with the NLF.

Minh's labors to terminate the fighting created powerful adversaries, because Washington opposed any move toward neutralization, which seemed tantamount to total defeat akin to the "loss" of China in 1949. While U.S. leaders feared the domestic recriminations that would follow a withdrawal from South Vietnam in an election year, Minh's efforts also alienated a number of ARVN generals who owed their positions and power to a continuation of the struggle and American financial support. Although a number of officers formed dissident organizations to challenge Minh, in the end, General Nguyen Khanh led the group that seized power and attempted to form a military dictatorship.[42]

Khanh's January 1964 coup temporarily ended any opportunity to stop the war through negotiations. A short, pudgy, goateed, jaunty character, Khanh seemed like a breath of fresh air when he told the Americans he had overthrown the government to prevent it from embracing a neutral solution to the conflict. He appeared forceful, energetic and dedicated to pursuing the war with vigor, and his government outlawed neutralism.[43] Thus, the United States threw its full weight behind Khanh and his argument that South Vietnam could not afford democracy while war raged in the countryside. General Maxwell Taylor, U.S. ambassador to South Vietnam during the second half of 1964, claimed that President Johnson's concern over the possibility of more coups in South Vietnam led him to instruct his policy-makers to advertise Khanh as the clear favorite of the United States. As Taylor remembered, "When it was all over, there was no doubt that he was the 'American boy,' at least for the time being."[44]

Yet the replacement of one dictator with another caused the country to seethe with discontent. While pleasing the United States with his get-tough attitude toward the war, Khanh could not bring political unity to South Vietnam. Over time, he moved closer to the United States and further from his own citizenry, setting the stage for an explosion of protest against his government, which he himself ignited in August 1964.

THE FIRST BUDDHIST CRISIS OF 1964
ANARCHY IN SOUTH VIETNAM

Like Buddhists, South Vietnamese Catholics also had to adjust to a new political situation. The fall of Diem and efforts to remove members of his Can Lao party from official positions threatened Catholics with a loss of their privileged position in South Vietnam. In addition, tension between Khanh and members of the largely Catholic Dai Viet party reflected their fear of the potential for radical political change in favor of groups less dedicated to carrying out the war.[45]

In May, Thich Tri Quang charged the government with a lack of commitment in removing former Diem bureaucrats and asserted that many government officials continued to persecute Buddhists. While Khanh unquestionably wanted to prevent renewed Buddhist protests, he understood that many of his most effective officials were fervently anti-Communist Catholics. By removing these elements, he would seriously undercut his ability to combat the growing NLF menace, create a severe reaction in right-wing groups like the Dai Viet and most likely provoke his American sponsors, who wanted the war prosecuted with greater effort.[46]

Khanh decided to mollify the Buddhists with other actions. As a partial palliative, he executed Ngo Dinh Can, Diem's brother and the virtual warlord of the Hue area, and decided to prosecute Major Dang Sy, the Catholic officer who had issued the order to open fire on Buddhist demonstrators in May 1963.[47] Vietnamese Catholic bishops, however, objected strenuously to the possibility of a trial, claiming that public opinion had been stirred up against Dang Sy through a concerted public relations campaign. Khanh also moved quickly to preempt Buddhist efforts to challenge his rule by repealing Decree #10, the hated law that declared Buddhism to be an association rather than a religious organization.[48]

Tensions coursing through the Catholic community contributed to growing opposition to Khanh. Objecting to perceived favoritism toward Buddhists by Khanh officials and Lodge, 35,000 Catholics demonstrated in Saigon on June 7, 1964. Most of the protesters objected to the removal of Catholic officials and claimed they were now subjected to the same discrimination they had been accused of by Buddhists when Diem held power.[49]

Increased activity by the Dai Viet party, however, created a much more dangerous situation for Khanh. A right-wing, nationalist party that formed in the 1930s, the Dai Viet absorbed many elements of the Can Lao party and thus hewed to a pro-Catholic, anti-Communist line. Many key army officers belonged to this group and watched Khanh closely in hopes he would falter and they could seize power. One of their leaders, Nguyen Van Thieu, eventually ruled South Vietnam from 1967 to the last days of the war.[50]

Through the adroit use of personal diplomacy and concessions, Khanh temporarily cooled the passions of Buddhists and Catholics. His ability to confront issues head-on and meet with opposition parties enabled him to continue in office, even with the deteriorating situation in the countryside and despite serious questions concerning the viability of his government and reservations over his ability to confront a concerted challenge. Indeed, although numerous hostile forces besieged Khanh during his early months in office, his ability to confront these groups contrasted favorably with Diem's moves the previous summer. In August, however, his political instincts deserted him when the Gulf of Tonkin incident emboldened him to increase his power.

Khanh declared a state of emergency on August 8, 1964. Claiming that South Vietnam needed a new martial spirit to combat increased Communist insurgency and wage a possible war with North Vietnam, he suspended a number of civil liberties and imposed a national curfew.[51] In seeking to divert attention from his power grab by focusing on the threat from the North, Khanh misjudged popular attitudes in calling for an expanded war from a society sick of conflict. This seemed particularly true in view of the fact that U.S. reprisals against North Vietnam after the Gulf of Tonkin incident had already inflamed Vietnamese emotions by signaling an increase in the fighting.

Nine days later, Khanh promulgated a new constitution and declared himself president of South Vietnam.[52] His seizure of increased power along with his suspension of civil liberties created a widespread belief that he wanted to establish a military dictatorship. Buddhists in particular understood this would wreck any chance to end the war. Suddenly, the burst of democratic activity that had been the fruit of the hard-fought victory against Diem seemed endangered. Thus, the country rapidly erupted into a state of frenzied anarchy and more instability as students carried out another round of ferocious demonstrations similar to those of 1963. While students engaged in violent protests, Buddhist leaders organized huge antigovernment demonstrations and worked behind the scenes to influence Khanh.[53]

Adding to the chaos in the streets, simmering tensions between Catholics and Buddhists exploded into religious warfare. On August 24, fighting broke out in Danang between large groups of Catholic and Buddhist students, while other Buddhist students roamed the streets of Hue, enforcing a school boycott. On August 25, some ten thousand Buddhists attacked and burned to the ground a Catholic village near Danang in what *Time* referred to as "an anti-Catholic pogrom." Danang soon witnessed large mobs of Catholic and Buddhist students surging through its streets in search of each other, resulting in horrific violence and atrocities. Soon religious violence spread to Saigon and other urban areas of

South Vietnam, contributing to an image that the country had descended into a primordial kind of anarchy. Press reports of soldiers and police witnessing rioting and violence with no response added an almost surreal quality to the apparent collapse of South Vietnamese society.[54]

Disregarding appalling violence and disorder, Khanh refused to move to restore order. The events of 1963 paralyzed him; a strong move against the rioters and more instability, he feared, might turn the Americans against him as with Diem. On the other hand, many high-ranking ARVN officers expressed astonishment over his refusal to confront the demonstrators. So did Ambassador Taylor, who urged him not to give in to the Buddhists, because concessions might encourage them to seek more accommodations from the GVN. This echoed the same reasoning Diem had used the previous year when he refused to grant Buddhist demands. Khanh certainly knew this; perhaps Taylor did not, but in light of Diem's experience, it is not surprising that Khanh ignored Taylor.[55]

Life in the cities contributed to the Buddhists' ability to mobilize mass action and the NLF's to recruit new members, since both groups competed for the same disaffected elements. Josef Reisinger, of the *Far Eastern Economic Review,* illustrated the effects of thousands of refugees moving to the cities when he characterized Saigon in August 1964 as a filthy city with garbage and litter lying uncollected, while in the streets, "[b]eggars were everywhere: old men, women, crippled and children." He described the malaise affecting the Vietnamese: "Two decades of terror, fighting and death have sapped the citizens of this country of their energy and will to struggle for an unknown 'freedom.' Sickened and demoralized, they have lapsed into an almost traditional fatalism: What Buddha wishes will come to pass."[56]

In addition, America's neocolonial assault on Vietnamese culture exerted an extreme psychological effect on many South Vietnamese so soon after independence from France. This was often illustrated by the orgy of senseless violence that raged through the cities of South Vietnam. In many cases, students joined leaderless mobs intent only on destruction. They focused on religious differences, which were simpler to identify, rather than on the pain they felt over the destruction of their culture. The anarchy in the streets convinced many U.S. officials that they needed to exert greater control over the GVN to carry on the war.

Khanh responded to the sudden expression of Buddhist political power by offering to meet with Buddhist leaders. The Buddhist hierarchy took advantage of the opportunity to press their cause by demanding an immediate cessation of the president's dictatorial powers, calling for a purge of Catholics in the GVN and advocating the formation of a government that followed the popular will.[57] Khanh quickly agreed, but damaged himself further in Vietnamese eyes when he told them that he had to check with the Americans before concluding an agreement.[58]

After five days of unparalleled violence and protest, Khanh withdrew the new constitution and resigned. Emboldened by Khanh's vulnerability and repelled by his weakness in confronting the rioters, a Catholic faction of the Military Revolutionary Committee (MRC), the group of generals who ostensibly ran the country, blocked him from regaining full power in the new government. On August 27, the MRC appointed a triumvirate of generals—Khanh, Minh and General Tran Thien Khiem—to form a caretaker government that would rule until a new government could be formed. The makeup of the triumvirate reflected the major power groups that emerged from the crisis: Minh, favored by the Buddhists due to his support for neutrality; Khiem, the Catholic leader of the Dai Viet faction in the army; and Khanh, supported by the United States but temporarily aligned with the Buddhists.[59]

An inherently unstable expedient sure to fade quickly, the triumvirate left the United States with no government to control. As a result, Americans began dictating to individual factions in the country. Hence, Buddhist efforts to remove foreign influences from their country had ensured that the only stable force left in South Vietnamese politics was an entity totally alien to Vietnamese culture: the United States. Thus, Washington, rather than Khanh, the Buddhists, the ARVN or the NLF, became the dominant factor in South Vietnamese politics.

Although Khanh's ineptitude had plunged South Vietnam into chaos, Taylor insisted that the United States would not support a government without him. Thich Tri Quang and Thich Tam Chau also endorsed Khanh to prevent a possible military coup.[60] As a result, Khanh continued to run South Vietnam, given that the support of the Buddhists and Americans meant he could rule without consulting the others.[61] Nevertheless, the Americans remained extremely concerned about the Buddhist alliance with Khanh, because the embassy could exert little control over them.

Finally, on August 29, the GVN moved to restore order. Despite the arrest of five hundred protesters, the rioting continued, leading troops to open fire on the demonstrators. The MRC declared martial law, with a curfew and the closing of all schools in Saigon. Police and ARVN leaders sternly warned students and other demonstrators that no further protests would be tolerated.[62]

The Buddhists appeared victorious. Their power had increased dramatically in less than two weeks, and they had paid an incredibly small price for their victory. No sweeping arrests of monks, no raids on pagodas, no repression and, most significantly, no self-immolations had accompanied their struggle. With virtually no support left besides that of the United States, Khanh quickly embraced the opportunity to gain the Buddhists' backing when they presented their demands to him on August 25.

AMERICAN RETORT

Concerned about the possibility of the GVN's imminent collapse and increasingly doubtful of Khanh's ability to rule, Washington reacted to the chaos in South Vietnam with great anxiety. At the height of the disorder, Washington announced its unqualified support for Khanh and indicated it would oppose any attempt to oust him. Bui Diem, a prominent South Vietnamese politician and later ambassador to the United States, expressed the irony of the American position by pointing out that U.S. plans to escalate the conflict seemed threatened by the increased instability in South Vietnam. Diem placed the anarchy in South Vietnam on America's doorstep, arguing that its preference for security over democracy had inflamed much of the urban populace of South Vietnam.[63] Having fought so hard against Diem for freedom, many South Vietnamese were astounded to see the champion of liberal democracy disregard their aspirations and support a military dictatorship.[64]

In the same fashion, many Americans turned on the Buddhists with a level of hostility formerly reserved for the NLF.[65] Admitting that Thich Tri Quang was not a Communist, the CIA nevertheless labeled him "a fanatic nationalist, undoubtedly anxious to see the U.S. out of Vietnam at the earliest possible moment."[66] Taylor ominously described him as "the most effective and dangerous politician in Vietnam" and warned that the Buddhist leader "may have ambitions extending beyond Vietnam."[67] General William Westmoreland, commander of American forces in South Vietnam, argued that Thich Tri Quang "wanted a dominant voice in the government,"[68] while the American secretary of defense, Robert S. McNamara, had referred to him several months earlier as "an ambitious, dangerous, unpredictable, powerful, political force antagonistic to Khanh's government."[69]

U.S. journalists also lashed out at Thich Tri Quang. In June 1964, *Time* called him "a frail, hot eyed monk . . . [who] has managed to confuse everyone about his political loyalties."[70] By September, the magazine viewed him as "an ambitious, probably neutralist and possibly pro-Communist intriguer."[71] *America,* a Catholic magazine indulging in the tortuous logic of the Cold War, charged falsely that Thich Tri Quang was a "former activist with the Communist Viet Minh and is therefore Communist trained."[72]

American journalists also found the events of August extremely unsettling. Peter Grose of the *New York Times* argued that the last week of August had represented "a shattering week for the present program of the United States to defend Southeast Asia."[73] *Time,* referring to the fall of the Khanh regime as "perhaps the most critical setback to date" for the United States, decried the actions of groups who seemed oblivious to the importance of the war against the Communists.[74] *Newsweek* argued that Buddhists no longer felt content with religious hegemony and now sought political power while complaining that they lacked a coherent political platform.[75]

The constant disorder in the country led Taylor to grow increasingly pessimistic over the ability of the GVN to defeat the NLF. He concluded that the instability and weakness of the GVN could in time force the United States to attack the Communists to free South Vietnam from their grip. Tragically for the United States and Vietnam, Taylor's assessment led him to advocate offensive action against North Vietnam to stave off a South Vietnamese collapse.[76] Thus, Buddhist peace efforts led the ambassador to conclude that only an American expansion of the war could forestall a GVN move to settle the conflict.

August 1964 constituted a stunning reversal for the United States as officials began to understand the depth of opposition in the country to the GVN and continued war. Increasingly, the GVN seemed hopelessly enfeebled and the Buddhists appeared almost invincible, leading American leaders and journalists to blame the NLF for the anarchy. While Buddhist power had been exaggerated by the United States and the GVN, Buddhist muscle-flexing genuinely concerned both governments, given that Washington could not accept that its presence in South Vietnam sparked the instability that it decried.

CONTINUOUS CHAOS

The perceived powerlessness of the Khanh regime and general ARVN dissatisfaction over his capitulation to the Buddhists soon created more volatility in South Vietnam. While Buddhists asserted themselves, ARVN generals seethed at Khanh's weakness. On September 13, dissident military officers attempted to overthrow Khanh. The coup lasted only one day, after Nguyen Cao Ky (then commander of the Vietnamese Air Force) refused to desert Khanh and threatened to bomb the rebels.[77] Nevertheless, the attempted overthrow indicated the deep concern many ARVN officers felt over Buddhist domination of Khanh.[78]

Some commentators, however, understood the Buddhist position. Following the coup, the *Far Eastern Economic Review* editorialized that "there is a growing body of opinion which holds that the war against the Viet Cong is anyway a hopeless one." It called on the United States to negotiate, because "it is undeniable that the neutralist solution would probably be the most accurate reflection of the desires of the majority of the South Vietnamese."[79] Historian Marilyn Young agrees, arguing that "[a]ny government in Saigon that aspired to popular support was likely to seek peace with the NLF and in time probably reunification as well."[80]

To forestall further coup attempts, Duong Van Minh announced the names of the High National Councilors (HNC) on September 17. This group, made up of distinguished South Vietnamese civilians, aimed to return South Vietnam to nonmilitary rule by writing a provisional constitution and selecting an interim legislature to govern until it took effect. On October 25, the HNC named Phan Khac Suu temporary head of the government.[81]

Meanwhile, Buddhists issued an appeal for peace, their boldest to date. On September 24, the journal of the UBC, *Hai Trieu Am* (Voice of the rising tide), published "Urgent Prayers of a Suffering People," which called for a negotiated settlement and for the combatants to refrain from killing each other. More importantly, the article referred to NLF cadres as brothers, a powerful indicator of the fratricidal nature of the steadily expanding war. The GVN promptly shut the journal down, leading Buddhists to launch a new publication.[82]

Thus, what the United States feared most had emerged from the Buddhist challenge to Khanh. He seemed increasingly under Buddhist control as the country lurched from military dictatorship to collective rule to civilian government to attempted government by coup ending in another seemingly bedeviled effort to return to legal constitutional rule in South Vietnam. Yet, this too was destined to fail. No government operating under U.S. control and advocating expanded war could survive if the populace had the opportunity to express its will.

THE SECOND BUDDHIST CRISIS OF 1964

Suu's appointment of Tran Van Huong, the mayor of Saigon, as prime minister of the provisional government and successor to Khanh, on October 30, 1964, soon incited significant opposition within Saigon. Some Vietnamese called for his ouster on the grounds that he seemed too old and lacked fresh ideas, while student groups objected to his proclamation that demonstrations would not be tolerated.[83] While many complained that Huong had not purged Diemist elements from his regime, others argued that by appointing civil servants with previous government experience rather than politicians espousing new ideas, the GVN ensured that nothing would change. By ignoring religious groups in making appointments, moreover, Huong quickly gained the enmity of both Catholics and Buddhists.[84] Unlike Khanh, Huong confronted agitators with force, threatening potential protesters with immediate conscription into the ARVN, a response remarkably similar to Diem's when faced with dissent in 1963.[85]

Within a week, the city again exploded in antigovernment fury. Although Huong blamed the disturbances on disgruntled political figures and insisted that religious organizations refrain from political activities, Buddhist leaders almost immediately joined students in demanding Huong's ouster, leading exasperated government leaders finally to use regular army units to quell the disturbances.[86] As in the disorders of August, the GVN threatened arrested protesters with trial and summary execution before military tribunals.[87]

After the GVN imposed martial law on Saigon, Buddhist leaders closed the headquarters of the UBC and organized a campaign of non-cooperation to topple the Huong regime.[88] On November 29, a spontaneous sit-down strike in Saigon led ARVN troops to wade into the crowd and disperse it with rifle butts. When authorities reported that a number of weapons had been seized, along with documents implicating the NLF in the protests, Huong claimed the march represented part of an NLF plan to seize control of the city or even overthrow the government.[89] Thich Tri Quang, Thich Tam Chau and Thich Tinh Khiet, the patriarch of the UBC, responded by initiating a forty-eight-hour hunger strike as part of their nonviolent retort to the Huong regime. On December 16, Buddhists intensified their opposition to the GVN when several hundred Buddhists joined the hunger strike.[90]

Once again, the absence of a popular government had sparked opposition to the GVN. Constant Buddhist references to the will of the people acknowledged what just about everyone in the U.S. government and the GVN knew but feared to say: few people wanted the war to continue. Nevertheless, Taylor worked assiduously to establish peace between Huong and the Buddhists. The irony was inescapable for anyone who noticed: The United States, which had opposed Diem because he rejected compromise with the Buddhists and objected to Khanh, who did compromise, now found itself saddled with another Diemlike figure who refused to grant concessions to the Buddhists. In this case, however, Huong received considerable encouragement from Taylor to stand up to the Buddhists.[91]

Other events soon temporarily swept aside U.S. concerns with the Buddhists. On December 20, ARVN generals dismissed and arrested some members of the HNC and granted additional authority to Suu and Huong.[92] When he heard about the coup, the latest manifestation of the instability driving him to distraction, Taylor exploded in a burst of anger, dressing down the coup leaders and demanding that Khanh report to the embassy to explain the latest takeover.[93] Khanh retorted that if Taylor wanted to talk with him, he should come to his headquarters.[94] The next day, in a barely disguised swipe at Taylor and the United States, Khanh announced that the ARVN wanted to fight for the Vietnamese people rather than to fulfill the aims of another nation. Young claims that, at this point, Taylor insisted that Khanh quit and Khanh threatened to ask for Taylor's recall.[95]

The struggle between Huong and the Buddhists now receded into the background as deteriorating relations between Khanh and Taylor moved to center stage.[96] For the remainder of the year, as they struggled privately and publicly, Taylor increasingly questioned Khanh's ability to rule, while Khanh threatened to have Taylor declared persona non grata. On a more fundamental level, Khanh began talking to the NLF about a possible negotiated settlement, which brought the full weight of the United States against him.[97]

BUDDHIST SETBACKS IN 1965

At the end of August 1964, Buddhists seemed the overwhelming victors as they moved from opposition to support of the status quo and restoration of civilian government. They discovered by year's end, however, that they had won a hollow victory. Like most popular grassroots movements, they remained more effective at expressing and directing resistance than at forming policy or leading a government. Their enhanced position resulted more from the weakness of the GVN than from their own power.

For Washington, 1964 ended worse than it had begun, with the GVN in complete disarray and the United States on the verge of attacking North Vietnam. Bui Diem saw this as the inevitable result of a decade of blunders in South Vietnam, where "[t]he American policy of boosting whoever happened to grab power, for the sake of elusive stability, was now reaping its harvest."[98] McNamara argues that at this stage, the United States should have pushed the GVN to the point where a decision to conform to U.S. plans became inescapable. Then, he suggests, the United States should have withdrawn from South Vietnam.[99]

27

Following the fall of Huong in January 1965, South Vietnam seemed close to realizing peace. Khanh increasingly identified with the aspirations of the Buddhists to create a neutralized South Vietnam, leading the United States to encourage ARVN generals to overthrow his regime. Even though the Americans successfully jettisoned Khanh, as historian David Kaiser points out, "remarkably, the pro-American anti-Communist political forces within South Vietnam had steadily lost ground since mid-1963 not merely to the Communists but also to non-Communist neutralists led by the Buddhists, the only non-Communist political force that could develop a mass following."[100]

After the expulsion of Khanh in February, South Vietnam embarked on a period of civilian rule under Dr. Phan Huy Quat. His zeal to lead the nation effectively and to slow the rush toward an expanded conflict suffered constant interference from the Armed Forces Council, which held real power in the GVN, and from the United States, which had decided to confront the NLF militarily in South Vietnam.[101]

Nevertheless, Quat attempted to bring a measure of stability to the GVN and end the fighting. Buddhists reacted by launching a "Peace above All" campaign, which demanded "an early end to this fratricidal war," the expulsion of foreign combatants and negotiations to end the conflict.[102] Quat's plan to parley with the NLF, however, provoked significant hostility among South Vietnamese Catholics and other anti-Communist elements. As a result, the generals dissolved his government during the summer of 1965.

In the interim, a number of indigenous peace movements arose. Increasingly sickened by the rising cost of the war, citizens launched three different peace campaigns simultaneously in Saigon during 1965. The GVN crushed all of these efforts, sending a clear signal to Vietnamese of the danger of outright calls for peace. Nevertheless, as journalist Takashi Oka argued at the time, "the simple, uncomplicated, totally understandable popular ache for peace remains."[103] In May, a Buddhist-organized peace rally in Saigon witnessed thousands of Vietnamese calling for the creation of a "peace cabinet."[104] In December, Thich Tinh Khiet implored the contending forces to open talks to end the war.[105]

Even the American CIA sensed the deep desire for peace on the part of many Vietnamese. It commented in February 1966 that a GVN plan to whip up more support for the war "well may backfire since the generals may find that the people really want peace and not war." Donald Ropa, a member of the National Security Council staff, predicted in January 1966 that the growing refugee problem and a drastic increase in civilian casualties could "generate resentment against the U.S. or the Saigon government, and pressure for peace-at-any-price by pacifist elements such as the Buddhists."[106]

Following Quat's overthrow, power devolved upon Nguyen Cao Ky. Known for his colorful dress, love of gambling, indulgence in late-night activities, imprudent statements and bravado, Ky immediately set a new course for the GVN, proclaiming a permanent state of emergency, declaring war on North Vietnam and placing the country in a heightened state of military preparation.[107] Aside from expanding the draft, an action sure to trouble restive student organizations, he announced a number of austerity measures and imposed capital punishment without trial for numerous offenses, particularly profiteering and black-marketing.[108]

More ominously for Buddhist peace activists, the United States in 1965 introduced ground forces and implemented a sustained bombing campaign against the Democratic Republic of Vietnam (DRV, or North Vietnam). William Colby, CIA station chief in Saigon, claims that GVN weakness had persuaded most American officials that without the introduction of American forces, the Communists would emerge victorious by the end of 1965.[109] Thus, U.S. leaders decided to bomb the DRV in February in retaliation for attacks on U.S. installations at Pleiku and Qui Nhon. Mounting worries about the safety of the Danang air base convinced Washington to land thirty-five hundred marines at Danang in March to guard the facility. Before long, American forces began patrolling to seek out insurgent military formations.

As combat operations expanded, Washington discovered that the People's Army of Vietnam (PAVN, or the North Vietnamese Army) and NLF forces easily matched the American buildup. In July 1965, Johnson decided on a major escalation in troop levels and the bombing campaign. Although the number of American forces rose to 200,000 by January 1966, the United States appeared no closer to victory, leading the American president to insist that more effort be placed on winning the political side of the war through pacification.

Thus, the United States engaged in a number of half-hearted attempts to pursue an accommodation with the DRV, up to February 1966. Most peace efforts, however, accompanied or preceded major U.S. escalations of the fighting, causing the DRV to doubt the sincerity of U.S. peace offers. In fact, as historian George Herring points out, "the United States had no real desire to begin serious negotiations at a time when its bargaining position was so weak." Nevertheless, a highly publicized bombing halt at the end of 1965 raised hopes that the United States could negotiate a way out of the war. Still, the persistent American position that a non-Communist regime had to emerge from the talks precluded any settlement with the NLF or the DRV.[110]

For Buddhist leaders, Ky's war preparations, along with the introduction of U.S. combat forces, represented a stunning defeat. Certain that a genuinely representative government would negotiate with the NLF and end the war, Buddhists now recognized that ARVN generals, with no real constituency of their own, would never allow an election in which the will of the people prevailed to end the war through negotiations. Believing that the war must eventually be settled at the conference table rather than on the battlefield, Thich Tri Quang and his followers concluded that they must challenge the GVN while the relative weakness of Ky allowed them one last chance to grasp peace from the jaws of war.[111]

The United States, which had stood by helplessly as the Khanh government collapsed in August and the Huong regime disintegrated in January, again faced the situation it feared most: more instability. The successful Buddhist attack on Khanh and Huong, moreover, destroyed any hope that future governments could retain domestic political support while expanding the war. In a search for stability, subsequent governments moved closer to the United States, surrendered their independence, and found themselves unable to counter American demands to broaden the conflict. Similarly, the upheaval and anarchy of the Buddhist crisis convinced many non-Communist Vietnamese that they must support an American-sponsored dictatorship rather than see South Vietnam descend again into chaos. Thus, in a totally unexpected way, the United States became the beneficiary of the Buddhists' victory. While some Buddhists demanded a transition to civilian rule as the price of their continued support of any government, realization of their goal of peace proved to be far more elusive than Buddhists originally thought. Their quest for reconciliation between the warring parties created more instability, revolving door governments and, as always, expanded U.S. intrusion.

While some Buddhists, particularly the Thich Tri Quang faction, wanted to establish a middle way between the violence of the United States and the NLF, their movement suffered from a fatal flaw. Given that they had no weapons or areas of refuge and had to operate within the territory of one of the two main forces, they could be destroyed at any time and had to maneuver between two more powerful adversaries. In a democratic political system, the Buddhists could have had a decisive impact due to the popularity of their antiwar position, but their vulnerability remained the most significant aspect of their movement. They understood that the absence of democracy posed great danger to the people of Vietnam. As a result, they exerted great efforts to establish a civilian government devoid of dictatorial elements. Although Buddhist power had been exaggerated by the United States and the GVN, Buddhist muscle-flexing genuinely terrified both governments. Yet Washington could not accept that its presence in South Vietnam sparked the instability that it decried. While Buddhist leaders rejoiced over the possibility of civilian rule and the opportunity to end the war, American officials viewed with foreboding increased manifestations of Vietnamese nationalism and Buddhist political power. Indeed, Thich Tri Quang and the UBC became the American scapegoats for their failure to understand events in the country.

A number of factors converged in 1965 to call forth the Buddhist Crisis of 1966. The initiation of sustained bombing operations against North Vietnam in February, the introduction of U.S. ground forces at Danang and the rise of indigenous peace movements within South Vietnam in March, the ascension of Air Marshal Ky to the premiership in June, and the return of Lodge as U.S. ambassador in August sparked a clash between Buddhists dedicated to ending the war through a transition to popular democracy and representative government and a GVN equally devoted to expanding the conflict. Indeed, the stage was set for a dramatic confrontation between the proponents of war and peace. Both sides realized that free elections and representative democracy could fundamentally alter the makeup of the GVN and establish a new course for South Vietnam. Soon Buddhists would risk everything on a campaign to bring representative government to their country.

1

Origins of the
Buddhist Crisis of 1966

We should be clear in our own minds that the Buddhist
leadership are our adversaries.
> —Embtel 3817 (Saigon), Lodge to Rusk, 4-8-66.

DISMISSAL OF NGUYEN CHANH THI

In February 1966, GVN and American leaders met in
Hawaii to strengthen ties and plan ways to defeat the
Communist insurgency. While the conferees saw this as
a milestone in U.S./GVN relations, many Buddhists
viewed the meeting with horror because it would assuredly mean increased fighting. Thus, they decided to risk
everything in a desperate challenge to end the conflict
before it grew even larger and more uncontrollable. They centered their
strategy on a demand for democratic reforms as part of their larger plan
to end the war and expel the United States. While Buddhists equated
democracy with peace, U.S. and GVN officials wanted no expression of
popular opinion in South Vietnam. The result was the Buddhist Crisis of
1966.

Upon his return from Honolulu, Prime Minister Nguyen Cao Ky
acted quickly to exploit his newfound prestige. Emboldened by the vote
of confidence from President Lyndon Johnson, and believing he had to

enhance his ability to withstand potential challenges from groups like the Buddhists, he confronted and dismissed his main rival in the Directory, General Nguyen Chanh Thi, providing the pretext for Buddhists to launch their campaign to end the war.[1]

A number of theories have been advanced to explain Ky's move. Kahin argues that Lodge pushed Ky to dismiss Thi because he feared a potential Thi-led secession of I Corps.[2] Pike partly agrees, claiming that the U.S. embassy worried about the possibility of central Vietnam declaring war on the South in 1966, particularly since Vietnamese consciousness seldom transcended regional identification.[3] Journalist Stanley Karnow claims Johnson persuaded Ky to dismiss Thi, while Westmoreland asserts that Thi's refusal to report to Saigon when ordered and Ky's fear of a coup led to his firing.[4] Bui Diem maintains that the break between the two men had been brewing for months and that the final rupture occurred when Ky visited I Corps in early March. According to Diem, Thi insulted Ky by saying loudly to an aide "What is this little man doing here anyway?" Ky took the injudicious remark as a challenge to his authority.[5]

The factor that pushed Ky to the edge of the precipice may have been a February 1966 *Time* article that referred to Thi as a more dynamic figure than Ky who could seize power at any time.[6] Whether Ky believed this or assumed that the United States had leaked it to encourage Thi or to pressure Ky remains unknown. But considering the intrigues that surrounded the generals and the extreme instability between 1963 and 1965, Ky may have decided to launch a preemptive strike.

At the time, Ky provided a number of reasons for his decision. He argued that Thi had abused his position by adopting a posture similar to that of Ngo Dinh Can, who had served as a virtual warlord over central Vietnam under his brother Ngo Dinh Diem.[7] In his memoirs, Ky claims that Thi used his relationship with Buddhists in Hue to enhance his power and that he had a propensity to conspiracy, left-wing leanings and a mistress suspected of being a Communist.[8] Finally, Ky may have dismissed Thi because he knew that Thi supported negotiations with the NLF since, as Vo Van Ai points out, Ky fired everyone who resisted militarization of the war, including Thi.[9]

Thi, however, saw his problems with Ky as a manifestation of the relationship between Ky and the U.S. government. To Thi, the military rulers of South Vietnam had no regard for the welfare of the people or any sense of the need for popular support to prevail against the Communists. Thi argued that the United States had picked Ky to run the country because he would take orders. He saw Ky as a man without honor who lived an opulent lifestyle while the people suffered from the impact of the American intervention. At the same time, Thi had a number of personal confrontations with Ky, warning him, "[W]e must do something to have freedom and democracy, we cannot be so dependent on the Americans, we cannot be puppets." Unfortunately, Thieu and Ky did not follow his suggestions, eventually becoming "tay sai [slaves] for [U.S.] dollars." Like Buddhist leaders, Thi asserts that most Vietnamese did not want war except for the generals who aimed to please the Americans.[10]

Whatever the reason, the United States became deeply involved. The night before Thi's firing, Henry Cabot Lodge Jr., who had returned to South Vietnam as U.S. ambassador in August 1965, urged Ky to make sure he retained enough backing to dismiss his rival, warning him that if doubts arose over his ability to pull it off successfully, he should back off and wait for a better time. Ky assured the ambassador that it would be no problem and that people would not react to the dismissal, which demonstrates how far removed he was from popular opinion in the country.[11]

Ky called a meeting of the Directory, the group of generals who ruled South Vietnam, on March 10 to dismiss Thi. Although he acted as a first among equals, the Directory publicly emphasized its unanimity to forestall possible coup plotters hoping to capitalize on divisions in the body. Thus, after Ky threatened to resign unless the Directory followed his lead, even Thi voted for his own ouster.[12] Thi claims he provoked his fellow generals by warning them that "as long as Vietnamese leaders send wives and girlfriends to Hong Kong for shopping and drive big cars bought with the people's money, no one will fight to defend them."[13] They responded by placing him under house arrest and ordering him out of the country.[14] At the same time, the Directory named Major General Nguyen Van Chuan, commander of the ARVN First Division, temporary chief of I Corps.[15]

Ky's action pleased Lodge. Although the CIA had warned him in February of the possibility of Buddhist-inspired agitation occurring later in the month, Lodge had encouraged Ky to take an action that seemed certain to provoke the Buddhists and threaten the existence of the regime.[16] Engaging in the wishful thinking that surrounded most analysis on the war, Lodge believed that Ky could fundamentally alter the delicate equilibrium on which the GVN had been constructed and emerge unscathed. Ky's move against the strongest member, Thi, enraged Buddhists, who were fed up with the political machinations in Saigon while the country seemed headed for destruction.

Power sharing, however, constituted an essential element in the makeup of the Directory and had led to the kind of warlordism Ky decried. As Frances FitzGerald argues, the legitimacy of the GVN rested on the military strength of the United States, backed by thousands of American troops, while the generals divided the country into feudal fiefs where each ruled independently. Ky retained the position of prime minister because he was the weakest of the generals and easiest to control.[17]

Ky greatly underestimated the impact of removing Thi. Firing him upset the fragile regional balance on which the GVN relied for the little legitimacy it could claim. Other recent dismissals led many South Vietnamese, especially Buddhists, to believe that Ky had adjusted the Directory to reflect the growing power of Northern Catholics, who remained the most fervent GVN supporters of the war.[18] Removing Thi, a man known for his honesty, also strengthened the elements in the Directory intent on continuing the graft that had developed from the American largesse lavished on the ARVN.[19]

An intense, confident leader, and a Buddhist, Thi was a native of Hue who remained very popular with Buddhists there. A short, jaunty figure with a pencil-thin mustache, he radiated authority and was always willing to hold forth on numerous subjects with little prompting.[20] In many ways, he seemed cut from the same cloth as Ky, but his tenure as commander of I Corps matured him and instilled a sense of responsibility for the people under his care. In addition, his commitment to social justice, his ability to communicate in the local dialect, his responsiveness to the people and his stern anti-Communism made him extremely popular throughout I Corps.[21] Adding to his credentials with the Buddhists, he had tried to overthrow Diem in 1960 and remained the only active-duty Vietnamese military leader trusted by Thich Tri Quang.[22]

Americans also gave Thi high marks. General Lewis Walt, commander of the Third Marine Amphibious Force (III MAF), regarded him as an honest and able commander who endeavored to cooperate with American forces in his region.[23] Colonel Howard Sinclair, Thi's senior American advisor from February 1965 to the eve of his firing, deemed him a tough, assertive, fearless, honest leader whose outspokenness caused him substantial difficulties. Sinclair also claimed that Thi's troops held him in high esteem and that Thi considered Ky his close friend.[24]

While the reasons for Thi's removal remain murky, it is clear that Ky felt confident in dismissing his rival after Honolulu. Nevertheless, it was a major error. Restive Buddhists sought an excuse to challenge the GVN, and Thi's popularity in the critical provinces of central Vietnam ensured an explosive reaction to his removal. At the same time, U.S. support for Ky convinced many Vietnamese that the move would result in expanded war, further encouraging Buddhists to overthrow the GVN and find a government willing to make peace with the NLF.

THE BUDDHIST CHALLENGE

To Ky's great surprise and Washington's consternation, Thi's firing ignited antigovernment demonstrations throughout South Vietnam. Soon after the news of Thi's firing reached Danang, protests broke out. Although Thi ostensibly resigned for health reasons, Buddhist leaders deduced that his dismissal could spark enough fury to allow them to renew their call for democracy and general elections, bringing down Ky in the process.[25] The speed and breadth of the growing agitation, moreover, betrayed widespread opposition and universal ambivalence to the police-state tactics of Ky's regime, reinforcing Buddhist beliefs that the time had arrived to challenge the GVN and end the conflict.

Civil disorder quickly spread to more cities in central Vietnam as Hue and Hoi An witnessed protests, and most of Danang shut down in a general strike.[26] Speakers exhorted demonstrators to oppose the GVN with charges that Thi had been removed because he opposed dishonesty and despotism, while Chuan, his successor, announced he would not confront protesters as long as their actions remained peaceful.[27] At the same time, Vietnamese and American military authorities confined U.S. Marines and members of the Vietnamese Air Force to their bases in

Danang to avoid clashes with a new group named the Military and Civilian Struggle Committee, later called the Struggle Force to achieve the Revolution.[28] As the general strike continued, American installations, such as the port through which supplies flowed for the marines, had to cease operations.[29]

On March 16, Ky sent Thi to I Corps, ostensibly to restore peace. Yet it remains extremely difficult to explain Ky's foolishness in allowing Thi to return to the area where just a week earlier he had wielded total control and where numerous civilian and military officials remained beholden to him. Ky claimed he acted to restore their friendship, mollify his supporters in the region, and fulfill a promise to allow Thi to visit the area before leaving the country. However, Ky planned to purge his supporters in I Corps as soon as Thi departed for the United States.[30] Hence, Thi appeared in Danang on March 16, giving a jocular and light-hearted speech full of sarcastic references to his removal for health reasons.[31]

The next day he returned to Hue like a conquering hero, not a chastened despot. Twenty thousand supporters greeted him with cheers, a potent indicator of both his popularity and the depth of feeling against the GVN, which, according to Neil Sheehan of the *New York Times*, "left no doubt that the ruling Saigon junta was in serious trouble in this region." Members of student organizations and the local Buddhist association followed his speech with calls for the dismissal of GVN Chief of State Nguyen Van Thieu and Lieutenant General Nguyen Huu Co, deputy premier and defense minister, both prominent Roman Catholic members of the Directory and notorious for their corruption.[32]

Thich Tri Quang quickly asserted leadership. On March 15, he argued that Ky had become even more despised in the aftermath of the Honolulu Conference due to his slavish adherence to American goals. He reasoned that continued U.S. support for Ky ensured a violent confrontation with Buddhists. On March 20, recognizing that Ky had given him a golden opportunity to press the case for free elections and representative government, the Buddhist leader returned to Hue to direct the struggle.[33]

Protests had already begun to spread beyond I Corps. On March 16, the Struggle Movement erupted in Saigon with Buddhists demanding the restoration of civilian rule, the return of armed forces personnel to purely military roles and an end to Ky's despotism and American domination of the GVN. By the end of the month, massive protests with heavy anti-American overtones reached Nha Trang and Dalat. In Hue, students seized the radio station, the location of the original Buddhist protest against Diem, turning it into a propaganda voice for the Struggle Movement.[34]

Struggle forces soon gained important allies. The mayor of Danang, Dr. Nguyen Van Man, abandoned the GVN, Buddhist chaplains encouraged ARVN soldiers to ignore their officers and follow the Buddhists, and Chuan deserted the GVN and openly supported the Struggle Force.[35] Adding to the "hallucinatory" quality of the agitation, a number of factors converged during the spring of 1966 to generate widespread support in I Corps for the Struggle Movement. As FitzGerald points out, a local desire for autonomy and a political uprising blended into an emerging peace movement, student demonstrations against government corruption, a dramatic increase in anti-Americanism and an intellectual and trade union revolt over cultural and economic upheaval in the country, leading the nation to the verge of collapse, similar to August 1964.[36]

On April 1, Ky sent Major General Pham Xuan Chieu, general secretary of the Directory and number-three man in the GVN, to I Corps to persuade Thi to return to the fold. When Chieu arrived in Hue to offer Thi a new position in the GVN, in a dramatic demonstration of the collapse of governmental authority in central Vietnam, Buddhist dissidents refused to let him leave the city.[37] The next day, when the city shut down completely during a general strike, Chieu could find no one to help him leave. The Struggle Force released him after another day, but they had made their point about the limits of GVN authority in I Corps and about Buddhists' determination to have their voices heard.[38] When Chieu returned to Saigon, he denied he had been held hostage, but his ordeal convinced Ky that he had to restore order.[39] Simultaneously, protesters in Dalat attacked the radio station, Buddhists marched in Pleiku and anti-American upheavals occurred in Qui Nhon.[40]

More seriously for Ky, large numbers of ARVN soldiers participated in the latest protests in Hue and Danang. No greater indication of the impotence of the Ky regime and widespread resistance to its war aims seemed possible than the wholesale defection of troops retained by the state to withstand the Communist threat.[41]

Once again, Buddhists had brought a government to the brink of extinction. Escalating protests in the country and demonstrations of widespread dissatisfaction with the GVN forced Ky to hesitate in putting down the disorder, while Ky's actions set off a series of protests that demonstrated the weak political base of his regime and significant opposition to the United States and the fighting.

KY'S VACILLATION

Obviously, some kind of concessions had to be granted for the generals to retain power. Yet giving in to Buddhist demands for free elections, an action that might end the war, could provoke U.S. opposition. Despite a pledge of support from the United States, Ky's caution betrayed his deep insecurity over his relationship with the generals, Washington and, most of all, the people of South Vietnam. He knew he could be jettisoned at any time, especially if he allowed the popular will to prevail. Thus, like Diem, Minh, Khanh and Quat, Ky had to choose between alienating the United States and violently confronting people calling for representative government in South Vietnam. Initially, he chose a course that pleased no one.

Although the Directory publicly refused to compromise with the Buddhists, government officials met privately with Buddhist leaders, allowing them to air their complaints. GVN leaders soon proclaimed that they would consider moving up the time of already promised elections since that did not constitute caving into illegal demands but rather the granting of a reasonable request.[42]

Ky also soon implied that he would advance the date of elections. The Directory, however, remained deeply divided over acquiescence to Buddhist demands. Some members, particularly Ky, took a belligerent stance toward the demonstrators, while moderates feared that a GVN/Buddhist confrontation would help rather than hurt the Buddhists.[43] Finally, Ky offered to call a constitutional convention staffed by appointees selected by the Directory, but Buddhists demanded popularly elected delegates.[44]

The GVN then agreed to sponsor a constituent assembly made up of delegates from regional and provincial councils. While this seemed like a major concession, it failed to satisfy Buddhist demands for a truly representative assembly.[45] Lodge supported the GVN proposal, fearing a popular assembly would allow the Buddhists to dominate the new government and end the war.[46]

On March 27, Ky denied that a cleavage existed between the GVN and the people. He noted that the political stability of the previous nine months had been the longest period of internal peace since the fall of Diem and that the aspirations of the people and the GVN were identical. Arguing that domestic tranquility remained essential to defeating the NLF, he claimed that the disorder in I Corps eventually would benefit the enemy and therefore had to be halted in the interest of the nation. Cautioning against a rush to democracy, he warned that U.S. aid could cease if stability could not be achieved in South Vietnam.[47]

Within a week, he extended an olive branch to Thi. In an interview on March 30, he termed Thi's presence in Hue as convalescing leave and claimed he would give him a new job upon his return to Saigon.[48] His statement pleased the American embassy and Washington, which had been urging Ky to maintain lines of communication with his rebellious subordinate.[49] Indeed, Ky was caught between his desire to please the Americans with a transition to democracy, which would give the GVN increased legitimacy and more ability to carry the war to the enemy, and a populace that wanted the same thing to end the fighting. Thus, South Vietnam seemed to be moving toward representative government, a system that might terminate Ky's regime.

LODGE PUSHES KY TO RESOLVE THE IMPASSE

Throughout the crisis, Henry Cabot Lodge Jr., like Taylor in 1964, used his press contacts to label the Struggle Movement as Communist-dominated. Even worse, Lodge knew the Buddhists were not Communists. They stood in his way and that of his government and thus, in his mind, had become foes of the United States almost on the same level as the NLF. The Buddhists alarmed Lodge because he could not understand them, and he despised them because he could not control them. Often during the crisis, he held meetings with his staff where he would inquire repeatedly, "[W]hat do they want?" The inability of embassy personnel to provide him with answers increased his frustration and drove him to loathe the Buddhists.[50]

U.S. Secretary of State Dean Rusk often pleaded with his ambassador to urge Ky to act with restraint. Yet, contrary to his instructions, Lodge bullied Ky into taking strong action in I Corps. Unfortunately, Rusk matched Lodge's independence with weak leadership. Rather than sitting on or replacing his headstrong ambassador, the secretary acted more like a cheerleader, cajoling, praising and pleading with him to adhere to the U.S. position. In fact, as Kahin argues, despite entreaties from Rusk, Lodge often refused to talk with Buddhist leaders, declining at one point even to call a conference of the opposing groups because it might lead to a rapprochement.[51]

Rusk inundated Lodge with cables suggesting ways to confront the crisis. Lodge instead pursued his own agenda, reporting to Rusk on March 23 that the Buddhist leader aimed to topple the government, a statement that ignored considerable efforts by Thich Tri Quang to reach an agreement with the GVN. At the same time, Lodge blamed the disorder in I Corps on a "VC Fifth Column . . . utilizing unmistakable signs of communist techniques."[52] Despite a dearth of evidence to support his claim, he informed Rusk that Thich Tri Quang wanted to create a Buddhist-dominated regime and later characterized Thich Tri Quang's plan to bring democracy to South Vietnam as a "classic Mao Tse Tung tactic to switch to politics when the military side is going badly."[53]

Despite Rusk's entreaties, Lodge's intimidation succeeded in the end. At first, Ky had seemed to capitulate to Buddhist demands. He declared that a constitution would be granted to the people within two months and that elections would take place by the end of the year.[54] On April 3, the GVN announced plans to create a constituent assembly. While vague about the actual makeup of the commission, the GVN promised that its makeup would be broad-based and reflect all elements of South Vietnamese society, a proposal unsatisfactory to the Buddhists, because they wanted a truly representative system wherein the people would elect a constitutional convention that would become a legislative body after drafting a constitution.[55] While the Directory moved to establish a commission to create a constitution, Ky and Co sternly warned civil servants and soldiers in I Corps of the consequences of further rebellion, threatening them with trial before military courts followed by stern punishment.[56]

No sooner than pledging a new constitution, Ky backed away from his promise. Under urging from Lodge, he speculated that the country would not be ready for elections in time and the voting would have to be delayed. Incensed over Ky's treachery, Buddhist leaders called their followers to action while other groups in South Vietnam also demanded the restoration of democracy.[57] Lodge, meanwhile, reported to Washington that Ky planned to fabricate an incident in Danang as a pretext to launch an invasion of the Buddhist stronghold.

Finally, on April 3, Ky attempted to restore control in I Corps. He announced that he had moved troops to Danang to relieve the city from hostile forces, whom he labeled Communists, and had also threatened to shoot the mayor of Danang.[58] The movement of South Vietnamese marines to Danang, however, sent Ky's American sponsors into apoplexy as they contemplated the consequences of another of his rash actions. Although Lodge pushed Ky into the move with dark reminders of the events of 1963, the United States remained keenly aware of the public relations debacle that could result from scenes of South Vietnamese units fighting each other in the streets of Danang while American marines battled the NLF just a few miles away.[59] Ky also established a phony radio station at the Danang air base that purported to broadcast Struggle Movement messages but actually sought to convince people that Communists dominated the movement, leading to the belief in later years that they had infiltrated the organization.[60]

Ky's actions had a dramatic effect. Upon hearing of his plans to attack Hue and Danang, "Buddhist students screaming anti-American slogans stormed the Saigon Radio station," and over ten thousand protesters marched in Danang. In Banmethuot, Buddhist students paraded while demanding an end to the military dictatorship of Thieu and Ky. Increasingly, protesters referred to Ky and Thieu as American puppets, while Ky, for the first time, responded to the agitation in Saigon with force, sending specially trained combat police to disperse the crowds.[61] In the words of Kahin, "[n]ever had any South Vietnamese government stood more naked of indigenous backing."[62]

Eventually, Lodge's intimidation worked. After offering a series of pseudo-concessions to the Buddhists, Ky again reversed course and announced an impending attack against Danang to end the agitation in central Vietnam. At a time when Ky's position seemed increasingly perilous and the Buddhists appeared on the verge of victory, Lodge goaded Ky into an attack on Danang.

VIETNAMESE NATIONALISM

It is no coincidence that open rebellion by Buddhists and their allies first occurred in Danang and Hue. The initial elements of American ground forces had landed at Danang a year earlier, and the area around the city witnessed the first interactions between Vietnamese peasants and American forces. No other event spurred the nationalism and desire for peace that lay behind the Buddhist movement more than the introduction of foreign soldiers into South Vietnam. The appearance of alien troops waging war against Vietnamese inflamed the community, leading to greater recruitment opportunities for the NLF, strong anti-American sentiment among much of the population and enhanced support for Buddhist efforts to halt the war.[63]

The city of Hue represented a special hotbed of Vietnamese nationalism. Hue is the heart of Mien Trung, the historic central area of Vietnam. Traditionally noted for their fiery tempers and food, fierce independence and almost total adherence to Buddhism, the people of the area felt great pride in their location as the imperial capital and cultural center of Vietnam for the previous century and a half. In addition, Hue embodied Vietnamese Buddhism, centered on Chua (Pagoda) Thien Mu, the most famous and beautiful pagoda in Vietnam.

Hue also had great strategic value because of its close proximity to the Demilitarized Zone (DMZ) between North and South Vietnam. American and ARVN military commanders worried constantly about a PAVN invasion across the demarcation line to split the region from the rest of the country, leading the first American combat troops in South Vietnam to operate in that area.[64] In later years, the region witnessed the most sustained and intensive combat of the war.

The U.S. propensity to disregard Vietnamese customs and traditions further aggravated relations between the people of I Corps and Americans. In February 1966, the Buddhist newspaper *Dat To* (Fatherland) argued that American actions had degraded Vietnamese traditions and diminished the ability of the GVN to pursue an independent course.[65] As American combat operations expanded in I Corps, augmented by the sustained bombing of North Vietnam, many Vietnamese, particularly Buddhists, expressed indignation over the increasing levels of Vietnamese civilian and military casualties.[66] For Buddhist leaders, this constituted additional proof that the war had to end to prevent the further slaughter of their people.

Feelings of nationalism among the people of I Corps increased as many Americans demonstrated condescending attitudes toward Vietnamese and blatant indifference toward Vietnamese lives and property. Some Vietnamese found especially galling American stereotypes about Asian ability to endure pain more stoically than Caucasians and the commonly held opinion that Asians placed less value on life than did Westerners.[67] Many Vietnamese concluded that American racism led to the use of napalm, chemical defoliants, white phosphorus and B-52 strikes, which, to them, confirmed that American leaders wanted to eradicate a new "yellow peril" in Asia.[68]

Vietnamese intellectuals particularly resented the way the American onslaught against traditional Vietnamese values had degraded the cultural fabric of the nation. To them, the role of Vietnamese women became especially charged and created enormous bitterness. Greed, increased consumerism, prostitution and the disrespect shown married women by American soldiers resulted from the U.S. presence in Vietnam and heightened feelings of shame over their occupation by a foreign power.[69] Adding to the humiliation felt by Vietnamese, ARVN troops never won the large battles or participated in the war in a meaningful way, and the spectacle of Vietnamese digging through American garbage dumps for food left an indelible impression.[70]

Confusion over the American crusade in South Vietnam abounded. Some Vietnamese viewed U.S. intervention with ambivalence based on the choice of the lesser of two evils: acceptance of foreign troops versus the necessity of defeating an ostensible foreign invader.[71] Buddhist leaders, while also at odds, still generally viewed the war as a disaster and understood that U.S. intervention had raised the stakes to unacceptable levels. Like their fellow Vietnamese, many monks and nuns remained deeply divided and troubled over the U.S. role in Vietnam.

Thich Tri Quang added to the perplexity with his propensity to make contradictory statements. In February 1966, he argued that the narrow political base of the GVN had created increased levels of anti-Americanism.[72] In March, he claimed only to oppose U.S. backing of the military dictatorship, with its heavily Catholic orientation, while expressing appreciation for American efforts to combat Communism in South Vietnam. At the end of 1966, he maintained that Washington wanted to colonize South Vietnam.[73]

Other Buddhists also struggled with the issue. Thich Nguyen An, who lived in a pagoda in Saigon in 1966, claims Buddhists wanted to express the people's desire for peace, human rights and freedom, but he also appreciated the American intervention against a foreign invader.[74] Human rights activist Vo Van Ai maintains that the GVN represented "Diemism without Diem," arguing that the Buddhists did not so much oppose American intervention as U.S. tactics and support of the GVN that drove many non-Communists to join the NLF. Vo believed that the Buddhists were the only group in South Vietnam that could end the war without a Communist victory.[75] Tran Hong Lien, a noted scholar and historian of Vietnamese Buddhism and a student activist in the 1960s, joined the student movement to resist a foreign invader—the United States. Thich Quang Lien, an American-educated scholar and a leading member of the Vien Hoa Dao, supported American actions as benevolent and kind toward South Vietnam but came to oppose the war because of heavy Vietnamese casualties. Ban Hoang, a lay Buddhist leader, reasons that a belief in nonattachment led many Buddhists to oppose both Communism and American-inspired capitalism and to seek a middle way that would reflect Vietnamese values.[76] Thich Nhat Hanh agreed, arguing that the attachment of some Vietnamese to foreign ideologies had helped plunge the nation into a destructive conflict.[77]

Historian Douglas Pike asserts that it remained impossible to ascertain the true nature of Vietnamese attitudes about American intervention, due to the clandestine nature of the Vietnamese people. By this, he means that the Vietnamese, through their long history of foreign invasion and occupation, developed a habit of self-survival in never telling foreigners what they really thought.[78] Kahin concurs, but modifies the statement to declare that they would not tell the U.S. government or the GVN their true intentions. Nevertheless, they remained very open and honest with Kahin and their fellow Vietnamese in expressing their dedication to end the war.[79] At the same time, revulsion at the high level of civilian casualties caused serious doubt even among those who actively supported the United States.

While significant opposition to the GVN existed before the introduction of American ground forces, U.S. intervention further inflamed nationalistic feelings in the country. Increasing resentment over the high cost of the war and the presence of foreign troops led many Vietnamese to turn to Buddhist monks and nuns, the intellectual and moral elite of the country, to provide a solution. Buddhist leaders hoped to tap the strong feelings to end the war and expel the United States.

DIVISIONS WITHIN THE UBC

The Buddhist movement fragmented badly after 1964. While serious arguments arose over the political activism of some monks and nuns, most dissent revolved around the issue of war and peace.[80] Even though the UBC represented a minority in the larger framework of South Vietnamese Buddhism, militant leaders believed that the people of South Vietnam wanted the war to cease and aimed in that direction.

The organization remained troubled by the ongoing struggle between Thich Tam Chau and Thich Tri Quang. Their ideological conflict developed along regional lines, with Thich Tam Chau's most vehement adherents living in Saigon among fervently anti-Communist northern refugees, while Thich Tri Quang's support remained strongest among extremely nationalistic central Vietnamese. Their philosophical and strategic differences reached the breaking point in 1966, with Thich Tam Chau, located at the Quoc Tu pagoda in Saigon, adopting a lower profile and Thich Tri Quang becoming the unquestioned leader of the movement and the most powerful advocate of democracy.[81] Increasingly, each leader stayed in his respective area, although Thich Tri Quang sustained a strong presence in Saigon through his close association with Thich Thien Minh and the An Quang pagoda.[82]

The two leaders adopted fundamentally different approaches toward the GVN. While Thich Tam Chau, as the leader of the moderates, continued his friendly relations with Ky throughout the crisis, Thich Tri Quang and the radicals argued that Vietnamese should not follow the DRV or the United States, a position sure to alienate many Buddhists opposed to the Communist presence in South Vietnam. Although Thich Tri Quang objected to Communism, he believed that GVN actions helped the NLF, blocked Buddhist efforts to find a middle way between the violence of the United States and the NLF and prevented Buddhists from launching their social revolution.[83]

Exacerbating the conflict, many Buddhists suspected that Thich Tam Chau remained a paid informant for the U.S. embassy. Douglas Pike claims that some of the young monks considered him an "Uncle Tom" and resented him for it.[84] Thich Dui Tri, a Buddhist monk who demonstrated against the GVN in Saigon during 1966 and followed Thich Tri Quang, argues that the GVN and the CIA used their resources to broaden the divisions in the movement.[85]

The well-known arrogance—some called it extreme self-confidence—of Thich Tri Quang turned off some followers and repelled many Americans who viewed him as a crass opportunist. Nevertheless, having brought down Diem, Khanh and Huong in less than eighteen months, Thich Tri Quang thought he could do the same to Ky. He did not, however, appreciate that the situation had evolved into something far different than 1963–64 because U.S. involvement in the war had dramatically raised its commitment to the preservation of a stable GVN. As a result, U.S. officials labored constantly to discredit Thich Tri Quang and enhance the prestige of his rival.

Determined to achieve popular democracy in the country as the first step toward peace, Buddhist leaders had to face both the hostility of the United States and the GVN and significant internal dissension within the UBC. At the same time, GVN and U.S. officials tried to exacerbate tensions between moderates and radicals in the movement so that the message of the radicals would be muted by the squabbles in their organization.

Importance of Democracy to the UBC

Buddhists genuinely feared a Communist victory in South Vietnam. In the summer of 1965, the Buddhist magazine *Dan Toc* (The People), posed the question, "Why do we struggle?" The journal answered: to save the nation from ruin. Many Buddhists assumed that if the ARVN suffered defeat in the field or the GVN collapsed, which surely it must if the war followed the same path, then the country would be lost and Buddhism destroyed. Hence, Buddhists held that representative government would grant badly needed legitimacy to the GVN, which could then gain the loyalty of the people. Although Buddhists viewed democracy as a way to reverse the immediate impact of the heavy U.S. presence, they also recognized that it could enhance the possibility of ending the war through negotiations. They believed that most Vietnamese wanted peace and a quick conclusion to the fighting.[86] Some Buddhists also thought that a democratic South Vietnam had the potential to defeat the DRV by giving Vietnamese an alternative to Communism.[87]

A remarkable Saigon press conference on March 13, 1966, set the stage for the struggle to follow. Much of the leadership of the Vien Hoa Dao, including Thich Minh Chau, head of the Vanh Hanh Institute; Thich Quang Lien; Thich Thien Minh; Thich Tam Chau; and Thich Phap Tri, leader of the Vietnamese Theravada Buddhists, called for the restoration of democracy and the return of all exiled generals, many of whom favored neutralism and had supported the Buddhists in the past.[88]

On March 17, Thich Ho Giac, assistant chief of chaplains, clarified the Buddhist position. Buddhist leaders had four goals: the establishment of true democracy in the country; the return of all ARVN officers to military positions, meaning the end of ARVN domination of the GVN; the restoration of all exiled officers; and the creation of a government that would realize the people's aspirations.[89] The clamor for the return of exiled officers, particularly Minh, easily the most prominent and popular ex-military leader in South Vietnam, was an explosive proposal, considering that many of the generals had conspired to overthrow him and expel him from the country in 1964. While the Buddhists remained coy about their reasons for returning these officers, they understood that a Minh government would move quickly to negotiate with the Communists to end the war. In fact, when Minh finally ran for president in 1967, the GVN denied his candidacy for the practical reason that he remained infinitely more popular than Thieu or Ky.[90] Although Buddhist leaders viewed Ky's government with disdain, they assured him privately that they wanted him to stay on rather than resign during the transition period to democracy, because they feared that the transfer of power to another general in the Directory could upset their plans.[91]

Profound changes brought on by the introduction of billions of American dollars increased Buddhist concerns for the welfare of the people and the need to gain a more representative form of government.

Thich Thien Minh went to the heart of the matter when he described the devastating impact of the war on Vietnamese society, which had caused grave economic dislocations while Vietnamese died to defend a system that exploited them. In a barely disguised swipe at American neocolonialism, he claimed to see little difference between a government of the franc or of the dollar.[92] At the same time, most Buddhist leaders understood that an American-dominated GVN could never muster the support necessary to resist U.S. destruction of the local economy, while the tremendous financial demands of the war worked against launching a social revolution.

The explosive growth of the cities, swelled by mounting numbers of refugees, also had a profound impact on Vietnamese society. While the movement of so many people to urban areas allowed the GVN to maintain better control over the population, it also created demands for additional services in the midst of a general deterioration of living conditions during a time of seeming prosperity, particularly as rampant inflation eroded wage increases among white-collar salaried workers.[93] Increasing urban populations created enormous slums, which became effective recruiting areas for the NLF. U.S. supplies earmarked to relieve the distress of refugees usually ended up on the black market, enabling GVN officials to enrich themselves from the misery of the people they allegedly served.[94]

In addition, a general breakdown in services plagued Saigon. Crime and prostitution soared, garbage was never collected, roads never repaired and buses never ran on time.[95] Lacking an effective way to object to these profound changes, a rage directed at the GVN and the United States simmered just under the surface of the collective psyche of the people. Buddhist attempts to confront the GVN and demand improvements in living conditions released the pent-up fury of the people, which manifested itself in growing civil disorder and a desire to get rid of Ky, who seemed too weak to negotiate with the NLF or stand up to the United States and end the suffering of the people.[96]

Buddhist calls for constitutional government, in many ways, disguised their true intentions. Afraid of a GVN that spurned negotiations with the NLF and a U.S. government dedicated to pressing the war in South Vietnam, Buddhist demands for democracy masked their real goal: "restoration of peace and negotiation with the NLF."[97] As Vo Van Ai argues, Buddhist leaders viewed an effective civilian government as the only alternative to the NLF able to carry out negotiations, since "by early 1966, it became obvious that the military rulers had no interest in negotiated peace but would crush all opposition by force." Many Buddhists viewed the conflict as a Cold War struggle, where the two Vietnamese sides represented the superpowers as proxies. Believing that the United States had to exit the country before the conflict would cease, Buddhist leaders seldom made these statements publicly for fear of arrest or assassination by GVN authorities.[98]

Ronald Beasley, president of the International Fellowship of Reconciliation, a group dedicated to bringing peace to Vietnam, contends that by 1966, the most important word in the Buddhist vocabulary had become "reconciliation." He argues that Buddhists understood that the war would eventually have to end in negotiations and that the GVN would have to participate in the talks to establish a lasting peace.[99]

The Buddhist Crisis of 1966 revealed problems more intractable than a mere power struggle within the Directory. Buddhist-led disturbances in the spring of 1966, the most severe crisis since the fall of Diem, pushed South Vietnam to the threshold of a suicidal civil conflict, revealed the vulnerability of the Ky regime and laid bare the insecurity of the huge U.S. commitment in South Vietnam.[100] Buddhist-motivated instability that year, moreover, brought the GVN to the verge of a total collapse, removed I Corps from the control of the government and exposed U.S. weakness and vulnerability in South Vietnam.[101]

Finally, the return of Henry Cabot Lodge Jr. played a critical role in the unfolding drama. His frustration with Buddhist attempts to limit the war led him to label them Communists, effectively masking the issues that drove the Buddhist protests and causing them considerable difficulty in 1966 and afterward.[102] Nevertheless, as demonstrations exploded across the country, the intensity of anti-Americanism fueled by objections to the introduction of foreign troops into South Vietnam, the grave concerns over rampant inflation and the severe strains of the war on the people soon became apparent to U.S. and GVN officials.

Once again, a seemingly small incident had provoked a major confrontation between the GVN and its citizenry. Obvious unhappiness with continued military dictatorship in the country combined with the widespread desire for peace impelled Buddhist leaders to confront the GVN in the wake of Thi's dismissal in a bold attempt to return civilian government to the country and end the war. For Buddhist elders, the events of early 1966 represented a continuation of their long-term strategy to bring to the country a government that would negotiate an end to the war. Thi's return to Hue, moreover, led fed-up ARVN troops to rebel against the central government, bringing the strategically critical central Vietnam to the brink of secession. The weakness of Ky's position caused him to hesitate early on in putting down the spreading upheaval, while Buddhist demonstrations of political strength terrified American officials. Eventually, Lodge persuaded Ky to move against the dissidents in Hue and Danang, leading to an even greater outpouring of public disapproval of the GVN.

As shocked American officials began to question their commitment to South Vietnam, the stage was set for a confrontation in Danang. Ky would suffer a humiliating reversal when dissident forces blocked his exit from the air base, while American officials began considering a withdrawal from the country and Buddhist leaders plotted the return to civilian rule. Buddhist political success, however, soon called forth opposition from various groups worried that they might be left out of the new political order in South Vietnam, creating even more instability.

2

Conservative Backlash

The strain on our political and economic life and the strain on the South Vietnamese is all but intolerable.
—Memo, Rostow to the President, 4-5-66.

 Responding to Lodge's pressure to settle the crisis, Ky flew to Danang on April 5 to resolve the impasse. Yet, despite the presence of four battalions of ARVN, including paratroopers, riot police, and South Vietnamese Marines, he found himself confronted by the Struggle Force, augmented by rebellious ARVN troops who threw up roadblocks and made clear they would fight GVN efforts to free the city. After a tense confrontation between his marines and the Struggle Force, Ky realized he lacked sufficient power to defeat the insurgents and wisely negotiated a political solution.[1] In a face-saving measure, Ky met with Chuan, Buddhist leaders, and representatives of Thi at the air base.[2]

Ky's attack on Danang led to one of the most confused and contentious periods in the troubled history of South Vietnam. Trapped between rebellious generals who demanded harsh measures against the Struggle Movement, Buddhists who called for a transition to civilian rule and democracy, and U.S. officials who required internal stability as the price for continued support, Ky had tried to end the crisis. In Danang, however, Struggle forces compelled him to carry out a humiliating retreat.

When he returned to Saigon, he reopened negotiations with the Vien Hoa Dao and extended an olive branch to the Buddhists.

Indiscreet GVN statements had stiffened resistance in I Corps, especially after Thieu asserted that insurgents controlled Danang, and Ky claimed that Communists had taken over the city.[3] The "Communist" designation struck particularly hard since many of those involved in the Struggle Movement had served on the front lines against the NLF. Thieu and Ky, however, knew which buttons to push with the Americans. Labeling the Struggle Force as Communist made it easy for the United States to rationalize the use of its air assets to transport Ky's force to Danang.

The next day, Ky returned to Saigon. Claiming the situation in I Corps constituted a political problem, not a military issue to be solved by force, he conceded he had erred in calling the rebellious forces in Danang Communists. This revelation occurred when he recognized his authority in central Vietnam extended no farther than a perimeter guarded by U.S. Marines.[4]

Ky's prestige in the country had suffered grievously. Adding to his difficulties, Chuan publicly claimed he had blocked Ky's forces with the threat of a bloody battle to defend the city, and the commander of the ARVN first division, General Pham Xuan Nhuan, maintained that his division would also contest efforts to retake Hue.[5] Despite Ky's pledge not to attack Danang, Vietnamese Air Force planes continually buzzed the city, causing tensions to rise even more, and ARVN Marines remained at the base rather than withdrawing to Saigon.[6] Struggle forces, meanwhile, continued to blockade the air base.[7]

Ky's diminished political status forced him to seek a temporary truce with the Vien Hoa Dao. Upon his return to Saigon, he met with Thich Tam Chau, Thich Ho Giac and Thich Thien Minh and promptly hammered out an agreement to soon hold elections for a constituent assembly.[8] The next day, Thieu announced that the Directory had approved a move to a representative government as soon as possible.[9]

BUDDHIST INTRANSIGENCE

Ky's retreat from Danang delivered more power to the radical wing of the Vien Hoa Dao. Soon afterward, Thich Tam Chau transferred power over the organization to Thich Thien Minh and Thich Ho Giac, since he had lost the ability to rein in the radicals within the Vien Hoa Dao.[10] With the militants ascendant, Thich Tri Quang asserted that one of the first questions the newly elected Assembly should ask was "whether the American presence [in Vietnam] is [still] desired."[11]

On April 10, dismayed by Ky's vacillation in implementing their arrangement, Buddhist leaders called for a new protest campaign against the regime. Recalling that the GVN had never met their March demands, the monks decided to drive Ky from office to achieve their goals of peace and democracy. At the same time, they announced the creation of "kamikaze" squads of Buddhist youth, designed to confront government forces.[12] In the most outspoken expression of their position yet, Thich Thien Minh "refused to rule out the possibility that the Buddhists, if they came to power, would negotiate with the Viet Cong and ask that American troops be withdrawn." While American leaders had suspected all along that this was the ultimate Buddhist goal, this public affirmation and the announcement of a new campaign against the GVN created more depression and trepidation among U.S. officials, who feared more instability in South Vietnam.[13]

Meanwhile, Ky called a National Political Congress of prominent South Vietnamese to decide on the most effective method to hold elections. Buddhist leaders viewed this as another delaying tactic and decided to boycott its sessions. Nevertheless, the congress ended up adopting the Buddhist program and sending it to the GVN for approval. Buddhist leaders also sent a telegram to Lodge demanding the United States cease its support of repressive regimes, arguing that U.S. policy might spark a civil war in the country.[14]

Faced with the prospect of renewed agitation, the Directory quickly acquiesced to Buddhist demands. On April 14, Thieu announced that elections for a constituent assembly would take place in three to five months.[15] The next day, Ky promised Buddhist leaders that no reprisals would be carried out against those who had participated in the antigovernment agitation and that all Vietnamese marines had been removed from the Danang air base.[16] Buddhist students in Hue, however, continued to call for Ky's resignation, speculating that his promises were a ruse to buy time while he built support for another assault on the Struggle Movement.[17]

New GVN pledges to hold elections led the leadership to request a halt to demonstrations. On April 18, the Vien Hoa Dao called for an end to antigovernment agitation after accepting GVN guarantees to move toward democracy, as well as American promises "that the U.S. would never allow a suppression of the Buddhists in central Vietnam . . . if the Buddhists agreed to put an end to their struggle."[18] Thich Tri Quang traveled through I Corps, arguing for a cessation of the struggle since the GVN had acceded to Buddhist demands. Claiming that South Vietnam did not want to become an American possession, he assured the country that the Buddhists wanted Ky to retain power until the elections created a new regime, ensuring stability during the interim.[19]

Thich Tri Quang claimed that the creation of a legal democratic process to change governments would prevent the kind of violence that had accompanied previous efforts to reform the GVN and end the war.[20] He viewed elections as a way to remove U.S. control of the GVN and bring peace to the country. During an interview in 1973, moreover, he admitted "that the struggle for democracy . . . was the external appearance of the struggle. The real issue was the restoration of peace and negotiation with the NLF."[21]

Aware that American hostility could wreck plans to bring democracy to South Vietnam, Buddhist leaders softened the anti-Americanism that had been an important part of the battle against the GVN. Thich Tri Quang publicly denied anti-American feelings or intentions to negotiate with the Communists. Instead, he argued that the creation of a national assembly would strengthen the forces committed to preventing a Communist victory in South Vietnam and that U.S. opposition to democracy negated the positive effects of American aid. He also rejected reports that the Buddhists wanted to gain control of the GVN or the National Assembly, claiming that monks would not run for office or attempt to dominate it from behind the scenes.[22]

His efforts to make up with the Americans, however, could only go so far. His ability to comprehend the dangers of continued fighting in South Vietnam led him to argue, "The Buddhist people do not want the war on either side. We do not like Communism because it is atheistic and we are against the government because it does not respond to the needs of the people."[23] Another time, he claimed that South Vietnam suffered oppression from both the United States and the NLF, while repeating his argument for a national assembly that would allow the people to resist the United States and the NLF.[24] Despite NLF, GVN and U.S. claims that they retained the support of the people, Buddhist success in mobilizing the population lay in its call for peace. By identifying with the aspirations of the people, Thich Tri Quang and the Vien Hoa Dao gained a measure of legitimacy long denied the GVN.[25]

Thich Tri Quang continued the campaign by granting rare public interviews to *Time* and *Newsweek*. He disavowed the idea that a representative government would necessarily expel the United States and asserted that the Vietnamese needed American help against the Communists. But he objected to the use of American war materials against the civilian population and particularly scored the United States for allowing its aircraft to transport ARVN Marines to Danang. Despite his effort at conciliation, he made clear that all conflicts end in negotiations eventually, implying that American military might would enable the GVN to bargain from strength.[26]

This statement went to the heart of the Buddhist position. At no time did they intend to surrender the country to the Communists.[27] While Buddhist leaders abhorred American actions in Vietnam, they realized that a temporary U.S. presence during peace talks would assure them a measure of security, although they remained sure they could control the NLF in a postwar government once American forces left.[28]

On May 2, Thich Tam Chau and Thich Quang Lien left Saigon for an international Buddhist conference in Ceylon.[29] Increasingly frustrated by his inability to control the demonstrations in Saigon or to make his voice heard in the Vien Hoa Dao, Thich Tam Chau decided to exit the country temporarily.[30] For the United States, the departure of the moderate Buddhist leaders meant that antiwar extremists now controlled the organization and that South Vietnam seemed on the brink of a revolution.

NEW LEADERSHIP IN I CORPS

Unable to defeat his opponents in a direct confrontation, Ky decided to place more loyal subordinates in I Corps. On April 15, Ky appointed General Ton That Dinh commander of I Corps, to replace Chuan. The third commander in less than five weeks, Dinh seemed an ideal choice.

A native of Hue, he had been a key figure in Diem's overthrow and had led the attack against Buddhists during August 1963.[31] Ky hoped that Dinh's readiness to move against the Buddhists in 1963 indicated he would be willing to do so again. But given Dinh's reputation for cunning and intrigue and a huge ego that needed constant stroking, his appointment represented a considerable risk that he could become another Thi.

A week later, Dinh announced that he had brought peace to I Corps. He had reestablished GVN control of the radio stations in Hue and Danang, asked Dr. Man to continue as mayor of Danang, implemented joint squads of Vietnamese Air Force (VNAF), ARVN, and National Police personnel and allowed the Struggle Force limited radio time daily as the price for restoring GVN control over the Danang radio station.[32] According to FitzGerald, Dinh's reaching out to the contending groups in I Corps "was the only intelligent move made by a government official for the duration of the crisis."[33] His actions, however, reflected more than a desire to rule the area effectively. Since many local people anticipated the imminent collapse of the Ky regime, the new I Corps commander joined what he perceived to be the winning side.[34]

Ky also replaced Colonel Pham Van Lieu as director of the national police force. His successor, Colonel Nguyen Ngoc Loan, signaled the growing influence of the Baby Turks.[35] Representing the faction who wanted to get tough with the Struggle Movement and end the crisis regardless of casualties, Loan, who later achieved international disrepute for his public execution of a suspected Communist during the Tet Offensive of 1968, constantly pushed Ky to attack the dissidents in Danang with threats to launch the assault unilaterally or head up a coup if Ky did not act.[36] Throughout the remainder of the crisis, whenever the GVN resorted to force, Loan was close by.

ROLE OF THE NATIONAL LIBERATION FRONT IN THE BUDDHIST MOVEMENT

Despite numerous U.S. government and press assertions to the contrary, little evidence exists of NLF involvement in controlling the Buddhist hierarchy at any time during the Vietnam War. Nevertheless, American officials and reporters clung to the fiction of Communist complicity, because acknowledging the strength of the Buddhist message would have undermined the whole U.S. effort in South Vietnam.

The NLF did benefit tremendously from Buddhist-inspired disorder and certainly hoped for its continuation. Truong Nhu Tang, an NLF agent who operated in Saigon in 1964, never mentions any contact with the Buddhist leadership but does claim that the NLF wanted to reap maximum rewards from the upheaval.[37] The appearance of widespread resistance to the GVN gave great strength to NLF claims that it had the support of the population and that the GVN constituted little more than an American creation, while the positioning of major elements of the ARVN around Saigon to guard against possible coups and put down riots meant that the NLF could operate with relative impunity throughout the countryside.

In some ways, the NLF and Buddhist clerics had much in common. Both sought to end the war and expel the Americans, appealed to and drew their main support from the people, and emphasized nationalism and saw neutralism, for different reasons, as the answer to South Vietnam's problem. Abhorrence at the idea of Americans killing Vietnamese, moreover, gave a huge boost to the nationalism that remained a critical component of both movements. Knowing the high esteem in which many of their rural followers held the NLF, Buddhist leaders remained reluctant to espouse anti-Communism publicly. American commentators, however, seized on this silence and labeled the Buddhist leadership, and particularly Thich Tri Quang, as Communist sympathizers.[38]

Although less apparent, differences between the NLF and Buddhists remained quite real. While the NLF succeeded in winning the battle for the people in the countryside, Buddhist leaders demonstrated an ability to stimulate mass action in the urban areas of South Vietnam that had eluded the NLF. Remembering the enormous triumph of the Viet Minh in provoking an urban uprising in August 1945, the NLF dreamed of replicating that event in South Vietnam. Buddhist success in directing urban uprisings contributed to an NLF misconception that it also could tap the urban masses to overthrow the GVN, leading to the destruction of a significant portion of its urban organization during the Tet Offensive of 1968.[39]

Buddhist demonstrations of urban political power, however, made the NLF wary of an alliance. The NLF faced a real dilemma: Buddhist leaders helped it tremendously by stimulating mass action, but they also appealed to a group the NLF considered absolutely critical to its success. Journalist Robert Shaplen saw these as distinct but corresponding movements, where each side had different goals but complemented the other unintentionally by weakening the government.[40] Both Buddhists and the NLF recognized the revolutionary potential in the urban proletariat, but Buddhists appeared more effective at tapping it, a source of increasing concern for the NLF.[41] The NLF remained in the uncomfortable position of hoping the Buddhists would succeed in disrupting the government but not to the extent that they could deny the NLF access to the disaffected elements of the urban population. This developed into a larger issue when the war caused a massive influx of peasants into the cities. Thus, the NLF saw more of its supporters fall under the sway of the Buddhists, whose plan for a coalition government seemed designed to deny the NLF the victory it sought on the battlefield.[42]

Buddhists, for their part, remained mindful of the danger of an alliance with the NLF. The bitter experience of Buddhism in Tibet, China and North Vietnam convinced them that they had no future under a Communist regime. In many ways, they feared more the establishment of a puppet organization, which had occurred in North Vietnam and China, over outright repression, the model in Tibet, since a Communist-controlled organization could confuse the people and lure them away from the leadership.[43] In addition, an alliance with the NLF would have brought the government of South Vietnam, the Americans, and non-Communist Buddhists to oppose the Buddhist movement. The only safe course remained in calling for neutrality and hoping for a coalition government representing all factions. In the final analysis, neither Buddhists nor the NLF desired an alliance; each wanted to use the other to attain its goals. Unfortunately, U.S. leaders did not realize that their presence, not the Communists or the Buddhists, had caused the agitation in South Vietnam and continued to drive the growth of the insurgency.

RESPONSE FROM THE RIGHT

Probably no group felt greater hostility toward the Vien Hoa Dao than did South Vietnamese Catholics. Mostly refugees from the Communist north, their position as a privileged elite disintegrated with the departure of the French and the ascension of the Viet Minh, only to be restored by Ngo Dinh Diem in South Vietnam and again diminished by the Buddhist movement in 1963. In addition, their hostility to the NLF as a representative of the ideology that had forced them to flee their homes in the north and threatened to overthrow the GVN established them as the cornerstone of anti-Communism in South Vietnam. Naturally, Catholics opposed actions that seemed to weaken the war effort against the Communists. They also suffered from a sense of insecurity after the fall of Diem, exacerbated by increased demonstrations of Buddhist political power.

During the initial stages of the crisis, Catholic groups also expressed opposition to Ky's military dictatorship. But as Buddhist protests grew and Catholics saw their position further threatened, they turned to Ky with support and demands that he check the growing violence and disorder in the country. Analogous to most opponents of the Vien Hoa Dao in the spring of 1966, Catholics feared Buddhist domination of a civilian government and possible NLF penetration of the elections, although a minority continued to support Buddhist efforts to end the war.[44]

When Lodge expressed concerns over NLF infiltration of the elective process, many Catholics fervently seized on the issue. Even without Lodge's misgivings, however, Diem and the French before him had ruled mainly by balancing the various factions in the country against each other. The prospect of a victory for any camp created apprehension among the others, although all would have had an opportunity to determine policy in an open electoral system. Perhaps they sensed, like the Vien Hoa Dao, that the people would demand an end to the war. To the mainly North Vietnamese refugee Catholic population of Saigon, ending the conflict with the Communists seemed unthinkable.

Catholic agitation soon began to match Buddhist-inspired disorder. On April 10, the Saigon University Catholic Students Association called for an end to demonstrations. Agreeing with Buddhist demands for representative government, the students supported Ky's suppression of urban disorder and condemned the anti-Americanism of recent demonstrations, because they feared that the radicals in the VHD would open talks with the Communists if they gained control of the GVN.[45] On April 14, Catholics announced the formation of a new organization, the Bloc of Catholic Citizens of Vietnam, a group that aimed to gather all

South Vietnamese Catholics under its banner.[46] On April 18, some three thousand Catholics paraded against recent GVN capitulations to Buddhist ultimatums and called for energetic actions to prevent Communists from gaining access to the proposed national assembly.[47] On April 24, Catholics demonstrated in three different parades in Saigon and Hue. Marchers, accompanied by black-clad youth armed with broken beer bottles to ward off Buddhist attacks, displayed banners expressing appreciation for American help and concerns about Communist penetration of the elections.[48]

Catholic demonstrations manifested increased hostility toward Lodge. On March 30, they charged that the ambassador had pressured them through the Vatican to refrain from protesting against the GVN. On May 2, an estimated five thousand Catholics carried out an anti-Lodge rally in Saigon. Consisting of mainly northern Catholics who had fled south in 1954, they demanded that Lodge leave the country, though they still expressed support for the American cause in South Vietnam.[49] At a time when Lodge advocated forceful actions against the Buddhists, Catholics, remembering his 1963 alliance with Thich Tri Quang, saw him as the source of their problems.

Buddhists also took advantage of May Day to press their cause. A large contingent of students chanting "Hoa Binh" (peace) and "Americans go home!" accompanied by marchers carrying signs that said "no more bombs," attempted to walk to the American embassy in Saigon, but government forces kept them away from the structure. Speakers addressed the crowd, calling for a halt to the use of herbicides and munitions on the part of American forces and for an end to the U.S. "race war of extermination in Vietnam."[50]

At the same time, tensions reached the flash point in central Vietnam. Remembering the religious violence of 1964, many Catholics feared for their safety among hostile Buddhists. Increasingly, Catholics in Danang and Hue armed themselves in anticipation of a Struggle Force attack on their enclave, while confining themselves to their areas at night for fear of a Buddhist attack.[51]

Other groups also objected to Buddhist domination of the elections. In a further manifestation of increased Vien Hoa Dao isolation, followers of the Hoa Hao Buddhist sect remonstrated against possible Communist infiltration in the forthcoming elections.[52] On May 8, the Cao

Dai, Catholics and the Hoa Hao joined other groups to create the People's United Front, an organization that called for a three-year moratorium on elections while also arguing for an expansion of the Directory by adding civilian members.[53] Because of their heavily anti-Communist orientation and former conflict with the Viet Minh, members of the Hoa Hao and Cao Dai feared a Buddhist-brokered accommodation with the Communists as much as Catholics did.[54]

The Vietnamese Kuomintang, a right-wing nationalist group better known as the VNQDD (Vietnam Quoc Dan Dang) party, also disapproved of Buddhist efforts to bring democracy to South Vietnam. Their fears seemed realized in April when conflict broke out between VNQDD members and the Struggle Force.[55] On April 19, fighting occurred in Quang Ngai between VNQDD and Struggle Force elements, leading Dinh to intervene forcefully to end the violence.[56] On April 22, the VNQDD accused Struggle forces of attacking their headquarters in Danang and Hoi An and demanded that the GVN clamp down on the Buddhists.[57] The same day, Lodge informed Rusk that VNQDD members in I Corps had drawn up a list of Buddhist leaders targeted for assassination, including Thich Tri Quang, in reprisal for the harsh treatment at the hands of Struggle forces.[58] Thich Tri Quang, moreover, accused the ARVN of supplying VNQDD members with weapons to use against the Struggle Force.[59]

Of greater concern to the radicals, the UBC suffered from a steady erosion of popular support. In moving away from the traditional role of the Buddhist priesthood to political activism, Thich Tri Quang and his followers sacrificed their greatest asset: the ability to claim the mantle of religious authority. Even though many Buddhists believed they had to follow the instructions of the monks, since "they came from the gods,"[60] the Buddhist movement alienated and caused great confusion among the faithful by engaging in overt political activity and civil disturbance.[61] Although personally nonviolent, the monks lost control of their movement, resulting in significant acts of hostility on the part of their followers, severely damaging their standing with the people of Vietnam.

In many ways, the radicals failed to move South Vietnamese society, because their message caused perplexity on the part of many Vietnamese. Just as the war produced great confusion for young Americans faced with the contrasting opinions of teachers, prelates and government officials about the importance and validity of the American commitment to South Vietnam, so too did Buddhists in South Vietnam suffer great moral confusion in trying to come to terms with the conflicting messages from authority figures in a culture that remained far more constrained by traditional roles than did the United States. Nevertheless, many teachers like La Thanh Ty, fearful of the impact on their students as future soldiers in the conflict, often led them out of classes to rally against the war.[62]

Yet in the end, challenging the government, the ultimate source of authority in a neo-Confucian society, proved too much for many tradition-bound Vietnamese. Even though the GVN remained illegitimate in usual terms, it retained a certain level of legitimacy because of the nature of Vietnamese society. In a culture that attributed the Mandate of Heaven to government, even the inept Ky regime retained enough authority to confront Buddhist monks who had violated societal norms. While most Vietnamese suffered from extreme war-weariness and held deeply ambivalent feelings about the GVN, many greatly feared the prospect of a Communist victory in South Vietnam.[63]

Many South Vietnamese, moreover, had tired of the continuing turmoil, an embarrassment to a nation claiming to be an alternative to Communist-imposed dictatorship. In addition, the violence that accompanied numerous demonstrations, reports of stockpiles of weapons in pagodas and the outright revolt in I Corps caused many Vietnamese to question the religious justification of the Buddhists; the constant American and GVN refrain that Communists lurked behind the movement aroused suspicion of their motives.[64]

Some Vietnamese, particularly Catholics, condemned the loose organizational structure of Buddhism. They believed that the ease of entry into the Buddhist priesthood and the absence of a formal church hierarchy or organization, comparable to their own church, created opportunities for monks like Thich Tri Quang to launch a movement that threatened the stability of the state.[65] While their organizational and doctrinal flexibility enabled Buddhist leaders to adjust their message and lead the struggle to end the war, when they seemed to go too far, "the natural order was violated and compensatory mechanisms—as natural as gravity or moonlight—redressed the balance."[66]

Unquestionably, support for the Vien Hoa Dao outside of central

Vietnam had slipped during the three-month crisis, due to the constant GVN assertions of Communist involvement and fanaticism. Ky, moreover, did not need the endorsement of the majority of his citizens to retain power; in fact, he never had it. He required only enough backing to provide the appearance of popular support, which he gained from Catholics, right-wing organizations and other non-Communist elements. When the government agreed to hold elections, much of the lay support for the Buddhists evaporated, while many non-Buddhists feared VHD domination of the voting. Hence, the factionalism and regional divisions that plagued South Vietnam from its creation ensured that one group could not gain sufficient power to end the war. At the same time, the consistent anti-Americanism of students in Hue and attacks on U.S. facilities in Hue and Danang also turned many Americans against the Buddhists.[67] Although the vocal minority who argued for Hoa Binh (peace) and Doc Lap (independence) ultimately suffered defeat in their confrontation with the GVN, and though "no one wanted to fight for a dictator," significant support for the war still existed among merchants, Catholics, northern refugees, anti-Communists, right-wing groups and others concerned with the Communist menace.[68]

DETERIORATION OF THE ARVN

The continued use of elite military forces to confront South Vietnamese civilians rather than the NLF contributed to a further erosion of the combat capability of the ARVN. The decline in ARVN effectiveness eventually led to the introduction of more U.S. combat units utilizing increased firepower, leading to greater manifestations of anti-Americanism and expanded civilian casualties. U.S. officials looked upon elite ARVN units as the backbone of the army and the core around which an effective military organization could be fashioned. Even though the United States bore the major cost of training and equipping the ARVN, Ky used ARVN Marines in his failed attempt to liberate Danang, Vietnamese Rangers to break up demonstrations in Nha Trang and ARVN paratroopers to combat students in Saigon.[69] By late April, Lodge disclosed that the war effort had experienced reverses due to the diversion of military assets away from the conflict, but he mainly attributed the setbacks to Communist influences in the disorders.[70]

The most pressing concern for U.S. officials remained the breakdown of discipline in I Corps. The CIA reported on April 16 that ARVN units had become more active in the Struggle Movement and that Dinh's negotiations with the dissidents had granted them a measure of legitimacy they had lacked previously. At the same time, it claimed that ARVN Rangers had joined Struggle groups to act as a police force in the area, often arresting members of other blocs, like the VNQDD and the VNAF, who opposed the movement.[71]

Buddhist chaplains contributed to the decline of combat effectiveness. Soldiers in I Corps often ignored their officers, preferring instead to follow the instructions of their chaplains.[72] Nor did the leadership confine its efforts to central Vietnam. On May 6, MACV reported increased activity on the part of Buddhist chaplains throughout the military. In a talk to soldiers outside of I Corps, Thich Ho Giac suggested that they should consider abandoning the fight since the "objectives of the war are those of [the] U.S. . . . why should Vietnamese soldiers die for such a cause?"[73]

The U.S. position on a return to civilian government remained closely linked to the problem of ARVN deterioration. Although Washington claimed to support the restoration of a nonmilitary regime, it constantly asserted that the South Vietnamese army remained the only power able to hold the country together and carry the fight to the Communists. Yet the ARVN represented an extremely unsettling force, with its constant intrigues, bullying of civilian administrators and propensity to overthrow governments not to its liking. The near collapse of the ARVN in I Corps and its further deterioration throughout the rest of the country undercut any stabilizing impact it might have had and demonstrated the ambivalence many soldiers felt about the war.

NEW CONFRONTATION IN I CORPS

A seeming calm descended on South Vietnam during the first two weeks of May. While other groups dominated the news, Buddhists waited for the GVN to fulfill its pledge for elections for a national assembly.[74] Ky seemed battered from every direction: Buddhists demanded a transition to civilian rule that would most likely end his tenure in office; right-wing groups pressed him to prevent Buddhist domination of the elections; young ARVN officers wanted a firm hand against the Buddhists; and the Americans wanted all of the internal problems to disappear so they could prosecute the war. Most U.S. commentators agreed that Ky's chances for survival seemed slim.

Realizing he had to act to rescue his government, Ky decided to launch a second attack against Danang. On May 7, he set the stage for another assault on Danang when he told journalists that he intended to remain in power for another year.[75] Although he had guaranteed elections by August 15, and an electoral commission stood in session in Saigon at the time to establish procedures for the transition to civilian rule, Ky had again backed away from his promises to the Buddhist leadership.[76] Believing that the population could not endure another year of war, Ky's comments filled Buddhists with dread.[77] In Danang, Dr. Man predicted, "We are in for a bad time."[78]

The next day, Rusk defended Ky, claiming that he had been misquoted.[79] Privately, the secretary of state could not believe that Ky had again inflamed a crisis that could lead to a Buddhist political victory.[80] Lodge, however, supported the new attack on I Corps, since he sensed that the ultimate goal of the Struggle Movement would be an end to the conflict.[81]

Ky recognized he had to attack Danang if he hoped to survive in office. Increasingly written off by the Americans and politically isolated in South Vietnam, he capitalized on growing opposition to the Buddhists and forestalled a possible coup attempt by striking quickly at the Struggle Force. After all, who would want to deal with an out-of-power Ky? As commander of the South Vietnamese Air Force, he would have remained well positioned to overthrow any regime that faltered and would be deeply involved in the ongoing intrigues in Saigon. He understood that if he fell, he would likely be expelled from the country, never to return. Thus, on May 15, he ignored his pledges to the Buddhists and launched a lightning attack on Danang.

What began as a bold gamble for Ky, when he had attacked Danang in

April, had ended in humiliating failure. The Struggle Force's stand, moreover, had demonstrated to the world the weakness of the GVN. Certainly, the legitimacy of the government seemed in greater question than at any time since the fall of Khanh.[82] Yet, the possibility of a Buddhist political victory created allies for Ky. The United States rallied to him despite severe reservations over his impulsive actions. In addition to transporting part of his force to Danang, American officials publicly criticized the Buddhist leadership for upsetting the fragile balance in the GVN and worked to solidify Ky's support among right-wing groups. Buddhist calls for democracy also drove Washington and Saigon closer together. The GVN and the generals who dominated it genuinely feared a popularly elected government, since it might enter into negotiations to end the war. In this, GVN and U.S. attitudes converged so that Washington assisted Saigon's efforts to terminate the democracy movement.

Through it all, the Buddhist hierarchy never lost sight of their ultimate goals: freedom from American domination, peace for South Vietnam and an end to the killing.[83] Moreover, as American peace activist James Forest points out, "had it not been for U.S. intervention at the crucial stage" the Buddhists most likely "would have brought down the military junta" and ended the war.[84]

Although the Vien Hoa Dao did not realize it, their near victory over Ky ensured their destruction as an organized force. Confronted by Catholics, the United States, the GVN and other groups fearful of their popular appeal, the Vien Hoa Dao faced a coalition bent on its destruction. Adding to their plight, their foes could call on the military power of the United States and the GVN to halt the last chance for peace in Vietnam. As FitzGerald points out, "The irony of the American position was now complete." By embracing Ky at the Honolulu Conference, U.S. officials were forced to back his increasingly erratic and impulsive actions against the "biggest popular movement ever to arise out of the Vietnamese cities and [oppose] what they had more or less favored all along—elections and a constitutional civilian government."[85]

Buddhist leaders could not know that their plan to end the war would fail. Their goal of free elections in which a government would come to power with a mandate to negotiate an end to the war would soon be crushed by an alliance of forces dedicated to carrying on the conflict. Despite a valiant effort, the Buddhist hierarchy failed to end the fighting because they spoke for a powerless citizenry, while those arrayed against them held political, military and financial control backed by the United States.

The final chapter in the Buddhist peace effort soon witnessed a military onslaught against the dissidents in I Corps and GVN determination to eradicate the Buddhist threat to continued war. Supported by his new religious and political allies, most ARVN generals, the Baby Turks, a group of field-grade officers increasingly fed up with Ky's unwillingness to confront the Struggle Force in I Corps, and the United States, Ky attacked Danang again in May to forestall Buddhist plans to end the war. At the same time, Ky's resolve to hold onto power brought him into conflict with U.S. Marines in I Corps, while exposing significant levels of hostility between the marines and Westmoreland.

3

Confrontation in Danang:
U.S. Marines and the
Buddhist Struggle Movement

Vietnamese history will never forgive these brutal acts.
—*Hoa Binh,* Interview with General Ton That Dinh

INTRODUCTION: DIFFERENCES IN TACTICS AND
MISSION CONCEPTS BETWEEN III MAF AND MACV

 Buddhist protests in central Vietnam during 1966 placed U.S. forces in an awkward position that, in time, raised serious questions about the U.S. role in South Vietnam and laid bare a simmering debate between U.S. Marines and the U.S. Army over American strategy in the conflict. For the U.S. Marines of the Third Marine Amphibious Force (III MAF), the rebellion in Danang came at a particularly delicate time. In the midst of rounding out their command and control structure in I Corps and initiating new tactics to confront local guerrilla units more effectively, the marines stood at the end of a frustrating year of trying to compel insurgent forces to face American units in open combat while dealing with significant hostility on the part of the local populace. In addition, considerable tension existed between the army-dominated Military Assistance Command, Vietnam (MACV)

71

headquarters in Saigon, led by General William Westmoreland, who functioned as the overall U.S. commander in South Vietnam and exercised authority over all U.S. operations in the country, and the recently created III MAF headquarters in Danang, commanded by Marine Lieutenant General Lewis Walt, who directed all U.S. Marines and other American forces in I Corps and also served as the senior advisor to the Vietnamese I Corps commander.

By 1966, a raging controversy had arisen between MACV and III MAF over the correct tactics and strategy to implement in I Corps, exacerbated by an unwieldy command structure, the firing of Thi, and differences in temperament and personality between the American commanders. Based on their long experience in conducting jungle warfare and combating insurgency in Latin America and Asia, marines insisted that the war could be won only in the villages. Aware that they merely controlled the ground they stood on, marine officers developed the Combined Action Platoon (CAP) program that called for small units of marines and ARVN to live and work beside the villagers in the hope that they could forge bonds with them and deny the insurgents access to the local populace.[1]

Westmoreland, however, demanded that the marines engage in search-and-destroy missions. Marine commanders considered this a waste of manpower that bled the marines by allowing guerrilla units to lure them into a continuous series of small engagements far from the population centers. Despite Westmoreland's later assertions that search-and-destroy would take the war to the enemy and lower civilian casualties, it removed the marines from the villages where they believed the war would be won or lost.[2]

Walt remained keenly aware of the importance of combating the insurgency at the village level. Upon landing at Danang in 1965, the general realized he had to win the loyalty of the local Vietnamese if he wanted to free himself from the danger of mortar attacks on his command and logistics area. From this early effort at self-preservation, he developed a strategy based on close interaction with the local populace. He later argued that captured PAVN (commonly called the North Vietnamese Army during the war) documents alerted marine commanders to a Communist plan to pull U.S. forces away from the inhabited districts, to deprive them of the critical intelligence to be gained there. Marine commanders bristled when they realized Westmoreland's search-and-destroy strategy matched their adversary's goal. Walt claims, moreover, that in his conversations with President Lyndon B. Johnson, he constantly stressed the importance of winning the war in the villages. However, if he convinced the commander in chief, the advice did not filter down to Westmoreland.[3]

Some marines complained that Westmoreland's attrition strategy mainly wore down U.S. forces rather than the enemy, a situation the overextended Americans could barely endure. To compensate for the lack of manpower, U.S. commanders resorted to the one thing they had in abundance—firepower—resulting in more civilian casualties and greater opportunities for the insurgents to condemn the GVN for introducing American forces into the country in the first place. Indeed, American combat operations continued in a constantly downward spiral, while marines rightly condemned Westmoreland for a strategy sure to lead to defeat.

The feud between Walt and Westmoreland, in many ways, betrayed the deep concerns felt by a number of U.S. officers over Westmoreland's flawed attrition strategy, poor leadership qualities, the U.S. role in South Vietnam and the viability of the GVN. Some military leaders embraced the concept of an enclave strategy to lessen casualties and protect the vital urban centers and the U.S. logistic pipeline. Others criticized the use of body counts, the one-year tour, the refusal of civilian authorities to call up the reserves or to mobilize the American public, and excessive civilian control of military operations. Many quietly worried about the prospects for an American victory in Vietnam.

An unwieldy command structure added to the conflict between MACV and III MAF. Westmoreland did not report directly to the Joint Chiefs or to the army chief of staff. Instead, he fell under the control of the commander in chief, Pacific (CINCPAC), a position held by a U.S. Navy admiral. As a result, marine commanders, exploiting their traditional relationship with the navy, often appealed MACV decisions to CINCPAC. The current CINCPAC in 1966, Admiral Ulysses S. Grant Sharp, remained far more familiar with marine doctrines and tactics and tended to favor them in conflicts with MACV. Army and marine commanders also shared operational control with their ARVN counterparts, while no overall command structure supervised military affairs in South

Vietnam. In the words of one high-ranking marine officer, "the lines of command were hopelessly convoluted." Finally, while conflicts between the U.S. Army and the U.S. Marines dated back to World War II, they reached new levels in Vietnam. Marines resented what they perceived to be the haughty West Point attitude of army officers, particularly Westmoreland. They compared their own poverty to the seemingly endless supply train that supported the army, while army personnel bristled over the self-proclaimed marine reputation for toughness and willingness to be "the first to fight."[4]

The personality of General Walt added to the sorry state of affairs. A man who believed to the depth of his being that the United States had to combat Communism at all costs, he enjoyed a close relationship with President Johnson, who awarded him a third star shortly before the Buddhist Crisis started. Walt also had a deeply compassionate side that rebelled against the excessive casualties caused by Westmoreland's flawed strategy of search-and-destroy. His sympathetic side, moreover, led him to develop a fatherly, protective attitude toward his ARVN counterparts, often siding with ARVN officers who opposed Ky and giving them false hope that the United States supported their opposition to the GVN. On the other hand, he frequently exploded in outbursts of temper, relieving commanders on the spot, ignoring the chain of command or overruling subordinates in front of their fellow officers.

Westmoreland seemed the absolute antithesis of Walt. He projected an image of "the cardboard general, always correct in his actions, [and] studiously polite" while expressing constant dissatisfaction with marine operations in South Vietnam. He considered marine units too heavy to carry out counterinsurgency in the countryside, measuring effectiveness by days spent in the field. Marine commanders, on the other hand, believed that Westmoreland was so focused on the American experience in World War II that he exhibited a woeful lack of knowledge of small-unit operations and conditions in Asia.[5]

Walt and Thi, on the other hand, enjoyed a close relationship. Walt liked Thi because of his willingness to fight the enemy, while he saw Ky as "a silky opportunist" disinclined to combat the insurgency. Comparable to many marine officers, Walt's operations officer, Colonel Edwin Simmons, distrusted the South Vietnamese government and felt the "U.S. was trying to pump plasma into the morbid body that was the GVN."

Having been on the scene with American combat troops longer than anyone else, the marines understood the deficiencies of the GVN from first-hand experience, particularly since their men had fought and died to defend a government run by a man most of them held in contempt.[6] When Ky dismissed Thi, Walt viewed it as part of Westmoreland's effort to undermine his command of I Corps.

III MAF AND THE STRUGGLE MOVEMENT

Despite Walt's effort to remain impartial, the Struggle Force soon collided with the massive American presence in I Corps. Not surprisingly, as members of a highly disciplined fighting force legendary for their esprit de corps, many marines expressed disgust at ARVN units engaging in outright rebellion against their government. Marines generally agreed that while they defended South Vietnam, the Vietnamese engaged in endless petty feuds, which added to their outrage. This feeling was exacerbated by the heavy anti-Americanism evident in local demonstrations and radio broadcasts.

On March 26, a marine enlisted man pulled down an anti-American banner displayed in Hue. While this seemed like a minor occurrence at the time, in the larger scheme of things, the reaction of everyone involved exemplified the tense atmosphere in central Vietnam.[7] Ever sensitive to the touchy nationalism of the Vietnamese and cognizant of the need to avoid a fight with the Struggle Movement in Hue, U.S. officials had to balance offending the students against humiliating a young marine for a perfectly understandable action. Buddhist student leader Buu Ton told U.S. officials that he wanted an apology broadcast over Radio Hue, insisting that the marine publicly put the banner back up. Ambassador Lodge vetoed these actions, insisting that "no public spectacle will be made of any U.S. Marine."[8] Despite a private apology by the marine, U.S. officials gave Buu Ton a written guarantee that military officers would do everything possible to prevent similar episodes and promised that the marine would be disciplined.

Nevertheless, there was considerable sympathy for the marine within the American camp. Given that his feeling about the anti-Americanism of the agitators mirrored those of many U.S. officials, they remained reluctant to condemn him for his misdeed. Westmoreland found the apology "a very distasteful action from [his] point of view because of the hotheaded attitude of the student leader who was either intentionally or unwittingly aiding or abetting the VC," pointing out that Buu Ton should be serving in the ARVN. Afterwards, Marine commanders significantly curtailed operations in the Hue area to avoid further confrontations.[9]

The situation escalated in early April when the Struggle Force bottled up Ky's invasion force and would not allow it to move into the city. Facing a difficult and dangerous challenge, Walt used his marines as a buffer between the two forces, hoping to dispose of the problem peacefully while imploring Ky to keep his troops on the air base.[10] Westmoreland, however, wanted the issue settled quickly, ordering Walt to remove U.S. advisors from all dissident ARVN units.[11] Thus, while Walt worked to cool off the adversaries in Danang, Westmoreland drove them to a higher state of frenzy, hoping to end the conflict swiftly.

Walt continued to try to keep the combatants apart. With combat seemingly imminent, he ordered that in the event that fighting broke out between the dissidents and GVN forces, all marines would remain in their quarters or at their posts, traffic (except for extreme emergencies) would be banned from the roads, an utmost effort would be exerted to protect American personnel and facilities, port operations would be suspended and U.S. personnel would not help or halt ARVN units involved in the fray.[12] Two days later, Walt placed two companies of marines on standby for a potential evacuation of U.S. civilians, put ten helicopters on alert for possible deployment, ordered two aircraft to observe Danang at all times, instructed the First and Third Marine Divisions to hold one battalion each on twelve-hour standby and forbade any external patrolling around the air base.[13] He also arranged for the Fourth Marines to establish an observation post along Highway 1 to report on Vietnamese troop movements towards Danang, and for a battalion of the Seventh Marines to establish defensive positions with tanks south of Hue. The same day, the U.S. embassy evacuated all American civilians from Hue and Danang, further straining the overloaded transport capacity of the marines.[14]

Walt's neutrality soon had a major test. On April 9, Colonel Dam Quang Yeu, commanding officer of the Quang Nam Special Sector and a fervent supporter of the Struggle Movement, moved toward Danang with a large force of dissident ARVN troops accompanied by armor and artillery. Walt ordered the new commander of the Ninth Marines, Colonel Simmons, to block their movement. Before his troops could intercept the dissident force, however, VNAF aircraft from Danang attacked the column, prompting a swift request from III MAF that the VNAF refrain from attacks on the rebels, since this could provoke an attack from Yeu's artillery on the marine air base.[15]

When Yeu's force continued toward Danang, Simmons set up a strong defensive position on one end of the Thanh Quit Bridge, nine miles from the airfield, while positioning a stalled truck in the middle of the structure. As the rebel ARVN force approached from the south, Yeu discovered his route into the city blocked and ordered his howitzers to establish firing points aimed at the air base. Walt responded by sending up marine fighter aircraft and directing marine artillery to lock onto the stalled troops. Wanting to prevent a fight between the allied forces, Colonel John R. Chaisson, Walt's new operations officer, exhibiting astounding personal courage, landed in the face of the loaded cannon of the dissidents and met with Yeu.

Chaisson warned the rebel commander that any move against the base would be viewed as an attack on American forces and that he should expect a vigorous response.[16] Finally, rather than risk a fight against the vastly superior firepower of the marines, Yeu wisely removed the artillery, but his troops remained just outside Danang.[17] The irony of the situation weighed heavily on the Americans, since U.S. forces had threatened to attack an allied army to prevent an ARVN attack on U.S. forces.[18] Walt arranged for a hasty meeting between Dinh and Yeu at III MAF headquarters, where the dissident colonel poured out his complaints against the GVN. Afterward, Yeu assured Walt that he would have no more problems with his soldiers.[19]

Concerned with the possibility of further confrontations, Walt bolstered his forces. The III MAF commander ordered U.S. aircraft to observe the approaches to Danang and Hue at all times, while other Marine units were alerted to protect the base.[20] At the same time, marine commanders beefed up security at all of the areas utilized by U.S. troops and reduced external patrolling around the air base to conserve their overextended forces.[21]

The troop movements had serious repercussions for the marines, especially because the use of American forces to prevent a destructive battle between contending ARVN units limited the ability of the marines to keep the guerillas from moving back into the villages around Danang. Indeed, the insurgents did not even have to fight their way in, since U.S. and GVN attention remained riveted on the events in Danang. Thus, by trying to create a fight between the opposing forces, Westmoreland further aided the NLF campaign to win the war in the villages. More importantly, the prolonged absence of U.S. and ARVN forces assisted the insurgents in convincing the local people that they could return at any time, despite the enormous firepower and mobility of the Americans.[22]

ARVN vs Strugglers vs Marines

Having sacrificed the element of surprise in April by announcing his designs in advance, Ky remained determined to avoid the same mistake with his second attack in May. Thus, unlike in April when ARVN leaders had laid out their plans for Westmoreland and Lodge before the assault on Danang, Ky launched his subsequent attack ostensibly with complete surprise. Ky's desire for secrecy meant that he also kept his intentions from III MAF. In fact, he claims that he held his plans so closely guarded that he surprised Marine officers when ARVN forces landed at the air base in May.[23] Nevertheless, he was confident that Lodge and Westmoreland would support him, because they had constantly urged him to resolve the rebellion in I Corps.[24]

On May 15, two battalions each of ARVN Marines and paratroopers, the elite forces of the South Vietnamese Army, landed at Danang early in the morning and quickly moved into the city. They promptly seized I Corps headquarters and soon after captured many other strategic positions in the city.[25] Unsure of Dinh's loyalty, Ky tagged Major General Cao Van Vien, Chief of the Joint General Staff, to lead the attack.

The intrusion of loyal ARVN units into the city caused sporadic fighting to break out in many quarters. Reports of small-arms fire, grenade explosions, and brief engagements poured into the III MAF command center while VNAF aircraft constantly cruised over Danang. By evening, GVN forces had seized the city, except for a number of dissident strong points, setting the stage for more armed conflict in the city.[26] Incensed by the attack, Walt contacted MACV and requested that Ky's forces be directed to vacate the city.[27]

While attempting to keep the contending forces apart, Walt remained far more interested in assigning blame for the ensuing debacle in the middle of his main logistics center. He easily concluded that the culprit was Westmoreland's protégé, Ky. The South Vietnamese prime minister maintained that Walt called his command center and demanded he end the operation. In response, Ky claimed he contacted Lodge and threatened personally to lead a strike against Danang. Ky contended, moreover, that despite Lodge's intervention, he still went to Danang, where he had a tense confrontation with the marine commander, threatening to destroy the American air base if the United States shot down his planes.[28]

On the other hand, Walt claimed that Ky could not adequately explain the attack, seeking refuge in his contrived cover story that loyal troops in the city had begged for help. Nor could Ky explain his reasons for not informing Walt or Dinh of the impending assault on the heart of their rear areas and the most critical military base in the country. In a blistering report to the National Military Command Center (NMCC), Walt stated his "personal opinion that certain factions in Saigon have carefully planned this attack in order to wipe out the Buddhist resistance and opposition. As a result, there is going to be bloodshed and a lot of bitterness among the population in the I Corps area."[29] Walt soon received a call from Washington informing him that that the GVN had complained about his interference in their operations. Upon hearing his explanation, he maintained that his superiors agreed with his actions and supported his moves in I Corps.[30]

The penetration of ARVN elements into the city ensured that more serious conflicts would occur between U.S. Marines and the adversaries battling in Danang. On May 15, several VNAF aircraft strafed ARVN units close to marine sites while VNAF planes buzzed U.S. formations. The III MAF issued a stern injunction to the VNAF to halt the hazardous confrontations, while also warning the VNAF not to attack ARVN columns approaching the city, since American advisors might be put at risk. Ky told Walt to remove the advisors, while also asking the U.S. embassy to explain Walt's orders concerning the conflict in Danang.[31]

Interestingly, the VNAF, commanded by Ky, seemed unconcerned about causing American casualties, while marine aircraft, led by Walt, had to protect marines on the ground from their ARVN allies.

Meanwhile, reports of Americans under fire poured in from around the city. Late on the night of May 16, U.S. Navy Seabees received small-arms fire, causing III MAF to dispatch marine MPs to pick up the sailors.[32] Early in the morning of May 17, Walt's beach house came under fire. At first, III MAF headquarters, thinking Walt was under mortar and small-arms attack, alerted a platoon of U.S. Marines supported by tanks to protect his residence, since he had gone there to spend the night. The mortars turned out to be friendly illumination rounds, but the dispatch of one platoon to patrol the area around Walt's home illustrated the extreme danger to Americans from the fighting in the city.[33]

On May 17 an encounter between U.S. Marines and the Struggle Force became deadly. As the new I Corps commander, Major General Huynh Van Cao, along with Brigadier General Jonas A. Platt, deputy commander of III MAF, and Colonel Archelus Hamblen, senior U.S. Army advisor in I Corps, prepared to lift off in their helicopter from a meeting in Hue, an ARVN officer, Second Lieutenant Nguyen Tai Thuc, fired two rounds at the aircraft from his pistol. The American gunner in the helicopter returned fire, killing Thuc and wounding several others in the crowd. Struggle forces were outraged over the lethal American response, further proof to them of U.S. backing for Ky. Thuc's death created a bitter legacy among many Buddhists who saw him as a martyr to their cause.[34]

The next day more disputes erupted between dissidents and U.S. Marines. The Struggle Force held one end, and ARVN Marines the other, of the Tourane River Bridge that connected Danang and the Tiensha Peninsula (called Danang East by the Marines) and served as the main artery for supplies to III MAF. As ARVN Marines tried to move across the bridge, they received fire from the dissident troops dug in at the other end.[35] The rebels warned the attacking force that they had wired the bridge with explosives set to blow up if any aggressor attempted to force its way across.

Chaisson rushed to the bridge to mediate the dispute and save the vital crossing for the marines. Directing his marines to replace the ARVN force on one end of the structure, he flew in his helicopter to the other side to negotiate with the dissident commander. Despite the insurgents' refusal to abandon their post, Chaisson ordered his heavily armed men to seize the other end of the structure. The Americans took the position without a fight, but the situation had been particularly scary since the marines had exposed themselves to potentially withering fire as they rushed across the bridge.[36]

Walt and Chaisson later confronted the rebel commander on the bridge and demanded he move his force. The dissident leader, however, gave the signal to blow up the bridge, telling Walt, "General, we will die on this bridge together." Fortunately for Walt and Chaisson, an American officer had climbed under the superstructure and disconnected the explosives.[37] As Walt recounted it, "there was no doubt that he (the Vietnamese officer) expected the bridge to blow on his signal. I shall never forget the expression on his face when his signal did not blow up the bridge and us with it."[38] When the device failed to detonate, the dissidents' will collapsed along with their defensive positions. The seizure of the bridge by U.S. Marines also ensured the defeat of the dissident forces, given that Yeu's substantial reinforcements could no longer move into the city to contest the ARVN Marines.[39]

After the latest flare-up, Walt took added precautions to safeguard U.S. resources. He deployed a marine rifle company to Danang to protect III MAF headquarters and ordered the dispersal of U.S. aircraft to other airfields in the area, again robbing American forces of critical assets to fight the insurgency.[40] Combined with the placement of USMC tanks around the airfield and at major crossroads leading into the city, the new dispositions further ate away at the already overstrained capacity of the marines to fight in the countryside and prevent a complete meltdown within the city.[41]

Tension among the Marines remained very high. On May 19 a report that ARVN Rangers had been observed moving toward the III MAF headquarters put the command center on alert while harried Marine officers attempted to discover their intentions.[42] The same day, Third Marine Division headquarters received a warning in English over its own tactical net: "We are Vietnamese airborne. We are ready to mortar the air base you know."[43] On May 20, Walt moved a full battalion of marines from Chu Lai to Danang to protect U.S. facilities in the city.[44]

The presence of rebel forces in Danang East soon led to more difficulties between the insurgents and American marines. The dissident commander, Captain Dinh Tan Thanh, threatened to destroy the ammunition dump if attacked by loyalist forces. While the loss of the ammunition had the potential to wreak havoc on marine operations, detonating the explosives could have caused severe damage and extensive casualties in the city among Vietnamese and American forces and the civilian population. In response, Walt moved a battalion of marines to the III MAF headquarters to act as a ready reserve in case the dump had to be seized by force. After three days of tense negotiations, marines took control of the facility on May 23.[45]

Allegedly unaware of the continuing movement of American marines into Struggle Force positions, VNAF forces launched a series of strikes against the marines. On May 21, VNAF aircraft attacked a marine placement with cannon and rockets, wounding eight marines, two seriously. Thus, VNAF planes utilized the huge American airbase to launch repeated attacks on rebel and U.S. Marine positions while their base received protection from the very marines being wounded by VNAF strikes.[46]

That the VNAF remained under the command of Westmoreland's proxy, Ky, drove Walt to greater fury. Warning the local VNAF commander that another assault would result in a marine attack on the VNAF planes, Walt commanded marine aircraft to circle over the VNAF aircraft that had remained aloft after attacking the marines. Upon learning of this action, the VNAF commander sent up more fighters to fly over the marine planes, further enraging Walt, who then ordered more U.S. aircraft to hover over the VNAF formation. Walt fumed in his headquarters for over an hour "with two phones in my hands—one to the Marine Air Commander and the other to the Vietnamese Air Commander. I kept warning the Vietnamese Commander that if his planes fired one round, one rocket or dropped one bomb we would shoot all of his planes out of the sky."[47]

Finally, after more stern warnings from Walt, the VNAF commander backed down and averted further bloodshed that day.[48] Nevertheless, Walt instructed the marine air wing to keep two fighters orbiting over Danang at all times, two on the airstrip with pilots in them ready to go at an instant's notice and another two to remain on five-minute standby. The aircraft on the ground, moreover, received orders to launch whenever

VNAF planes took off, to ensure they did not attack U.S. positions.[49] Yet the danger for the marines did not end there. The same day, dissident units, aiming at the airfield to retaliate against the VNAF aircraft that had attacked them, wounded two U.S. airmen and mortared marine positions at III MAF headquarters, leading to eight more marines wounded.[50] On the twenty-third, Struggle forces collapsed, and the city fell to ARVN units. For the marines, at least, the war inside Danang had ended, but the cost remained high—150 Vietnamese killed along with 700 wounded and 23 American wounded.[51]

WESTMORELAND'S RESPONSE

Unlike Walt, Westmoreland had the luxury of observing events in I Corps from afar. From March to June, however, the agitation in I Corps occupied more and more of his time. Westmoreland claims he kept a close eye on the Buddhist Crisis of 1966, since it could drastically affect U.S. operations in the country, a statement confirmed by the documentary record. However, Westmoreland could not admit that the demonstrators might have legitimate complaints. Instead he assumed they must be under Communist domination. On March 23, he received reinforcement from his deputy commander, Lieutenant General John A. Heintges, who argued that the GVN should come down hard on the student demonstrators, since "these young punks up there are doing as much damage to the overall cause in this country as the VC."[52] The next day, Westmoreland reminded Lieutenant General Nguyen Huu Co, deputy premier and defense minister of the GVN, that a number of students had draft deferments, implying that the time had come to lift their exemptions. Although Co promised Westmoreland that the GVN would force the student leadership into the army as soon as the crisis passed, Westmoreland despaired of the possibility of GVN action against the students.[53]

Unable to get the demonstrators drafted, Westmoreland tried to convince the GVN that the students followed the NLF. In a conversation with Co, he warned darkly that Communist forces in "four columns [were] marching into Quang Tri and Thua Thien Provinces . . . [while] fifth column activities [were] rampant in Danang and Hue." At the same time he reminded Co of the high level of American casualties and speculated on their impact on American public attitudes toward the war, again demanding that the GVN revoke the deferments of the students and draft them into the army. Westmoreland reported that his words had a strong impact on Co, who promised to relay his statements to other members of the GVN.[54]

Westmoreland also sought to sway his fellow Americans. He pointed out to Lodge that "228 Americans had died in the I Corps region fighting for South Vietnam during the three weeks that this 'foolishness' . . . had been going on, and the American people were bound to be upset."[55] When Westmoreland learned of Ky's plans for an attack in April, he warned Walt to stay out of the fray. Simultaneously, he expressed satisfaction with Ky's actions, while hoping the GVN would accomplish its goal.[56]

Unsatisfied with the reporting from III MAF, Westmoreland sent Brigadier General John F. Freund to I Corps to advise Walt and report back to MACV. Westmoreland instructed Freund to do everything "possible to put the struggle forces in a bad light by blaming the entire situation in I Corps on the group of young hotheaded students, emphasizing the suffering by the merchants, the increase in prices, the shortage of gasoline and food, and other problems resulting from the virtual closing down of the city." He further urged him to use American advisors to encourage dissident troops to rejoin their outfits.[57]

Westmoreland left Saigon on May 12 for meetings in Hawaii and did not return until May 20, with the GVN suppression of the Struggle Movement well under way. While claiming it was a coincidence that Ky's attack occurred while he and Lodge were out of the country, he initially decided to remain in Hawaii rather than rush back to Saigon, clearly indicating that he wanted the rebels destroyed before he returned. The next day, General Earle Wheeler, chairman of the Joint Chiefs of Staff, ordered Westmoreland back as soon as possible.[58]

Upon his return and under intense pressure from Wheeler, Westmoreland decided to end the agitation in Danang. While he had urged Walt to remain neutral, he now advocated all-out support for the GVN, including a psychological warfare campaign to woo dissident soldiers back to ARVN, seizure of ammunition and petroleum stocks in I Corps, establishment of food kitchens for Vietnamese suffering from hunger due to the breakdown in port operations, and guidance and support for the GVN.[59] With Westmoreland back in the country and exercising greater scrutiny over his actions, the III MAF commander had to abandon his former neutrality and support the GVN, no matter how distasteful he found his orders. The rebels collapsed, however, before Westmoreland could put any more of his plans into action.

Westmoreland expressed pleasure at the outcome. While admitting that the "American public sending its sons to die in Vietnam saw these events in Danang and Hue as distressing," he viewed the continuing strife in the country as unavoidable and part of the growth process of any new nation.[60]

New and Old Leadership in I Corps

The day after his attack on Danang, Ky chose a new chief for I Corps, Major General Huynh Van Cao, Ky's minister of psychological warfare and a Catholic who had served as IV Corps commander during the Diem regime. Although Cao was generally disliked in central Vietnam and extremely reluctant to accept his new assignment, Ky brushed aside his attempts to decline the new post.[61] Westmoreland, however, expressed dismay over the replacement of Dinh with Cao, because he considered the new commander of I Corps unsuited for the critical task assigned him.[62]

By mid May, Dinh had demonstrated a distressing level of independence from the GVN. Realizing that a reluctance to fight for American war aims underlay much of the ARVN support for the Struggle Movement, he had refused to order South Vietnamese units to return to their previous level of combat.[63] Although he had received hearty endorsements from Lodge and Westmoreland for the job in central Vietnam because of his former willingness to move against the Buddhists, he had also learned when he arrived in I Corps that Walt wielded ultimate power in I Corps and that great animosity existed between Walt and Westmoreland.[64]

As April wore on and his isolation increased, Dinh established tentative contacts with the Struggle Movement. His complete break with the GVN and move to the dissidents in Hue occurred when Ky attacked Danang. Upon learning that Dinh had gone over to the rebels, Westmoreland demanded that Ky remove him from Hue, where he had sought refuge. Ky responded by blaming the imbroglio on Walt: "Let me tell you frankly that this was the fault of your American commander. He supported Mr. Dinh or told him that the Americans were strongly behind him, and this caused difficulties."[65] Still smarting from Westmoreland's support for Thi's dismissal and determined to exact revenge, Walt "closed his eyes and let Gen. Dinh make life difficult for Thieu and Ky" and Westmoreland and Lodge. Unfortunately for Dinh, he misunderstood Walt's actions, believing them to be an expression of support by the Americans.[66]

Ky, however, remained determined to rid himself of the mercurial Dinh. After Ky decided to fire Dinh, Co called Heintges to inform him that Dinh had been dismissed. Co acknowledged that Walt would disagree with the decision, but he argued that the marine commander remained unaware of conditions in I Corps. The next day, Dinh still had not received official confirmation of his dismissal, but the GVN labeled him a dissident anyway when he refused Vien's order to report to I Corps headquarters. When Co expressed concern that Walt would not recognize a new commander for the area and continue to support Dinh, Heintges pointed out that Walt rightly supported the official head of I Corps until notified that a change of command had been ordered by the GVN.[67]

Despite Dinh's efforts to resolve the explosive situation in I Corps, he realized that Ky's attack would also sweep him up along with the Struggle Force. During an interview in 1972 with *Hoa Binh* (Peace), a South Vietnamese newspaper that followed a moderate Catholic line, Dinh discussed the fateful day Ky sent his forces crashing into the middle of his headquarters. Discovering the evening before that an ARVN attacking force was approaching Danang by air, he tried to determine their intentions but could not communicate with the air base. The next morning, after ARVN Marines and paratroopers had launched their invasion of Danang, Dinh frantically called Walt, who "said he did not know what was going on . . . but it seems that it's unfavorable for I Corps and especially for the Corps Commander."[68]

Frustrated with the lack of information from MACV, Walt decided to circumvent the chain of command. He invited Dinh to his office and suggested they call the U.S. secretary of defense to find out who had authorized the raid on their major logistics and operational base. Upon reaching McNamara, Walt asked whether the operation against Danang had been sanctioned by the U.S. government or had been the work of Westmoreland. Dinh reported, "Suddenly I heard General Walt raise his voice: 'That's something I can't accept even if it's you, Mr. Secretary, who are saying it. I don't approve of the nature of this operation. This is why I'm determined not to let the American Marines in Danang get involved in this.'"[69] Walt then put Dinh on the line. McNamara assured Dinh that the attack on Danang had not been aimed at him and would not be expanded past Danang. While McNamara demonstrated an amazing amount of knowledge about an operation for which U.S. leaders claimed they had no forewarning, his assurances failed to soothe Dinh, who told him that Americans were involved in the attack on the Struggle Movement.

Philip Habib, an officer in the U.S. embassy in Saigon, later confirmed Dinh's suspicions. He told Dinh that the United States wanted the agitation ended and planned to see the termination of the Struggle Movement through to the end, assuring Dinh that President Johnson had given the go-ahead for the attack on Danang.[70] Suddenly, the reason for Lodge's and Westmoreland's absence during the assault became clear; Washington could claim plausible deniability while Ky destroyed the Struggle Movement.[71]

Walt had every reason to resent Westmoreland's and Lodge's actions. By encouraging Ky to subdue the dissidents with violence, they had placed him in an impossible position and endangered numerous American and Vietnamese lives. In addition, the extent of disruption in the center of the most critical tactical area in the country seems almost criminal in retrospect. To Walt, it represented another example of Westmoreland's interference.

Walt did not really care why Ky had invaded Danang. It remained in his Tactical Area of Responsibility (TAOR) and therefore fell under his control. He told Dinh he suspected Westmoreland had been behind the attack: "These plans of action, General Walt himself said, were [carried out] under the secret orders of Americans, in particular of General Westmoreland, which had been issued to General Ky." Walt went on to confide to Dinh that he "had intercepted secret orders and this is why he had told me to be on guard." Dinh now saw Walt's actions as part of a stance where he ostensibly followed instructions from MACV but then worked to undermine Westmoreland.[72]

Dinh had heard enough for one day. Having fled to Walt's headquarters earlier in the morning while being chased by Vietnamese armor, he now wanted out of Danang.[73] Walt agreed, pointing out that ARVN units had already tried to kill the I Corps commander.[74] As a result, Walt granted Dinh asylum until he fled Danang in the marine commander's helicopter to the relative safety of the rebellious First ARVN Division in Hue.[75] Before leaving, Dinh told Walt, "Vietnamese history will never forgive these brutal acts. And I'm sure that Americans with [a] conscience will be angry because the weapons that the U.S. has supplied to be used against the Communists are being used to shoot at innocent civilians."[76]

Adding to the chaotic situation in Danang, Dinh's successor quickly demonstrated an inability to perform his duties. Cao's nerve broke when Loan ordered the higher-ranking Cao to attack the pagodas where the remainder of the dissidents had taken refuge, while another ARVN officer held a gun to Cao's head, threatening to shoot him if he refused.[77] Colonel Hamblen happened upon the scene and rushed the terrified I Corps commander out of the room, perhaps sparing Cao from a summary execution.[78]

On May 18, Cao requested asylum in Walt's military compound. Efforts to entice him to leave III MAF headquarters or assume his duties failed.[79] Claiming that Loan threatened to kill him if he did not attack the Tinh Hoi and Pho Da pagodas in Danang, Cao called Ky and reminded him that Cao's parents lived in Hue and that a direct attack on the pagodas could lead to retaliation against Catholics all over the country. Ky expressed surprise over Loan's role and promised an investigation.[80] The next morning, Ky flew to I Corps headquarters and promised Cao extra troops to ensure his protection. By this point, convinced of a plot to kill him and too paralyzed by fear to perform his duties, Cao declined and expressed his desire to stay at III MAF headquarters, protected by Walt and his marines.[81] Ky then appointed Brigadier General Du Quoc Dong, commander of the paratroopers, to carry the fight to the rebels.[82] The collapse of the Struggle Movement in Danang, however, quickly robbed Walt of his ability to defy Ky and Westmoreland by allowing their adversaries to stay in his area.

In the spring of 1966, two rebellions had occurred simultaneously in I Corps. While the Struggle Force challenged the GVN, U.S. Marines chafed under what they considered a ruinous strategy in South Vietnam. Adding to the strained relationship between the two commands, Westmoreland favored Ky in his confrontation with the Struggle Movement while Walt remained loyal to Thi, and later Dinh, and was reluctant to move forcefully against either.

In the process, one of the strangest series of events in the history of the Vietnam War unfolded when the prime minister of one of America's closest allies launched an attack against the main operational and logistics base of III MAF without notifying Walt or any of his subordinates. Eventually, a triangular conflict arose between the Struggle Movement and its ARVN allies, ARVN units loyal to the GVN, and U.S. Marines in the I Corps area, exacerbated by considerable hostility between Walt and Westmoreland. The growing upheaval had a significant impact on marine operations in the countryside, while the efforts of the Struggle Movement to resist ARVN incursions into Danang eventually forced a number of confrontations with III MAF, an organization inclined to support the dissidents due to its own disenchantment with MACV.[83] Ky and Westmoreland smashed the Buddhist revolt because both men remained determined to quash the rebellions within their organizations and continue the war.

The fighting in Danang had a serious impact on all concerned. While the defeat of the Struggle Movement cleared the way for the GVN to continue the war, it also exerted a great effect on the confidence of U.S. Marine officers and enlisted men, who saw their ally tearing itself apart. When Simmons observed the bitter internecine strife in I Corps, he realized that the United States would not prevail in Vietnam, due to the internal tensions at work in the country. At the same time, "there was disgust and bitterness on the part of individual American soldiers and Marines" over the near civil war in I Corps. Like the American people back home, marines asked themselves "what the hell is going on," adding to the pervasive feeling that the task of fighting the war had fallen completely on their shoulders.[84] Marine Lieutenant Philip Caputo, who witnessed much of the fighting in Danang, later insisted, "I knew then that we could never win . . . To go on with the war would be folly—worse than folly: it would be a crime, murder on a mass scale."[85] Earle Wheeler, chairman of the Joint Chiefs, reasoned that "we must recognize that we have lost irretrievably and for all time some of the support which until now we have received from the American people. In other words, regardless of what happens of a favorable nature, many people will never again believe that the effort and the sacrifices are worthwhile."[86]

For III MAF and MACV, the events of 1966 set the stage for a full-blown fight over American strategy two years later. During the Tet Offensive of 1968, relations between the two commands reached a new low as they fought over issues like the defense of Khe Sanh, the relief of Lang Vei and MACV control of marine air assets. These, however, seemed mild compared with the recriminations that followed the American defeat in Vietnam and the efforts of both services to assign blame for the U.S. failure in South Vietnam.

The agitation in I Corps also caused a dramatic drop in combat operations, a situation sure to benefit the insurgency. On another level, the movement of marines to the city to protect American installations, replace missing ARVN units usually assigned to defensive positions and to stand ready to intervene if the fighting involved Americans, significantly degraded marine efforts to pacify the countryside.[87] The outbreak of fighting had an even greater influence on CAP operations in I Corps, since resupply was limited by the conflict in Danang, while medical treatment for villagers, an important component of the pacification effort, also tailed off.[88]

Many historians and commentators have questioned why the insurgents did not become more entangled in the Struggle Movement. Others assert that the NLF controlled and drove the movement. Yet the NLF understood, like Walt and the marines, that at that point in the war the conflict would be won in the villages, not in the cities. While the guerrillas remained committed to an urban uprising, they made sure they secured the vital lifeline with the people, while the marines tried to keep the peace between contending ARVN forces.

American officials saw the low level of attacks during this period as evidence that the NLF did not take advantage of the disorder in central Vietnam. The insurgents did not need to attack, however, since they could operate in many areas of I Corps with complete impunity after many ARVN and U.S. Marine formations had moved to the city. In many ways, the three-month respite granted by the contending forces in I Corps allowed NLF and PAVN units time to recover from the initial shock of confronting the awesome military power of the United States while re-establishing their control of the villages. At the same time, PAVN units also took advantage of the absence of the marines to increase infiltration across the DMZ into South Vietnam, leading to heavy combat in the ensuing months.[89] Although the Struggle Movement had not been controlled or heavily influenced by the NLF, GVN repression drove some members to join the insurrection and, of course, kill more young Americans.[90]

Lodge expressed satisfaction with Ky's handling of the crisis. Relieved that they had avoided a potentially disastrous collapse in I Corps, Lodge and Westmoreland sensed the vulnerability of the Buddhists and pushed Ky to finish them off.[91] Thus, Ky had not only survived the challenge to his rule, but also emerged with increased confidence in U.S. support for his final assault on the Struggle Movement in Hue and Saigon. The fighting in I Corps, however, also had an enormous impact on American public opinion and congressional attitudes toward the war and contributed to the pall of depression that had descended on members of the Johnson administration. Although Buddhist-inspired instability had once more allowed American officials to gain a greater hold on the GVN and force it to continue the war, Ky's "victory" also allowed U.S. officials to continue pursuing a strategy some had begun to question seriously.

4

American Reassessment of Its Role in South Vietnam

It's damned easy to get in a war but it's gonna be awfully hard
to extricate yourself if you get in.
—President Lyndon B. Johnson to McGeorge Bundy

 Throughout the Vietnam War, Washington constantly affirmed its support for representative government in South Vietnam. The United States, however, never could complete the process, for fear that exposing popular attitudes could terminate the American position in South Vietnam. Washington followed a consistent course during the war: despite their rhetoric about the need for elections in South Vietnam, American representatives consistently urged GVN leaders to choose order over democracy. Nevertheless, the United States remained committed to a return to civilian government, since the existence of the military dictatorship proved increasingly embarrassing as it attempted, with growing frustration, to convince people around the world that it followed the aspirations of the Vietnamese populace in resisting the Communist threat.[1]

Vietnamese opposition to U.S. intervention in the spring of 1966, moreover, sparked feelings of resentment, outrage and consternation on the part of American leaders, rather than a desire to move South Vietnam toward self-determination.[2] The U.S. response to the agitation in central Vietnam spoke volumes about how it viewed itself in South Vietnam. Washington engaged in a painful reassessment of the U.S. position in South Vietnam while calling on all American personnel to maintain low profiles, acknowledging that its very presence in the country constituted an affront to Vietnamese nationalism.[3] Further increasing the distress of American officials, Vietnamese marchers often chanted "Da Dao My! [Down with Americans!]" as they paraded past the U.S. embassy in Saigon,[4] while the constant anti-American rhetoric put out by the Hue radio station particularly troubled U.S. officials.[5]

Furthermore, resentment over Vietnamese ingratitude, fear of a Buddhist political victory and Cold War ideology prevented American leaders from seizing an opening to escape from Vietnam in 1966. Even though U.S. leaders repeatedly expressed their resolve to press on in South Vietnam, the agitation in central Vietnam during the spring of 1966 presented an opportunity for the United States to disengage from its disastrous commitment to the GVN because of growing opposition to the war in the United States. While the antiwar movement had entered its early stages at this point, the recent self-immolation of two American antiwar advocates, the emergence of the teach-in movement and growing unrest on college campuses gave powerful indications of the spreading anger in America over Johnson's policies. Increasing draft calls particularly drove the growth of the emerging antiwar faction.[6]

AMERICAN ATTITUDES TOWARD THE UPHEAVAL IN SOUTH VIETNAM

According to journalist Stanley Karnow, the continuing disorder in South Vietnam shocked U.S. personnel in the American mission, who believed that their clients were insufficiently grateful for U.S. actions on their behalf. Karnow described the connection between the United States and the GVN as a parent/adolescent relationship, wherein Vietnamese leaders constantly rebelled against the domination of the United States, leading to astonishing levels of frustration among U.S. officials who could not understand why the Vietnamese insisted on waging internal battles rather than focus on the fight against the insurgency.[7]

American indignation did not remain confined to Saigon. President

Johnson demanded answers from his subordinates for the anarchy in I Corps, bombarding the White House Situation Room with requests for the most recent information from South Vietnam.[8] He directed Secretary Rusk to tell Ambassador Lodge that the continuous turmoil in the country could negate any of the positive aspects of U.S. aid to South Vietnam.[9] Rusk, Johnson, and the American embassy clearly did not recognize that many Vietnamese felt a greater need to be saved from the U.S. military than from the NLF or the DRV.

Even though U.S. policy makers remained torn over their approach to the unrest in South Vietnam and wanted to appear impartial, they needed ARVN to retain power, because civilian governments invariably sought an accommodation with the NLF. Hence, ignoring Rusk's pleas to refrain from taking sides, Lodge provided transport to move Ky's troops to Danang on April 5, which served as additional proof to many Vietnamese of the destruction of their sovereignty that accompanied U.S. actions in South Vietnam.[10] Lodge's action remained crucial to Ky's survival since, as George Kahin points out, American aircraft flying to and from U.S. air bases enabled Ky to move his troops from one American-protected enclave to another, while the presence of the airfield in Danang, guarded by U.S. Marines, allowed Ky to establish a base in the middle of the dissident stronghold from which he could strike at the rebels in I Corps.[11]

Rusk found ways to rationalize Lodge's actions. Despite his injunction to the ambassador not to assist the GVN, he congratulated Lodge on the embassy press release claiming that the United States had ferried troops to Danang to defend South Vietnam. He implored the ambassador, however, to prevent Ky from making any more inflammatory statements about I Corps being in the hands of Communists or about shooting the mayor of Danang.[12]

Buddhist leaders never forgave the United States for supporting Ky. Lodge's decision seemed a particularly sinister betrayal, given that they believed in his evenhandedness based on their experience with him in 1963. Thus, the agitation took on greater anti-American overtones, which created even stronger feelings among American leaders that the Vietnamese failed to appreciate the tremendous sacrifices being made on their behalf.[13]

Despite their concerns about appearing to take sides, American officials continued to make public statements that indicated more interference in South Vietnamese affairs. After Ky's retreat from Danang, Washington attempted to widen the spilt between Thich Tam Chau and Thich Tri Quang with a spirited and public attack on the latter. In an amazing display of frustration, a Johnson spokesman openly attacked Thich Tri Quang as a political opportunist who wanted to control subsequent South Vietnamese governments.[14]

Though some U.S. officials had resented Thich Tri Quang and the radical Buddhists since 1964, the agitation of 1966 increased their hatred of the Buddhists. The main Buddhist demonizers included Walt Rostow, Johnson's recently appointed national security advisor, Lodge, Maxwell Taylor, and, most importantly, Johnson himself. All four men had a huge personal stake in the outcome of the crisis in central Vietnam. Rostow, new to his position, wanted to establish his credibility with the president, while the Buddhist upheavals in South Vietnam had driven Lodge and Taylor to distraction. Johnson, on the other hand, feared the destruction of his beloved Great Society and a repetition of the domestic political bloodbath that had occurred in the 1950s over "the loss of China."

Rostow knew how to ensure a powerful American reaction against the Vien Hoa Dao. In a memo to Rusk and Secretary of Defense Robert S. McNamara on April 9, he characterized the Buddhist movement as "a classic revolutionary situation—like Paris in 1789 and St. Petersburg in 1917," arguing that Thich Tri Quang and his followers had to be curbed even if it meant the use of American forces.[15] The employment of Communist imagery worked well in exploiting Johnson's dread of a Communist victory in South Vietnam. Lodge and Rostow's ability to manipulate the deep-seated fears of U.S. officials by casting the Vien Hoa Dao as Communist-controlled or dominated retarded the ability of American policy makers to rationally judge events in South Vietnam. Instead, they usually reacted emotionally, making critical decisions more on the basis of illogical fears than on coherent thinking.

Taylor joined Rostow in calling for war against the Buddhists. At one point, Taylor advocated eliminating Thich Tri Quang in the political sphere, arguing that Washington and Saigon should expose the Buddhist leader's Communist connections.[16] Taylor soon advised the president that a "'whiff of grapeshot' . . . may be necessary . . . if the . . . [GVN] is to survive." He called for police raids on pagodas to prove Communist complicity in the movement and for a reasonable utilization of power against the Buddhists.[17] Taylor's memo struck a responsive chord with the president, who phoned Rostow demanding to know if American officials had followed Taylor's suggestions.[18] Thus, Johnson's inclination to use violence against the Buddhists received legitimation from his hawkish advisors. Rusk argued against force, insisting that GVN brutality would impel many Buddhists to join the insurgency. At the same time, he implored Lodge to prevent Ky from launching another attack on Danang that could seriously damage the U.S. position in South Vietnam.[19]

Fearful that the Vien Hoa Dao would use elections to seize power, Lodge desperately sought ways to dilute their political strength since he saw the month-long struggle as "a naked grab for power." Realizing that a full-scale onslaught against the dissidents in Danang might create a public-relations disaster for the United States, he instead advocated moderate but forceful action to end the Buddhist agitation.[20] American policy toward the Buddhists called for the GVN to allow some movement in the political sphere while cracking down on violent demonstrations, a process it hoped would preserve the Directory and cement groups like Catholics to the GVN.[21]

EARLY MISGIVINGS—JANUARY/FEBRUARY 1966

Late in 1965, Johnson responded to growing reservations in the United States about the war. During Christmas, he approved a bombing halt and initiated a "peace offensive," in part to cover a planned escalation of the war and convince an increasingly skeptical Congress and American public that the United States had not foreclosed the possibility of talks with the Communists.[22] Reacting angrily to the DRV's refusal to negotiate on American terms and agreeing with those who feared the impact of increased infiltration by PAVN forces, however, Johnson resumed and escalated the air offensive on January 31, 1966.[23]

J. William Fulbright, Arkansas Democrat and chairman of the Senate Foreign Relations Committee (SFRC), responded furiously to the decision to renew the bombing. Convinced that the administration remained a "prisoner of the Munich analogy," he held hearings on the war in early February. The hearings became high drama as Fulbright and some members of the SFRC attacked U.S. policy in Vietnam before a national television audience. When Rusk appeared before the committee, he and Fulbright clashed in a heated exchange that riveted public attention and raised awareness that sober, mature people also opposed U.S. actions in Vietnam.[24] The most dramatic testimony came from the so-called father of containment, George Kennan, who questioned American involvement in Vietnam, arguing that the conflict seemed peripheral to American interests in the region.[25]

The president agonized over the hearings. Always wanting to limit discussion on the war, Johnson sensed that publicity about congressional skepticism could increase opposition to his policies. Johnson had become ensnared in a prison he had constructed because of his fear of the political damage that would result from any move to disengage from Vietnam. In addition, he believed that the conflict in Vietnam represented an assault on his masculinity and America's status as a great power.[26] The hearings worried him so much that he arranged a hasty meeting in Honolulu with South Vietnamese officials to distract public attention, appealed to the head of CBS to take the Senate proceedings off the air, had Fulbright and other members placed under FBI surveillance and asked FBI head J. Edgar Hoover to determine if members of the SFRC had received Communist support.[27]

The SFRC hearings and increased popular demands for a reassessment of U.S. policy in Vietnam also influenced American public opinion. At the end of February, White House Press Secretary Bill Moyers informed Johnson that his approval rating on the war had plunged 14 percentage points between January 26 and February 26.[28] While support for the war still remained relatively high, the hearings had raised important concerns about Vietnam and legitimized opposition to the conflict.[29] Recent peace moves by the administration and its emphasis on elections in South Vietnam also left many business leaders uncertain how Washington could seek peace with the Communists while increasing troop levels and appropriations for the war. Some asked, "Why don't we get out now, if all we are going to have is elections which the Commies will win?"[30]

Even before the onset of the Buddhist Crisis, some administration officials sought to avoid the impending quagmire of Vietnam. In his 1995 memoirs, McNamara admits that he had grave doubts about the war by late 1965 and became convinced that the United States could not win. He was not alone. Former National Security Council (NSC) staffer Chester Cooper claims that McNamara and his closest associate, John McNaughton, assistant secretary of defense for international security affairs, both questioned the ability of American forces to prevail. Realizing that the policy of graduated pressure had failed, McNamara forecast that the United States could be in the same stalemated position three years later. Thus, he considered the possibility of the U.S. opening talks with the Communists.[31]

With Johnson coming under increasing fire from critics, one wonders what the outcome would have been had McNamara and McNaughton confronted him with their growing disillusionment over the war. As David Halberstam points out, however, the president had become so angry about the growing antiwar criticism in the country that by early 1966 pessimists or doubters lost access to Johnson.[32] Thus, McNaughton, like McNamara, held his questions so closely that they came as a great surprise to officials who searched through his files after his untimely death in a plane crash the following year.[33]

On January 19, McNaughton penned a perceptive and thoughtful memo in which he argued, "Vietnam 1966 is not Cuba 1962." One of the original architects of U.S. policy in Vietnam, McNaughton had left Harvard Law School to become McNamara's assistant and most loyal subordinate.[34] He reasoned that the tough stand taken by President John F. Kennedy during the Cuban Missile Crisis properly reflected America's vital interests in the region, as opposed to the peripheral concerns of the Soviets, and that the close proximity to its soil allowed the United States to easily establish military dominance. He maintained, however, that the United States did not have vital interests in Vietnam and had overestimated its ability to project power in the area. Thus, he argued, the United States had "in Vietnam the ingredient of an enormous miscalculation."[35]

To McNaughton, the reasons for U.S. entry into the conflict no longer seemed important. He insisted that avoiding humiliation had become the main rationale for the U.S. presence in Vietnam, suggesting that the only remaining justification for the American commitment to the GVN was demonstrating American credibility in the international realm. Arguing that Washington had entered into a mounting armed impasse, he admitted that the United States probably would not prevail in the conflict, asserting that it did not have to defeat the NLF to salvage its honor. Hence, the creation of a coalition or neutralist government in Saigon, or even a decision by the GVN to seek an accommodation with the Communists, would not constitute an American defeat.[36]

On the other hand, he maintained that an increasingly exhausted GVN and ARVN showed little prospect of carrying on without U.S. help. The problem, he contended, derived from the U.S. refusal to recognize legitimate Communist complaints about GVN and American actions in Vietnam, leading to an inflexible American posture that precluded attempts to find peace. Because the stalemate in Vietnam had escalated beyond a reasonable level, he suggested that the U.S. push for talks between the contending parties while adopting an enclave strategy, wherein U.S. troops would only protect large cities and essential military bases, to lessen casualties and protect the vital urban centers of South Vietnam. He concluded that Vietnam represented only one facet of the U.S. effort to confront Communist China and that an end to the fighting through negotiations should be seen in the broader context of the wider struggle in Asia that would likely occupy the United States for the next two decades.[37]

McNaughton was not alone in perceiving the American dilemma in Vietnam. In the spring of 1966, Moyers, Undersecretary of State George Ball, McNamara, Johnson's close friend and confidant Clark Clifford, Assistant Secretary of State for East Asian and Pacific Affairs William Bundy and Johnson's aide Jack Valenti all harbored serious doubts.[38] More importantly, although not a majority in the administration, they still retained much influence with the president. Arrayed against them were Johnson, Rusk, Rostow (who also advocated talks with the NLF), Taylor and Lodge. But given Rusk's nonconfrontational style and tendency to defer to McNamara, Rostow's newness on the job, Taylor's waning influence after his stint as ambassador to South Vietnam and Lodge's distance from the scene, a strong move from the doubters might have been able to end the war.[39]

ROUND ONE—MARCH/APRIL 1966

After the outbreak of the Buddhist Crisis in March, senators from both sides of the aisle on the Vietnam issue weighed in to the discussion.

Most focused on the strident anti-Americanism of the protesters in I Corps and the persistent problem of political instability in South Vietnam. Like Johnson's advisors, some members of Congress sensed the GVN's narrow political base and realized that it lacked legitimacy and widespread support from its citizens. Richard Russell, Georgia Democrat, close friend and mentor to Johnson and a consistent skeptic about the war, argued that if it became obvious that most Vietnamese wanted an American exit, the United States should depart.[40] Later in the month, he recommended polling the South Vietnamese people to ascertain if they wanted the United States to remain. Claiming that it would be easy for the United States to withdraw militarily, he suggested that a lack of popular support would doom any American effort to save the country from the NLF.[41] So did Johnson, who feared that "if our people got the idea that the Vietnamese are insulting our men—Marines up in that northern area that are dying for 'em—why they'll . . . tell us to get the hell out of there. . . ."[42]

Soon, both hawks and doves joined the chorus. John Sherman Cooper, Kentucky Republican and a dove, argued that a desire on the part of the Vietnamese to terminate the conflict should lead to a U.S. withdrawal, because the United States could not protect a nation unwilling to fight for its own freedom.[43] John Stennis, a Mississippi Democrat and a supporter of the war, joined Vance Hartke, Indiana Democrat, and Jacob Javits, New York Republican, in calling for a U.S. exit if requested by a newly elected GVN.[44] Wayne Morse, Democratic Senator from Oregon and Johnson's most persistent Senate critic on the war, declared that "the sad fact is that my Government and yours is supporting a tyranny in South Vietnam, a brutal military junta that has not the slightest conception of the word freedom."[45]

Democrat Mike Mansfield, the Senate majority leader, publicly called for negotiations to end the war because of the worsening state of affairs in South Vietnam. He suggested that the agitation should alert American officials to the danger of a Vietnamese backlash against the U.S. Senators Claiborne Pell of Rhode Island and Frank Church of Idaho, both Democratic members of the SFRC and doves, echoed Mansfield's call.[46]

Nor was the issue confined to the Senate. Complicating the growing political problems of the Johnson administration, House members reported mounting bewilderment and dissatisfaction with the people in their districts over U.S. policy in Vietnam. They noted that the electorate, while still generally supporting the government's program in Vietnam, seemed impatient to end the conflict and bring the troops home.[47]

Adding to the urge for a reassessment of America's role in South Vietnam, U.S. casualties exceeded those of ARVN for the first time in the spring of 1966.[48] While the dramatic growth in casualties also related to the sharply increased number of U.S. soldiers in South Vietnam, the information came at a time when some Americans expressed ambivalence about the growing cost of the war. This reinforced those who favored withdrawal and magnified the feeling that the South Vietnamese did not appreciate the enormous sacrifices of the United States.[49]

On April 2, Johnson met with Rusk, McNamara, Rostow, Moyers and Valenti to discuss the deteriorating situation in South Vietnam. Rusk informed him that I Corps had moved out of the government orbit while other areas seemed ready to join the struggle against the GVN.[50] According to McNamara, Johnson seemed resigned to failure in Vietnam as a result of the agitation in I Corps, commenting that the United States might have to retreat to Thailand if the Buddhists succeeded in their rebellion. He insisted that his staff examine options that could mean a departure from South Vietnam. In response, McNamara called for the United States to dispose of Thich Tri Quang.

While it is impossible to know how serious Johnson's threats were, little doubt remains that he had contemplated an American withdrawal from Vietnam if the Buddhists overthrew Ky. McNamara, who had started to question whether the United States could win in Vietnam, argued most forcefully for action against the Buddhists.[51] While he had growing questions about the war, he remained unable to express his doubts in front of the president. Indeed, he often attacked other officials who advocated positions he had privately embraced.

Given that Johnson had staked his and his country's credibility on halting the spread of Communism in Asia, his despondency had a powerful impact on his subordinates, increasing the doubts that had begun to assail them. On April 4, Valenti proposed that the United States consider withdrawing from South Vietnam if the Ky regime fell. An announced intention to leave the embattled country might allow Johnson and his advisors to "rid ourselves of the Vietnamese bone-in-our-throat," while still maintaining U.S. credibility. Valenti felt sure that these actions would show "that we will stick with an ally and a commitment until the one becomes insane and the other no longer has real meaning."[52]

Reacting to the crisis atmosphere in the administration, McNaughton wrote a memo on April 4 titled "Observations about Vietnam." He argued that the United States had two options in responding to the disorder in I Corps: Fix it or get out of Vietnam. He insisted that the recent agitation represented an opportunity for the United States to escape from its commitment to South Vietnam.[53] The same day, Johnson met with Vice President Hubert Humphrey, Rusk, McNamara, Rostow, Taylor, William Bundy, Supreme Court justice Abe Fortas and Valenti. Expressing doubts that Ky could win in Danang, Johnson again raised the prospect of an American pullout.[54] Interestingly, Johnson considered withdrawal twice in one week. One must wonder what would have happened if his advisors had used his suggestion to push for a departure from South Vietnam rather than discussing the best way to ensure the survival of the GVN.

The Department of Defense also contemplated an American exit during April 1966. Staffers prepared a "Possible 'Fall Back' Plan," which McNamara reviewed on April 9. Among the options considered was a "[p]residential decision to seize upon the I Corps troubles as the vehicle for disengagement by the United States." Along with considering an American retreat, they also included plans to convince American and world opinion that the United States could no longer stay in South Vietnam due to the unreliability of the GVN and that an American retreat would not lessen the U.S. role as guarantor against Communist aggression. Even the Joint Chiefs of Staff seemed ready to accept an American withdrawal. While arguing that the United States should continue the conflict as long as it retained GVN support, the chiefs directed that planning go forward on an American withdrawal from Vietnam "if required" by a regime that demanded its exit.[55]

On April 8, shortly after Ky's failed attack against Danang, administration officials met to consider a U.S. response to the upheaval in South Vietnam. Moyers notified Johnson that the participants at the meeting would attempt to calculate presidential options in South Vietnam.[56] On the ninth, higher-ranking administrators met to formalize the process. They asked George A. Carver Jr., a CIA specialist on Vietnam, to argue for maintaining the same course in Vietnam, and McNaughton and Leonard Unger, deputy assistant secretary of defense for Far Eastern affairs, to discuss a middle-of-the-road compromise position, with McNaughton taking the pessimistic line and Unger arguing the optimistic scenario. They assigned Ball the task of examining the case for withdrawal and supervising preparation of the reports.[57]

As a result, the officials wrote papers speculating on the future of the GVN, with some assuming that the Buddhists would form a nonaligned government. On April 11, Unger asked if the United States could tolerate a neutralist GVN. If not, he wondered whether the United States could install a military dictatorship in South Vietnam or a regime totally under U.S. control. At the same time, he wondered how the United States could easily escape South Vietnam with its international reputation intact.[58]

On April 12, Carver prepared an essay titled "Consequences of a Buddhist Political Victory in South Vietnam." He distributed his paper to Bundy, Rostow, Moyers, Unger, Ball, McNaughton, Deputy Secretary of Defense Cyrus Vance, and Robert Komer, Johnson's new chief of pacification for Vietnam. Carver suggested that a Buddhist triumph might actually benefit the United States, because it would provide the GVN with a measure of legitimacy and respectability that it lacked. He saw three choices for the United States: conspire with other groups to overthrow the government; get out of Vietnam; or attempt to coexist with the new government while keeping its options open. Analyzing the three choices, he concluded that only the last provided the United States with any opportunity to retain its position in South Vietnam.[59]

On April 16, McNaughton, speculating on a worst-case scenario, indicated that a new regime might negotiate with the Communists to form a coalition government. He argued that this could create a more complex challenge for the United States and could force Washington to accept a number of disagreeable outcomes. While suggesting that the United States had a number of responses, including "Simple Opposition," overthrowing the government, or accepting the new arrangement, he viewed the possibility of a neutral GVN with dismay. Reasoning that there was "no cause for optimism," he claimed that any coalition government would eventually order the United States out of the country, while American troops would have to face tough choices over how much force to use in disengaging from the enemy, how to protect allied forces in Vietnam, and what to do with excess military supplies. With no island enclave like Taiwan, McNaughton suggested that the United States could find itself forced to grant asylum to thousands of Vietnamese. On the other hand, he maintained that a U.S. refusal to evacuate Vietnamese would seem racist and make its allies question the U.S. commitment to their survival while "[b]ad publicity would be inevitable."[60]

Other White House operatives sought to influence Johnson. Rostow argued that the enormous strains caused by the war and the resultant political upheaval in both countries compelled the United States to find a way "to shorten this war without doing unwise or desperate things." Trying to preempt the doubters in the White House, he suggested the United States notify the NLF it should open talks with the GVN, an action that drove the American government to the edge of hysteria when Vietnamese Buddhists advocated it and which had led to the ditching of several South Vietnamese leaders. Skeptical about the chances for successful talks with the Communists, Rostow lobbied for military escalation. He asserted that compelling the Communists to sue for peace through the use of military force remained the best way to end the conflict.[61]

In many ways, he was advancing the counterview of conservative Democrats and Republicans who called for much more aggressive action in Vietnam. While this probably constituted the least likely method for the United States to prevail in Vietnam, Rostow's advice had the desired effect on Johnson, who also believed that the insurgents would negotiate only after being defeated in the field. Thus, Rostow played to Johnson's hard-line outlook on the war in calling for intensified military action at a time when many Vietnamese and Americans preferred to halt the conflict.

OPTIONS—APRIL 1966

According to William Bundy, U.S. officials considered "a collapse in the South a real possibility" in the spring of 1966.[62] As Ky's position became more tenuous after his failed attack on Danang, the desire for a policy reconsideration gained momentum in the White House, while worried advisors produced memos and reports detailing Washington's precarious position. Johnson directed that contingency preparations take place and that Rostow keep him apprised of the group's progress. At one point, Rostow reported that while McNamara wanted to continue attacking insurgent forces and the DRV, Rusk seemed less eager to see negotiations begin between the NLF and GVN. Thus, Johnson and his top officials had actively considered and discussed overtures to the NLF and the possibility of a negotiated solution to the conflict in Vietnam.[63] Even Rostow, while advocating escalation, called for peace talks.[64]

Meanwhile, Carver produced a memo on April 16 titled "How We Should Move" that became part of "Option A." He argued that the American commitment to South Vietnam had been misinterpreted, leading many officials to assume that the United States had to acquiesce to GVN actions to press the fight against the NLF. Carver characterized this as "an intolerable position for a great power." He urged his colleagues to present the GVN with a clear statement that the U.S. commitment remained linked to sensible political performance by the Vietnamese and the knowledge that they wanted the United States to continue its efforts in South Vietnam. Finally, he suggested that the United States encourage the GVN to seek peace talks with the NLF as a possible way for Washington to extricate itself from Vietnam.[65]

In a second essay, "Option A," he called for U.S. forces to exert maximum military pressure on NLF/PAVN forces to allow the GVN breathing room to restore order. He also advocated a policy of gradually escalating pressure to make the GVN conform to U.S. wishes, a plan that seems remarkably similar to the ineffective U.S. strategy against the DRV. Finally, he called on the United States to sustain the GVN while attempting to weather the political storm caused by Thi's dismissal.[66]

McNaughton and Unger's essays combined to present "Course B." They called for negotiations with the NLF to end the war, hoping an independent GVN could survive within a coalition government. Insisting that the United States prepare the GVN for talks with the Communists while Washington contacted Hanoi, they suggested that the GVN would have to grant amnesty to members of the NLF and bring them into the government in a limited fashion. In return, the NLF must acknowledge the GVN as the legitimate government of South Vietnam, a very unlikely concession, and renounce the use of terror and military action. U.S. and PAVN forces would be required to leave the country. Fearing that the NLF would continue to resist U.S. pressure, McNaughton and Unger advocated that the United States assure the NLF that it would not conclude a deal that had the potential to deny it power. Yet they remained so wary of GVN strength and stability that they worried it would collapse when talks were announced, not even lasting long enough to negotiate its future. The authors suggested that if the GVN refused to cooperate or failed to broaden its base and enhance its legitimacy, then Washington should threaten to reduce military aid to the GVN. They recognized, however, that it would be close to impossible to reverse course or for the GVN to survive once it became known that the United States wanted out of South Vietnam.

A U.S. withdrawal, McNaughton and Unger argued, would allow the United States to escape much of the international criticism heaped on it because of the war, improve relations with the Soviet Union and satisfy growing domestic opposition. In a statement that should have made everyone pause, McNaughton and Unger conceded, "*Sentiment today in the United States appears overwhelmingly to favor the Government's pursuing negotiations and seeking a peaceful settlement*" (italics added). At the same time, they realized that recriminations would certainly follow because of increased American casualties.[67] A later draft of "Course B" advocated that the United States link its continued backing of the GVN to its "working out a peaceful settlement with the VC/ NLF even on relatively unfavorable terms."[68]

Ball's "Course C" called for the United States to get out of Vietnam. Ball, Johnson's designated Vietnam policy critic, argued that the internal divisions in South Vietnam remained so profound that it could not weather the present storm. He pointed out that because the United States "cannot give South Viet-Nam a government as a foreign aid grant—we should concentrate our attention on cutting our losses." Like the others, he emphasized the basic premises of U.S. activity in South Vietnam: the GVN had to be able to prosecute the war, and the Vietnamese people had to want the United States there. He concluded that the United States had fulfilled its responsibility: "It is the South Vietnamese people who have failed, not us." He demanded that the United States issue an ultimatum to the GVN that failure to achieve stability would compel the

United States to begin limiting military operations in the country and force a U.S. withdrawal. Dismissing concerns about the impact on U.S. allies, he argued that most American allies would approve.

Like Unger and McNaughton, Ball claimed that U.S. public support would be favorable. In a remarkably prophetic statement, he argued that U.S. officials had to "face the fact that there are no really attractive options open to us. To continue to fight the war with the present mushy political base is . . . both dangerous and futile. It can lead only to increasing commitments, heavier losses, and mounting risks of dangerous escalation."[69] Although Ball was carrying out his role as Johnson's designated devil's advocate on the war, as historian Fredrik Logevall points out, many other members of the administration agreed with this stance.[70]

William Bundy conveyed the pessimistic attitudes of U.S. leaders with a cover memo that summarized the options and tried to predict the outcome of the Buddhist Crisis. While happy that the GVN had thus far avoided a collapse, he averred that further upheaval in South Vietnam could easily damage American public support for the war, increasing pressure on Washington to withdraw. He cautioned that "with steady or probably rising casualties, the war could well become an albatross around the Administration's neck at least equal to what Korea was for President Truman in 1952." Thailand, he predicted, would be lost, and countries like Korea, Japan, Taiwan and the Philippines would be in grave danger.[71]

The president and Rostow reviewed the three options on April 19. Five days later, Rusk reviewed the options and then told Johnson that both he and McNamara felt the situation in Vietnam did not warrant the implementation of "Course C." Rusk suggested that they "stay on Option A."[72] The next day, the president and his staff met very briefly to discuss the alternatives. The shortness of the second meeting implies that a more thorough review had taken place at an earlier time, perhaps on April 19.[73]

In the end, the president rejected the calls for an American withdrawal. Although no notes from the two meetings exist, historian William Gibbons reports that Johnson declared that "we shall stay on course," and Bundy claims that Johnson "categorically thrust aside the withdrawal option."[74] For Johnson, an insecure man who valued loyalty above everything, the dramatic change in attitude on the part of some of his advisors must have been disturbing. After all, many of the people who had encouraged him to send combat troops to South Vietnam now questioned the conflict on which he had staked his reputation and integrity. While the options reflected the growing disillusionment of many administration officials, Johnson refused to move, chiefly because he accepted the Cold War premises on which American intervention had been predicated.[75]

The failure to reverse U.S. policy in Vietnam must be attributed mainly to Johnson, an intensely political man who failed to move even when his political life seemed threatened by a war he never wanted. Logevall argues that Johnson's attitude toward the war had been for the most part shaped by the danger it could inflict on his domestic programs and on historical judgments of his presidency.[76] As Karnow points out, Johnson always feared being called a coward or unmanly by his political enemies. Hence, his dread of appearing timid prevented him from summoning the courage to stop the war.[77] His greatest nightmare was a possible conservative backlash over an American withdrawal. However, he may have greatly overstated it in his own mind because of the grief that Democrats had given the GOP over the "loss of Cuba" in 1959.

Yet on another level Johnson had consistently supported an independent South Vietnam. From the day he took office in November 1963, he had declared, "I am not going to lose Vietnam. I am not going to be the President who saw Southeast Asia go the way China went."[78] Johnson also believed in using military force to halt the spread of Communism. Throughout his Senate career he had supported expanding military expenditures, and after he became president, he constantly chose escalation over disengagement in Vietnam.[79] While he understood the political danger of American intervention, he never challenged the fundamental tenets of U.S. Cold War thinking, particularly containment and the critical importance of demonstrating American credibility.[80] Johnson ardently believed in the principles that undergirded that philosophy. Doubts among many of his advisors and their desire to open talks with the NLF could not shake his conviction that the Communists had to be defeated militarily before the United States could successfully conclude the war.

Nor did he use rhetoric that would have indicated to his subordinates that he opposed military action to halt Communism in Vietnam. In the wake of the first American air attacks against the DRV in August

1964, Johnson did not sound like a man reluctant to use force when he bragged, "I didn't just screw Ho Chi Minh, I cut his pecker off."[81] After an NLF terrorist bombing in December 1964, he told Taylor that he thought efforts to defeat the DRV with bombing appeared overrated and that ground forces would have to be utilized to put down the insurgency.[82] On another occasion, he assured his advisors that he was "determined to make it clear to all the world that the U.S. will spare no effort and no sacrifice in doing its full part to turn back the Communists in Vietnam."[83] In fact, he preferred that U.S. forces "find 'em [Communists] and kill 'em."[84]

Nothing had changed by 1966. He still dreaded a domestic political backlash to the point that he lost sight of the fact that many Americans would have been relieved by an American exit. The turmoil and instability in South Vietnam most likely would have muted what might have been a brutal but short-lived reaction. After all, conservatives remained generally unsatisfied with American strategy in Vietnam and demanded a major escalation to bring victory, a course Johnson also would not follow because of his anxiety over a potential Korean-style intervention by the PRC. Thus, his fear of forces he could not control drove him to stay a course that ultimately destroyed his presidency and brought the country to the brink of a meltdown in 1968. He felt the same way about growing calls for neutralization in South Vietnam and America, ordering Lodge to "stop neutralist talk whenever we can by whatever means we can."[85]

While much has been made of Johnson's efforts to resist pressure from the Joint Chiefs of Staff to escalate, a lot of his rhetoric aimed at eliciting pity from subordinates, and possibly later historians, so that he could cast himself as a hapless victim of overly aggressive advisors. As Logevall argues, moreover, the presidency is not a committee.[86] Johnson followed advice to escalate and expand the war while falling back on the convictions he had developed in a lifetime of political activity. The next month, during a National Security Council meeting, Johnson worried "that an unusually large amount of time was spent considering new proposals or changes in policy. Our strategy has been the same for three years. . . . We are committed and we will not be deterred. We must accept the fact that some will always oppose, dissent and criticize. We want results."[87]

McNamara argues that at this point he should have forced a reevaluation of American policy. But he claims that he and Johnson feared the political and diplomatic price of withdrawal.[88] In the end, U.S. leaders concluded that despite the strong urge to pull out, that option appeared to be unacceptable. William Bundy put it this way: "[H]owever discouraged we were, 'we must carry on with it' was the feeling."[89]

Rostow maintains, however, that policy-makers never seriously considered a pullout from South Vietnam, a statement that flies in the face of substantial documentation. In a 1969 interview, he conceded that "[e]veryone was unhappy about Vietnam" by 1966, but few wanted to withstand the political heat a decision to withdraw would have generated. In fact, he argues that those who attacked U.S. policy, such as Fulbright, were unwilling to publicly pay the political price of an American retreat from Vietnam. After looking at various options, U.S. leaders concluded that staying in South Vietnam remained the safest course.[90]

Although Johnson and his subordinates had rejected an American withdrawal, some advisors still had doubts about the war. Ball's biographer, David DiLeo, argues that Ball could never overcome the counterarguments of Rusk, McNamara, McGeorge Bundy and, later, Rostow. Yet, as he points out, the defection of one of these advisors to Ball's side might have changed history. Valenti agreed, claiming that if Ball could have found supporters in the administration, his arguments would have been greatly strengthened. Despite McNamara's behind-the-scenes maneuvering and the growing doubts of people like McNaughton, Unger and Bundy, the "ally to which Valenti referred proved to be distressingly elusive."[91]

Believing he had contained the doubters in his administration, Johnson quickly moved to shore up public opinion. Three days after the April 19 meeting, he called an impromptu news conference to stem the growing uneasiness in the country. Agreeing that the rebellion in I Corps had been unsettling, he pleaded for support for the American stance in South Vietnam. Concerning the cascade of bad news coming out of South Vietnam, he declared that the Communists "hoped the American people would get tired and change their course." He confidently predicted that their efforts would ultimately fail. His purpose, however, seemed as much to instill confidence in his increasingly despondent advisors as in the American public.[92]

Despite Johnson's directive to continue the conflict, McNamara pressed others in the administration to initiate talks with the Communists. On May 4, he called Ball to inquire if he had made any progress in opening talks with the NLF or the DRV. When Ball answered in the negative, McNamara pressed him to exert a greater effort.[93] In mid-May, McNamara suggested to American diplomat W. Averell Harriman that the United States should contact the NLF and the DRV and urge them to move forward with plans for a coalition government in South Vietnam.[94] Revisiting the topic in late May, he told Harriman that "the U.S. should let the South Vietnamese decide their own future even if it [means] a coalition government with the Viet Cong, which might or might not take over."[95]

ROUND TWO—MAY/JUNE 1966

Ky's second attack on Danang left American leaders exasperated by the latest of his impulsive acts but hoping that he could still pull it off and end the civil strife in I Corps. American leaders particularly remembered the 1963 public-relations debacle when the GVN launched assaults against pagodas around the country, leading to the decision to discard Diem.[96] By 1966, after three years of chronic instability and increasing manifestations of anti-Americanism in South Vietnam, many U.S. leaders considered that decision to have been the worst one made by the United States in South Vietnam.[97] Thus, they viewed Ky's attack on the Struggle Movement with great trepidation, fearing it would ignite a civil war in the country or a backlash in the United States similar to that of 1963.

Particularly disquieting to American leaders, the political situation seemed headed for a peaceful resolution resulting in elections for a constituent assembly, when Ky upset the fragile peace that Dinh had constructed in Danang. Adding to their discomfort, Ky attacked Danang to destroy a movement whose platform called for popular democracy and elections, a position the United States could hardly oppose publicly. Forced again to acquiesce to Ky's actions because of their huge investment of money, prestige, and American lives, U.S. leaders quickly mounted an intensive damage-control campaign, claiming to have no foreknowledge of the attack and calling for nonviolent means to end the conflict.[98]

American leaders rapidly became aware of their limited ability to control events. Despite entreaties by Rusk, Porter, and Lodge, Ky refused to talk to Buddhist leaders and denounced Thich Tri Quang as a Communist.[99] At the same time, he declared that he had not informed the United States in advance of his suppression of the Struggle Movement because it was a domestic matter. Thus, even though totally dependent on the United States for his survival, Ky also felt the need to lash out at American domination of South Vietnam.[100] American leaders, however, retained few illusions about their ally. As Thich Tri Quang pointed out, "today, the Vietnamese and the Americans are like a couple who do not love each other anymore, but who cannot obtain a divorce because they have a child—their common fight against the communists. So they continue to live with each other, but without love."[101]

Washington saw elections as a way to rob the Buddhists of their main point of contention with the GVN. Thus, when Ky announced plans for balloting in the fall, U.S. leaders breathed a huge sigh of relief, particularly because they knew that neutralists, Communists, and pacifists would be excluded. At the same time, Thieu and Ky expanded the Directory by adding a number of civilians who represented non-UBC factions in the country, strengthening their government by making it appear more inclusive while also further isolating the radical Buddhists.[102]

Fed up with the machinations in South Vietnam, Rusk also tried to circumvent Ky. In a terse cable, he ordered Porter to convey to Thieu that the "time has come when he must be impressed with our utter disgust with the way [the] Vietnamese leadership [is] behaving and risking throwing away what may be their last chance to preserve their country's independence." To the secretary of state, the latest flare-up in I Corps represented another example of the Vietnamese failing to uphold their part of the effort to combat the insurgency while U.S. soldiers did the fighting.[103]

On May 20, Rostow met with Bui Diem and the South Vietnamese ambassador to the United States, Vu Van Thai. Diem assured Rostow that Ky and the generals would hold the promised elections and had no plans to launch an attack on Hue similar to the assault on Danang. While glad that the Vietnamese had shared their plans with the United States and remained committed to defeating the Communists, Rostow explained that "the Vietnamese should understand that our support was tendered at heavy political costs. American boys were dying. Our balance of payments situation was worsening. Domestic programs could not receive the attention we would like to give them." Echoing the views of many Americans, Rostow pointed out that the Vietnamese had forgotten the war while "killing each other in what looked from a distance as a struggle for privilege and power."[104]

Ky's invasion of Danang in May also ignited new protests in the United States as grave doubts about the whole enterprise in South Vietnam again seized the U.S. Congress. In mid-May, Missouri Democratic senator Stuart Symington "confided to a colleague that he . . . [had] never felt so discouraged about developments in Vietnam" as he did during the months of unrest in the spring of 1966. Senator John Sherman Cooper, the Kentucky Republican, wondered how long the United States could continue to prop up the Ky regime. Democratic senator Albert Gore of Tennessee questioned how free elections could ever be held in South Vietnam after the recent events. Democratic senator from Washington Henry Jackson "found most of his colleagues simply throwing their hands in the air in frustration."[105] Javits of New York warned of a possible American withdrawal if the Vietnamese failed to resolve their disputes and achieve stability.[106] Mendel Rivers of South Carolina, the Democratic chairman of the House Armed Services Committee and a consistent hawk, speculated that if the Vietnamese could not put their house in order, the United States might have to withdraw completely.[107]

By the end of June, Johnson had to face the first inklings of a full-scale rebellion in his own party when Senator Mansfield convened two meetings with Democratic senators to discuss confidentially the impact of the war on their political futures and to measure public attitudes toward the conflict. Afterward, he sent a sobering account to Johnson. Almost every senator reported that public support for the war had slipped badly during the internal squabbling in South Vietnam and urged Johnson to find a way out of the conflict.

Many advocated neutralization as a first step to withdrawal. Although it is not entirely clear what they meant by the term, it seems obvious that most saw it as a way for the United States to depart from South Vietnam without suffering a humiliating defeat. Little support existed for a unilateral pull-out. One senator pointed out: "The only moral reason we have for being in Viet Nam is the contention that the South Vietnamese want us there, but have we tried to find out whether this is really so or not—whether, in fact, the people want us?" One participant argued, "We are becoming the colonial power in this situation in spite of ourselves." Another claimed, "There is greater confusion on Vietnam than on any other issue in many years. People are too sophisticated to accept the idea we are there at [the] invitation of [the] Vietnamese to stop aggression from [the] north. [The] [p]ublic is asking questions we cannot answer." All of the discussants expressed uneasiness with the situation in South Vietnam and demanded a new course that would bring peace or victory, and the vast majority favored negotiations. Others severely criticized Johnson's advisors, who they believed had not provided the president with adequate information or viable options, except escalation.[108]

Deteriorating public support particularly concerned administration officials. On May 10, Rostow warned Johnson that recent polls showed the American public evenly split between a desire for escalation and peace.[109] Thus, a solid majority of Americans already disagreed with Johnson's middle-of-the-road policy. Rusk informed the U.S. embassy in Saigon on May 15 that the agitation in central Vietnam had badly damaged public backing for the war.[110] While some White House advisors called on Americans not to be swayed by press reports into believing that American policy was close to collapsing, pollsters reported rapidly plunging support for the war from April to June 1966.[111]

The next month, Johnson's free fall in the polls continued. A June 1966 Gallup poll showed backing for his policies in Vietnam slipping from a June 1965 poll—that had shown 66 percent for, 20 percent against and 14 percent undecided—to 47 percent for, 35 percent against and 13 percent undecided. Remarkably, over one-third of those polled now favored an American withdrawal, even before the United States had experienced the heavy combat that occurred in later years.[112] On June 24, journalist Hugh Sidey pointed out that Johnson's approval rating had "fallen to 46% . . . the lowest since Harry Truman hit 23% in 1951." Sidey attributed Johnson's decline to the war and domestic economic issues.[113] Of course, Sidey or few others understood at this point that the "dislike" would soon turn into contempt and hatred because of the war.

Thus, the Buddhist Crisis of 1966 represented a turning point in

Johnson's presidency. Johnson's approval rating on the war dropped from 65 percent in the summer of 1965 to 50 percent in February 1966 and then to 42 percent in September 1966. Despite a few temporary upward spikes, he never recovered his former popularity. In June, Moyers reported to the president that the pollsters had discovered that "the people are in a foul mood over Vietnam" and that the administration's position seemed sure to continue declining.[114] Johnson acknowledged the decline in a phone conversation with Senator Russell in early June, observing, "We got a pretty disastrous poll coming out on Vietnam. About 35–36 percent want to get out. . . . About 41 percent approve of the way I'm doing it, and about 36 percent disapprove." When the Georgia Democrat suggested that Johnson follow McNamara's advice to escalate, Johnson responded, "Well, he's not advising that now."[115]

Ever sensitive to criticism and concerned about the widespread questioning of the U.S. commitment, Johnson appealed to Americans to endorse his policy and lashed out at his critics. On May 18, he called for national unity, asking "every American to put our country first if we want to keep it first." Within a week, Johnson pleaded "for patience and understanding in both Vietnam and the United States," while urging the contending parties in South Vietnam to settle their differences peacefully.[116]

During the week of fighting in Danang in mid-May, the idea of a U.S. withdrawal again arose within the administration. Bundy claims that there was "a brief flurry of similar feelings when Ky moved against Hue and Danang. . . . But in the end he won, and so we all relaxed."[117] Yet the morale of embittered U.S. officials in Saigon and Washington had been dealt a painful blow.

Although the authorship remains unclear, McNaughton's files contain a number of memos produced that week that again advocated negotiations to end the war, increased military pressure on the DRV, the possibility of American aid to the DRV as an incentive to bring it to the negotiating table, the issuing of American statements to encourage the DRV to believe that it could gain control of the GVN peacefully, and the deployment of U.S. forces along the DMZ and in Laos to stop infiltration from the north. More importantly, his files contain a copy of a proposed UN Security Council resolution arranging for negotiations to end the war through the reconvening of the 1954 Geneva Conference. In addition, he had a draft of a presidential statement announcing an American stand-down as the first step in a U.S. withdrawal from South Vietnam.[118] Johnson never delivered the speech that could have changed his place in history and established him as a leader able to make a difficult but correct decision.

Playing on his fears of the impact of an American pullback, Rostow throughout this period advised Johnson to reject renewed calls for American retrenchment. At one point, he characterized demands for an enclave strategy in South Vietnam as trying to negotiate "from the Pusan perimeter in 1950," an obvious play on LBJ's Cold War attitude toward the war in Vietnam.[119] Presenting Johnson with a series of options to pursue in Vietnam, he urged "more than our present course . . . but less than a major escalation," which fit well with Johnson's habit of choosing to escalate gradually in the face of turmoil in South Vietnam.[120] On June 29, American aircraft attacked installations in the Hanoi and Haiphong areas. "When Johnson was shown photographs of the raid he was ecstatic, remarking to Rostow that 'them sons-of-bitches are finished now,'" hardly the response of a reluctant warrior. That same month, the president decided to increase U.S. forces to close to 450,000 by the middle of 1967.[121]

Historians of the Vietnam War have usually focused on Ho Chi Minh's overtures to the United States in 1945, the Geneva Conference in 1954 or Buddhist-inspired upheavals in South Vietnam in 1963 and 1964 as periods when the United States might have escaped from its eventual commitment to combat Communism in Vietnam. In the same manner, many historians have argued that Lyndon Johnson's policies enjoyed widespread support during the early years of the war, while some have also characterized Johnson as a reluctant warrior pushed into Vietnam by hawkish advisors. In some ways, he has been seen as a "dawk," a man who exhibited both hawkish and dovish tendencies.[122] An examination of the 1966 Buddhist Crisis, however, demonstrates that American public support was far softer in the early years of the war than is commonly believed, that Johnson's reputation as a dawk should be rethought, and that 1966 constituted another significant opportunity for America to escape the war.[123]

Johnson was the most important hawk in his administration. Not that he particularly wanted to get involved in Vietnam, but he proved unable to transcend his Cold War attitudes toward containment and the importance of halting Communist aggression in Asia. Moreover, as Herring argues, "once committed to it [the war] he had invested his personal prestige to a degree that made it impossible to back off."[124]

In the end, fear of the domestic and international repercussions of an American withdrawal rendered U.S. leaders incapable of overcoming Johnson's desire to prosecute the war and carrying out an American exit from Vietnam. Thus, 1966 differed little from 1945, 1954, 1963 and 1964: after briefly questioning their covenant with South Vietnam, U.S. officials, following Johnson's lead, returned to what they considered their distasteful duty and renewed their commitment to the GVN.

In rejecting the withdrawal option, Johnson and his advisors missed another opportunity to get out of Vietnam. They might have been able to withdraw in the spring of 1966 with far less political damage than some in Washington believed, because of widespread discontent in Congress, growing questions among American citizens and realization among some officials that the nation had become hopelessly stalemated in a war few wanted to fight. Indeed, some U.S. officials sensed the futility of their endeavor in Vietnam, realizing that disaster lay in the future.[125]

With growing U.S. concerns about the war and increasing questions among Johnson's subordinates, a bold move by McNamara and the other doubters in 1966 might have tipped the scales toward peace. Had he expressed his doubts to the president or publicly aired his declining confidence in the use of military force to achieve U.S. objectives, the defense secretary might have spared many Americans and Vietnamese from the deep pain of war. However, McNamara's hesitancy in expressing his concerns kept him from attaching his name to any of the memos produced during this period and giving them the weight to perhaps move Johnson toward a settlement. In fact, in a 1997 letter to the author, McNamara maintained, "It would have worked if those of us who were skeptical of our ability to win had presented our views more effectively and forcefully."[126] William Bundy agrees. "Negotiations were on everyone's minds during the spring of 1966," he argues, and "if we had presented it in a different way," it might have succeeded.[127]

However, powerful arguments for staying in Vietnam persisted. It may simply have been too close to the introduction of U.S. troops to withdraw, particularly given Johnson's insecure nature and the urge to justify the deaths of American soldiers in the field. Yet, as Logevall argues, even though support for the war seemed to exist after American troops landed in South Vietnam in 1965, there had been little enthusiasm for escalation. Thus, even though Americans "tended to rally behind the troops," the very weak backing for intervention throughout 1965 indicates that Johnson could have pulled out and still retained popular support.[128]

Given that the war threatened his presidency, withdrawal should have been considered. Unquestionably, strong opinions held by many Americans about the importance of credibility and containment would have led to severe criticism of the Johnson administration at first. Certainly, the Republican Party would have relished the opportunity to repeat another political bloodbath like the "Who lost China?" debacle for the Democratic Party in 1949. Yet, despite the political risks involved, Johnson might have pulled it off had he acted decisively. After all, by 1966, many Americans had become extremely weary of the constant instability in Vietnam, and an increasing number had started to question why Americans should die to defend a nation that seemed unwilling to fight for itself.

If the United States had pulled out in 1966 rather than in 1973, what would have been different? By the time U.S. forces eventually withdrew, little had changed in the tactical situation except for the death of untold numbers of Vietnamese and the destruction of much of the country. Certainly, the United States emerged from the war far weaker than when it entered. Moreover, the inability of Johnson to withdraw plunged the nation into its greatest moral crisis since the Civil War. At the same time, the war separated many Americans from the ideological moorings that tied them together, setting the collective American psyche adrift in a desperate, and as yet unfulfilled, search for self-meaning.[129]

To some U.S. officials, challenges to their posture on South Vietnam bred stubbornness rather than reconsideration. They became even more firmly entrenched in their positions despite their own doubts and a tidal wave of criticism from around the world and at home. Whether this resulted primarily from overwork, as McNamara argues in his memoirs, or from an urge to protect their reputations, as Kahin claims, or as part of a historically deterministic process, as Herring suggests, is hard to say. In the face of heavy international and domestic criticism and clear evidence that many non-Communist South Vietnamese opposed American interference in and domination of South Vietnam, however, American officials should have implemented a total reevaluation of their policy and acted on their instincts to terminate the struggle.

Kahin and Herring seem correct: the main concern of U.S. policymakers was national and personal credibility. Logevall points out, moreover, that their conception of credibility operated on three levels, namely personal and political credibility as well as the credibility of the Democratic Party. Nothing, however, was more important than their personal credibility.[130] Hence, no one in the Johnson administration faced the growing quandary about U.S. war aims by publicly advocating withdrawal. Having come so close, they followed the president's lead and chose what seemed to them the proper and necessary path, staying with the American commitment to South Vietnam rather than risking the heavy criticism that a retreat would have fostered. Afraid to embark on a bold and politically risky strategy of withdrawal, they chose to stay with the safe course in defining the war as a way to contain international communist expansion.

Yet the critical question remains: Why did the United States find itself unable to withdraw from Vietnam in 1966 despite ample evidence that the war might be unwinnable and could destroy the Johnson presidency? In the end, LBJ could not transcend the convictions he had acquired over a lifetime to make the only decision that could have saved his presidency. Alas, he was a victim of a fervent Cold War ideology that overpowered his keen political instincts. He supported calls for escalation because they resonated so closely with his deeply held beliefs. He had been elected in 1964 with the largest majority in history by purporting to be a "peace candidate."[131] Had he followed his own election rhetoric, he might have salvaged his public career and spared the United States and Vietnam the trauma of an expanding war.

The Vien Hoa Dao now represented the only obstacle to a renewed American commitment to South Vietnam, since all that remained for the GVN and the United States to carry the fight to the enemy was the eradication of the Struggle Movement in I Corps and Saigon. Thus, Ky moved to suppress the Vien Hoa Dao and buttress his relationship with Washington as Buddhists exhibited increasing strains of anti-Americanism in Hue and Saigon.

5

Resolution

They woke me this morning to tell me my brother had been
killed in battle. . . . When can I break my long silence? When
can I speak the unuttered words that are choking me?
  —Thich Nhat Hanh, *Call Me by My True Names*

 Ky's May 15 attack on Danang caught the Buddhist lead-
ership by surprise. Sure that he would soon fall from
power like the string of dictators before him, and trust-
ing American guarantees that no more attacks would be
launched against the Struggle Force, Buddhist leaders
had underestimated Ky's staying power and the new level
of American commitment to a stable GVN.
  Probably no one received as big a shock from the assault on Danang
as Thich Tri Quang. With assurances from Lodge that the United States
backed the GVN-Buddhist agreement on elections, the Buddhist leader
suffered a severe jolt when he realized he had been double-crossed by
the American ambassador.[1] Even worse for the dissidents, Thich Tri
Quang had served as an unwitting accomplice for Ky. Believing that the
Americans would hold Ky to his promise of elections and allow an or-
derly transition to civilian government, the Buddhist leader had recently
traveled through the area, sometimes in a helicopter provided by General Walt, urging moderation and encouraging his followers to tear down
the roadblocks and barricades that could have blocked the ARVN thrust
into Danang. Particularly painful for Thich Tri Quang, Struggle Force

leaders had been reluctant to follow his advice, because they believed that Ky would not honor his pact with them. The Buddhist helmsman persuaded his fellow dissidents to lower their guard mainly because he miscalculated Ky's staying power, his own influence with the GVN, and the heightened level of U.S. commitment to continued military rule in South Vietnam.[2] According to Frances FitzGerald, when Thich Tri Quang recognized he had been betrayed, he "shut himself up in his cell for several days, crying out and beating his head with his fists."[3]

Stanley Karnow, however, visited the Buddhist leader at the Dieu De Pagoda in Hue during this period and found him unruffled and under control. While Karnow described the city as tense following the GVN attack on Danang, he realized from Thich Tri Quang's calm demeanor that the monk did not grasp the true desperation of his situation. Karnow argues that Thich Tri Quang failed to sustain the Struggle Movement because he lacked the sophistication and acumen of a normal political leader. Instead, his leadership focused on preserving traditional Vietnamese values, which had been ruptured by the conflict between the United States and the Communists.

Thus, what Lodge and others characterized as a naked grab for power by the Buddhist leadership really constituted an effort to preserve time-honored ideals and a way of life being destroyed by the war. Karnow saw Thich Tri Quang's challenge to the GVN as something many Vietnamese admired. Certainly, for central Vietnamese fed up with a war run by mercenary generals from an increasingly westernized capital, their stand in Hue seemed like a last grasp to hold onto a Vietnam in the process of passing from the scene forever.[4] Hue, the beautiful, peaceful, graceful city along the Perfume River, had emerged as the last bastion of Vietnamese self-identity under assault from America. Its pastoral quality was now marred by mobs of students who surged through its streets in waves of anti-American and anti-GVN outbursts, awaiting the certain retribution that would follow a GVN victory in Danang.[5] At the same time, the Hue radio station forgot its earlier bitter denunciation of U.S. interference by calling on the Americans to join the Struggle Movement in ousting Ky and Thieu.[6] Like many Vietnamese, the students who had seized the station still believed that, in the end, the world's greatest democracy would support their egalitarian aspirations.

Thich Tri Quang acted swiftly to bring the United States into the conflict on his side. Still naively believing in Washington's good faith, he petitioned President Johnson and Lodge for assistance against the GVN and demanded that Ky and Thieu leave the government.[7] To his consternation, he soon discovered the United States not as ready to jettison Ky as it had been Diem and Khanh. In fact, the president refused even to send him a return cable, instead ordering the local consul to deliver a noncommittal answer.[8] Finding the American silence particularly disturbing, Thich Tri Quang wondered at one point if all of his followers would have to die for the United States to restrain Ky.[9]

The Buddhist leader did not understand the new American attitude toward his movement. By this time, the United States increasingly saw its allies in the fight against Diem as the source of the instability it deplored in South Vietnam. Nevertheless, his "appeal put the United States in a dilemma. Many American officials . . . saw the justice of his argument that the Buddhists had kept their end of the recent political truce and that Premier Ky had not."[10] Thich Nhat Hanh also appealed to Americans to allow the Vietnamese people to settle their problems without foreign interference, pointing out that the GVN attacked anyone who advocated peace in South Vietnam. The monk's courageous stand meant that he could not return to South Vietnam; his life would be in constant danger for calling for reconciliation in a country exhausted and sickened by decades of conflict.[11]

In the end, the United States rejected the monks' request for assistance. In a reply meant to make the Vietnamese pause and contemplate the repercussions of an American withdrawal from South Vietnam, Dean Rusk argued that the U.S. public was increasingly fed up with the political infighting in the country. Instead of supporting the Buddhists, he called for the contending parties to put aside their differences and focus on defeating the Communists.[12]

While Buddhist leaders groped for a strategy, the dissidents' situation in Danang grew increasingly desperate. After loyal ARVN forces overran insurgent roadblocks in Danang, the rebels retreated into the Tinh Hoi, Tan Minh, and Pho Da pagodas in the southern section of the city, vowing to fight to the death. The besieged Buddhists stockpiled wood in preparation for threatened self-immolations if ARVN units attacked the religious sites.[13]

Despite the military onslaught in Danang and the heavily armed forces on both sides, Buddhists continued to demonstrate nonviolently. At one point, ignoring the heavy fighting close to the pagoda strongholds, "150 Buddhist youths and priests and girl and boy scouts sat praying on the pavement in front of a major pagoda 800 yards up an adjacent street."[14] On another occasion, while dissident troops fortified and consolidated their positions in the pagodas, "[a] group of about 20 gray robed Buddhist monks carrying Buddhist flags came marching up one street toward [ARVN] marine positions." Remarkably, the loyalists did not shoot at the monks but continued to exchange sniper fire with rebels. The same day, the *New York Times* displayed a dramatic photo of a lone Buddhist monk sitting in the street, blocking the path of an ARVN tank.[15]

Buddhist leaders sought outside help to restrain Ky's forces from a final onslaught on the pagodas. Thich Tri Quang called on the United States to send American Marines to protect the besieged Buddhists, and Thich Don Hau contacted the International Red Cross, asking for assistance in treating Buddhist casualties who had been denied access to medical care by Ky's troops.[16] Desperate Buddhist leaders appealed to U Thant, secretary general of the United Nations, President Johnson and General Walt to stop the ARVN offensive, to no avail. Neil Sheehan reported, moreover, that many women and children were wounded in the fighting. As the ARVN noose tightened, the scene at the Tinh Hoi pagoda became grim: "More than 40 bodies, draped with Buddhist flags, lay in an anteroom off the sanctuary of the pagoda . . . [including] an infant about 2 years old."[17] Unable to receive help from the outside, the interior of the Tinh Hoi pagoda had become "a scene of bedlam . . . [where] trucks, jeeps and ambulances flying Buddhist flags roared out carrying wounded to the hospitals."[18]

On May 21, the Tan Minh pagoda fell. One of three pagodas that anchored the rebels' defensive perimeter, its loss constituted a major blow to the dissidents. Loyal ARVN elements seized the religious site after heavy fighting while VNAF aircraft attacked the pagoda, inflicting several casualties, including two dead monks. In the end, ARVN forces took seventy-five military and forty civilian prisoners from the pagoda, leaving the temple "deserted except for two monks wearing white mourning bands . . . who chanted prayers and beat wooden blocks before the gilt statue of [the] Buddha." All that remained of the Buddhist resistance were "[p]ools of congealed blood."[19]

The last stronghold fell on May 23, when the remaining four hundred rebels surrendered the Tinh Hoi pagoda without a fight. As Jerrold Schecter points out, it had taken three thousand elite ARVN troops a week to subdue eight hundred dissidents.[20] The CIA estimated that the Struggle Force suffered about one hundred fatalities and hundreds more wounded in the fighting.[21]

LODGE RETURNS TO SOUTH VIETNAM

Lodge's arrival in South Vietnam on May 20 significantly changed the tenor of American reporting on the crisis, because he constantly endeavored to show the Buddhists in the worst light. Although his tough talk and exasperation with the Buddhists resonated with Walt Rostow and appealed to Johnson, it flew in the face of Rusk's instructions. Despite Rusk's desire to bring the opposing sides together, Lodge approved of Ky's violation of the American-guaranteed truce between the Buddhists and the GVN, while Lodge continued to refuse to meet or communicate with Thich Tri Quang.[22]

Lodge also persisted in identifying the NLF with the Struggle Movement. He argued that Communist "agents are at work, in the Struggle Forces and in the mobs . . . and they know how to intimidate, terrorize, propagandize, and agitate."[23] Lodge made these remarks despite the fact that two weeks earlier, the CIA had reported that Communists had failed to exercise any degree of influence in the upper echelons of the movement.[24] Assigning the uproar in Danang to the NLF, however, fit the mind-set of government leaders who wanted to believe that the Communists stood behind the opposition to the GVN. Accepting that genuine complaints against the GVN existed within much of the population would have undercut the very logic of the U.S. mission in South Vietnam.

Because of Lodge's reputation for political savvy, many people respected and listened to him, although in any real analysis, a number of his statements seem lacking. His ability to hang onto his critical post stemmed from the fact that his Cold War mentality matched the immature and politically unsophisticated thought processes at work in the White House, particularly those of Johnson and Rostow. Hence, at the same time that Rusk forbade Americans from taking sides in the conflict, Lodge, with his constant public references to the difficulty of holding free elections in South Vietnam, alerted Ky that the United States would not really mind if the military retained control.[25]

Lodge wanted to prevent any discussion of a possible neutralist solution to the war. Defending the GVN decision to exclude neutralists from the upcoming election, he argued, "As far as [the] majority of anti-communist Vietnamese are concerned, a neutralist solution to [the] present problem is merely [a] way station on [the] road to eventual Communist takeover."[26] He told Ky that the term "neutralist was defined completely differently in the United States from what it was in Vietnam. Here it means someone who was a crypto-Communist or worked actively against the national interest."[27]

KY MOVES TO DESTROY THE VIEN HOA DAO

After the storming of Danang, Ky's stance toward the Buddhists became more militant than ever before. He made clear that no more civil disobedience would be tolerated, ringing the Vien Hoa Dao with ARVN troops, closing the Buddhist Youth Headquarters, and moving a division of reinforcements from the Mekong Delta area to Saigon to act as a reserve for troops stationed in the city.[28] Ky had caught the Vien Hoa Dao off guard, with Thich Tri Quang in Hue and Thich Tam Chau out of the country, while de facto leadership in Saigon fell to Thich Thien Minh. Always before, the Buddhist leadership had acted collectively during crises. Now their physical separation robbed them of important decision making at a most critical moment.

Despite Ky's harsh new measures, the unrest continued. On May 21, Buddhists poured into the Vien Hoa Dao. Prevented from protesting in the streets, Buddhists staged a massive sit-down strike to show their dissatisfaction with the GVN. Despite the large gathering at the Buddhist headquarters, heavily armed police turned back every effort to march into the city, prompting Buddhist leaders to demand Ky's resignation.[29]

Another incident soon occurred, between a U.S. soldier and Buddhists. On May 23, an American infantryman discharged his weapon outside the Vien Hoa Dao, killing Sergeant Nguyen Van Ngoc, a member of the Popular Forces who had stopped to observe the antigovernment agitation. In a spontaneous and violent response, crowds of Buddhists attacked American vehicles, burning two trucks. As children outside the Vien Hoa Dao called for their fellow Vietnamese to "kill the Americans," anti-American banners again appeared in the city. One demanded that the "Americans should go home and take the dirty shooting war with them."[30]

Security forces greeted every attempt to march into the city. On May 23, demonstrators collided with ARVN troops with fixed bayonets, who drove them back into the Buddhist headquarters and then threw tear gas grenades into the compound. The dissidents responded with a barrage of rocks. The fracas continued until monks left the Vien Hoa Dao to negotiate with Loan and Major General Le Nguyen Khang, the military governor of the city. The officers agreed to withdraw their troops when Buddhist leaders promised to close the Vien Hoa Dao.[31]

The next day, ARVN forces watched two thousand Buddhists stream out of the surrounded Vien Hoa Dao as one thousand university students paraded through the city chanting "Down with Ky!"[32] Two days later, despite strenuous GVN efforts to halt the protests, another two thousand agitators, operating in smaller groups to evade security forces, tried to protest against the United States and the GVN and free the Buddhist headquarters. Police, backed by ARVN Marines and paratroopers, again used tear gas to disperse the marchers. One band attacked an American military jeep, sending the two occupants fleeing before security forces could respond.[33] On May 28, four separate groups of agitators, led by monks, attempted to parade but again collided with police and ARVN troops.[34] Upon hearing the news of the first immolation in Hue on May 29, enraged Buddhists in Saigon once more attempted to march into the city. ARVN troops, who had established roadblocks to keep the approximately twenty thousand marchers out, launched volleys of tear gas to drive them back and deny them access to American or GVN buildings. As the crowd scattered from the tear gas, ARVN Marines attacked the fleeing demonstrators.[35]

On June 1, Loan struck at the Vien Hoa Dao. Terrorists under his direction threw a grenade into Thich Thien Minh's car, seriously wounding him.[36] Although Thich Ho Giac called for moderation in the wake of Thich Thien Minh's wounding, Buddhists in the city blamed the United States and the GVN for the attack against their leader.[37] The appeals for restraint seemed to work. On June 3, some twenty thousand Buddhists marched peacefully in a funeral procession for Thich Vien Ngoc and Ho Thi Thieu, two Buddhists who had immolated themselves.[38]

The next day, the GVN announced it would add ten civilians to the Directory. Ky, however, assured Lodge that the military would retain control and that while the new members of the Directory would reflect regional, occupational, religious and other factions in the country, no radicals would be invited to join.[39] Soon afterward, the expanded Directory, which had no representatives from the Vien Hoa Dao, decided not to allow the Constituent Assembly to turn into a popular assembly after drafting the new constitution. This, of course, had been a major Buddhist demand, because they wanted popular elements to predominate in the assembly.[40]

Increasing the radicals' woes, Thich Tam Chau's imminent return to South Vietnam reopened the split in the UBC. Even before his departure for South Vietnam, the moderate monk appealed for an end to the protests. The militant monks in the Vien Hoa Dao defied Thich Tam Chau, however, refusing to halt the agitation and demanding Ky's removal as the price for peace in Saigon.[41]

Thich Tri Quang worked to have Thich Tam Chau removed as the titular head of the UBC. On May 28, the radicals chose Thich Thien Hoa as acting chairman of the Vien Hoa Dao to replace Thich Tam Chau, who was due back in Saigon the next day. The new chairman quickly promulgated the radical position, demanding an end to U.S. support for the Ky government.[42] On May 31, Thich Tam Chau met with the radicals in the Vien Hoa Dao and promised to support their struggle, while also pleading for moderation in the movement. Thich Phap Tri threatened to immolate himself if the Buddhist leadership embraced a temperate position toward the GVN.[43]

Thich Tam Chau met the same day with Thieu and Ky. Reasserting his role as leader of the Vien Hoa Dao, he assured government leaders that the Buddhists did not want them to resign and claimed that the uproar would soon cease.[44] Any opportunity for the radical Buddhists to challenge the GVN successfully and end the war evaporated with Thich Tam Chau's return, since the presence of the pro-GVN leader in the city served as a rallying point for moderate Buddhists and a lightning rod for criticism of the radical elements who had brought the wrath of the GVN on Buddhists around the country. On June 3, Thich Tam Chau was forced to resign as head of the Vien Hoa Dao. The day before, he had again asked members of the UBC to cease demonstrations against the GVN. For the fed-up radicals in the movement, this constituted the final straw, because Thich Tam Chau continued making overtures to the government that had attacked them in Danang and Saigon.[45]

Yet it was the radicals who were finished. With Thich Thien Minh in the hospital and Thich Tri Quang in Hue, and confronted with the police power of the GVN in Saigon and the loss of public support from a significant segment of the populace, the movement began to falter. Despite the resignation of Thich Tam Chau, moderates soon gained ascendancy in the UBC and persuaded most followers to reorient to the pagoda rather than risk total destruction.[46] On June 7, Thich Tam Chau arrived in the capital and rescinded his resignation. Calling on Buddhists to cease demonstrations and self-immolations, Thich Tam Chau bided his time as the radical position deteriorated throughout the month, waiting in the wings to regain control of the UBC after Ky had crushed the movement.[47] In the end, Thich Tam Chau triumphed over his rival Thich Tri Quang by conspiring with the GVN and the American embassy to destroy the radicals in the movement who wanted peace.[48] On June 19, the GVN arrested Thich Tri Quang, transporting him to Saigon and placing him under house arrest. Sensing his rival's precarious position, Thich Tam Chau launched a verbal attack on his rival, which signaled Ky that he could finish off the radicals. On June 23, police raided the Vien Hoa Dao, effectively ending the insurgents' stand.[49]

THE FINAL STAND IN HUE

With the collapse of the dissidents in Danang and the suppression of the movement in other parts of the country, Hue remained the most important center of resistance. Ky hesitated before attacking the city, because of its well-known sympathy for the Struggle Movement and the combat potential and doubtful loyalty of the large ARVN First Division stationed there.

Moreover, upon hearing about the GVN's storming of Danang, dissidents in Hue prepared for the inevitable ARVN attack. Troops from the First ARVN Division and Buddhist students threw up roadblocks at all approaches to the city and fortified key positions.[50] As students demonstrated against the GVN, decrying Ky's slaughter of the inhabitants of Danang, the Hue radio station toned down the heavy dose of anti-American broadcasts that had been its daily fare for the previous two months.[51]

Before long, Buddhists in Hue had occasion to attack the United States again. After the shooting of Second Lieutenant Nguyen Tai Thuc on May 17, U.S. officers expected an explosion of protest.[52] Thich Tri Quang, however, ordered an end to the agitation. Still hoping the U.S. government would come to the aid of the embattled dissidents in Danang, he wanted no more confrontations between Buddhists and Americans in central Vietnam.[53]

Nevertheless, the incident led to an agitated face off between Thich Tri Quang and the American representative in Hue. While assuring James Bullington, acting U.S. consul in Hue, that he had saved many lives by his timely intervention, Thich Tri Quang dismissed the story that an ARVN officer on the ground had precipitated the incident. Instead he blamed it on the inflammatory nature of Cao's visit to the city, which the monk claimed he had cautioned against while the Struggle Force remained under GVN attack in Danang. The consul replied by asking Thich Tri Quang to exercise his influence to maintain calm in the city. Years of frustration boiled out of Thich Tri Quang. "How can we remain calm," he exclaimed, "when Ky oppresses people, American soldiers shoot friendly Vietnamese and [the] U.S. support[s] [the] present government in its actions?" Despite his outburst, Thich Tri Quang agreed to help defuse the explosive atmosphere in Hue.[54]

On May 26, Buddhists in the city conducted a public funeral for Lieutenant Thuc. Immediately afterward, enraged over Thuc's death and Johnson's refusal to respond to Thich Tri Quang's pleas for assistance, students sacked and burned the USIS library, destroying close to ten thousand books. Soldiers sent to protect the U.S. installation "helped the Buddhists push aside barbed wire barricades" while "[t]wo monks cut their chests with razor blades and wrote in blood messages to President Johnson protesting American policies" in South Vietnam.[55] Firefighters refused to put out the blaze, and local security forces observed the attack but would not confront the demonstrators.[56] The same day, Buddhist monks and nuns launched a hunger strike at the American consulate and six thousand Buddhists demonstrated against Ky and the United States. The next day, the United States evacuated most personnel from Hue.[57]

The United States reacted sharply to the attack on its facility. Lodge expressed concern over the safety of the U.S. consulate and staff in Hue after the attack on the American library. Again pushing Ky to act, Lodge warned him that the Americans would respond forcefully if any U.S. personnel were injured by the rioters. Ky pledged that the Americans would not be hurt.[58]

On May 31, Ky stepped up the pressure on the dissidents by directing the ARVN First Division to commence operations in Quang Tri province north of Hue. The absence of the First Division stripped the Struggle Movement of its main defensive power as Ky positioned his forces for an assault on the city. U.S. officials also demanded that the GVN protect American installations in the city, providing Ky another excuse to smash the Struggle Movement in Hue.[59]

On June 1, an enraged crowd destroyed the American consulate in the city, despite Thich Tri Quang's pleas to avoid violence. "A screaming mob of about 1,000 students sacked and burned" the most visible manifestation of American neo-imperialism in their city while ARVN troops assigned to guard the American structure departed the area rather than confront the students.[60] On June 2, Ky ordered the mayor of Hue and chief of Thua Thien province, Lt. General Phan Van Khoa, to move against the students and any remaining rebels in Hue, since by this time "all semblance of governmental authority had vanished from the streets of Hue, and the city had drifted into a state of anarchy."[61]

ARVN armor entered Hue on the third to end the rebellion. Nhuan, however, still held back from attacking the dissidents, although they continued to storm the homes and offices of people associated with the GVN and the United States. Even though significant ARVN elements now resided in the city, they did nothing to break up the crowds of students who roamed the streets. Eventually, loyal troops seized key points in the city, prompting the *Saigon Post* to declare, prematurely, that Hue had been liberated.[62]

The people of Hue refused to yield. With the departure of the ARVN First Division, Buddhists in Hue resorted to a powerfully evocative form of protest: they placed their family altars in the streets to block ARVN vehicles. Unwilling to give the GVN further cause to kill innocent people, Thich Tri Quang initiated a hunger strike of his own while ordering an end to the demonstrations but called on his followers to carry out the symbolic act of moving their family altars into the streets.[63] Vietnamese understood the depth of revulsion this act signified in view of the fact that "[by] placing the family altar before an approaching tank, one sym-. bolically placed one's ancestors, the embodiment of the family, before the tank. In other words, one risked everything."[64]

The decision by Vietnamese to place family altars in the streets indicated a profound rejection of the GVN. When GVN and U.S. forces moved against the dissidents, they found themselves greeted by family altars in the streets of Hue, Danang, Quang Tri and Qui Nhon. Unable to compel regular ARVN units to disregard or run over the altars, Ky sent ARVN airborne and Marine units into the city under the command of Loan to break the movement.[65] At first, they also hesitated rather than destroy the altars that blocked their paths.[66]

U.S. officials considered these actions provocative. Lodge protested to Ky about the Buddhist action, claiming it was designed to incite a confrontation with the Americans. At the same time, he informed Ky that along with the altars, some people in Qui Nhon had lain down in the road to block the movement of troops and vehicles. To Lodge, this "seemed an unacceptable interference with military operations, and was obviously a Viet Cong tactic. It was being loudly praised on the Hanoi radio." Ky agreed with Lodge that Communists lurked behind the new form of protest.[67] Westmoreland also complained to ARVN authorities about the impact of the altars on U.S. combat operations.[68]

In the end, ARVN soldiers politely and reverentially moved the altars to the sides of the roads, paving the way for the subjugation of Hue. By June 19, government troops occupied the city with little resistance. On June 22, security forces moved Thich Tri Quang from Hue to Saigon and restricted him to the Duy Tan Maternity Clinic.[69] A week later, the GVN announced that Thich Tri Quang could receive no visitors in Saigon, except for Vien Hoa Dao leaders. Effectively isolated, he could no longer head the movement.[70] The GVN did not direct the same lenient treatment for other members of the Struggle Movement, "[i]mprisoning many of them in their foulest political camps . . . [leaving] the rest no alternative but to join the NLF."[71] On June 22, ARVN forces seized the city of Quang Tri, the last stronghold of the Struggle Movement in I Corps.[72]

SELF-IMMOLATION

Fenced in on every side, Buddhist leaders resorted to their most potent response: self-immolation. Self-immolation goes to the very heart of the Buddhist effort to end the war in South Vietnam. While most historians agree that the people of Vietnam paid a ghastly price for the American obsession with confronting Communism, few acknowledge the presence of an independent peace movement in the country. Why is it that historians can accept the deaths of millions to fight the war yet find it so hard to believe that some died for peace? Buddhist lore tells the story of a mother tiger so ravaged with hunger that she prepared to eat her cub. When a Buddhist observed this condition, he gave himself to the mother tiger to save the cub. Buddhists use this story to illustrate the importance they place on saving lives. Seen in this light, it becomes easier to understand self-immolation, although the grim nature of the act gives additional evidence of the anguish felt by Buddhists over the war.

Nonviolence and self-immolation are linked, because compassion and a dedication to peace impelled Buddhists to oppose the war even when they understood the power of the United States would be arrayed against them. Unable to respond violently to American provocations, Buddhists sacrificed themselves in the most dreadful fashion to shed light on their predicament while honoring the Buddha's injunction to practice compassion.[73] While many Americans dismissed Buddhist self-immolation as another unexplained act by a people they seldom tried to understand, the willingness of monks, nuns, and laypeople to die for peace serves as a poignant and lasting testament to the depth of feeling some Vietnamese held about the impact of the war on their people.

In many ways, self-immolation represents the highest manifestation of the Buddhist concept of nonviolence, given that the person committing the act chooses to harm himself or herself rather than harm another being. In addition, the Buddha's injunction always to act with compassion could be fulfilled by a person willing to sacrifice himself or herself to call the attention of the world to the plight of Buddhism in South Vietnam. Thus: "By demonstrating in this way the suffering of the war, the self-immolator hoped that those who supported or perpetuated the war would likewise become unable to bear the pain of war and stop the actions that allowed it to continue."[74] Finally, while the positive karma gained from dying for Buddhism seemed certain to benefit the people, Vietnamese Buddhists argued vigorously that self-immolation did not represent suicide. Rather than being the act of a despondent person fleeing the problems of the world, it sought to liberate the people from a ruinous war.[75]

The phenomenon of self-immolation seemed to defy rational explanation to Westerners. Yet destruction of the physical self by fire has a long tradition in Buddhism. When Alexander the Great invaded India in the fourth century B.C., for instance, a Buddhist monk immolated himself before Alexander's force.[76] As Douglas Pike points out, self-immolation constituted "an ancient gesture . . . against actions by the state seen as against religion." Buddhists also utilized it against the French and the Chinese during their occupations of Vietnam.[77]

Vietnamese Buddhist history contains numerous stories of monks who sacrificed themselves by fire. On occasion, monks continued an old practice of burning off a finger to "aid their liberation from the world," while, before the development of gasoline, "monks who decided to immolate themselves would eat fatty foods for a couple of years so they would burn better."[78] In present-day Vietnam, young Buddhist acolytes place burning incense on their heads as a part of their examination process to achieve full membership into the monastic society. Certainly, the Buddhist belief in self-negation and nonattachment to the physical self, combined with the relationship between concepts of fire and purity, could evolve into a belief in the importance of achieving a state of physical non-self through self-immolation, particularly after achieving enlightenment. Finally, self-immolation exerted a profound impact on other Buddhists, who vowed to carry on the fight for peace despite GVN repression and U.S. hostility.

In 1963, the self-immolation of Thich Quang Duc and others highlighted the discredited nature of the Diem regime, making it easier for Washington to write off Diem.[79] Three years later, a wave of immolations in South Vietnam failed to move the U.S. government or the American people. By this time, many Americans believed that fanatical Buddhists no longer deserved sympathy, and U.S. leaders saw the self-immolations as a cynical attempt to manipulate the press rather than the expression of deeply held religious and political beliefs.[80] Publicly, however, Washington remained extremely reluctant to make any statement on the issue.[81] Astonishingly, Lodge claimed that Buddhists had duped the press into projecting their political line by the "current cynical campaign of hunger strikes, letters in blood and suicides."[82]

Part of the U.S. media reflected this trend. *Time,* for instance, characterized the deaths as politically motivated, arguing that most Vietnamese were unmoved by the immolations "because the monks do not have a just cause now." Both *Time* and *Newsweek* claimed, moreover, that the lack of public outrage in South Vietnam indicated that the movement had lost the broad backing it enjoyed in the beginning.[83] Yet the loss of support did not prevent monks and nuns from sacrificing themselves for peace, because they knew that many people suffering from the war had not had their voices heard.

On Memorial Day, President Johnson spoke at Arlington National Cemetery about the recent immolations. Referring to the Buddhist sacrifices for peace as heartbreaking and futile, and calling on the Vietnamese to avoid fanaticism, he assured Americans that the upheaval in South Vietnam merely represented part of a maturing process for the young state. He called on Americans to support his policies in a war that seemed increasingly confusing to most of them and promised his audience that South Vietnam was making the transition to democracy.[84] Because they feared a U.S. backlash to the immolations more than the reaction of the Vietnamese, Thieu and Ky found solace in Johnson's remarks. At the same time, Thieu assured Lodge that the Buddhists remained in the thrall of the NLF, who wanted to bring about a neutral government that would kick the Americans out of South Vietnam.[85]

The first self-immolation of the 1966 crisis occurred on May 29. A Buddhist nun, Thich Nu Thanh Quang, set herself on fire in front of the Dieu De pagoda in Hue in a dramatic attempt to make the world hear "the tragic voice of [her] people." Condemning Johnson for "approving the massacre of our monks, nuns and Buddhist followers," she bemoaned the fact that "[f]or twenty years . . . much of the blood of our compatriots has flowed because of a war without reason." Upon learning of her death,

Thich Tri Quang compared the role of the United States in suppressing the movement in Danang to the American attack on Hiroshima in 1945 and vilified Johnson for continuing to support Ky. Nor did the Buddhist leader shrink from assigning blame for the horrible course his followers set themselves on: "Burning oneself to death is the noblest form of struggle which symbolizes the spirit of non-violence of Buddhism. The Vietnamese Buddhists have no other means to protest against the United States President than by sacrificing their own lives."[86] More sacrifices quickly ensued. The same day, a Buddhist laywoman, Ho Thi Thieu, immolated herself at the Vien Hoa Dao in Saigon to show her opposition to the GVN and the Americans, and a thirty-year-old monk, Thich Quang Thien, immolated himself in Dalat.

In spite of Thich Tam Chau's appeals, more immolations followed. Thich Nu Vinh Ngoc, a nineteen-year-old Buddhist nun from Hue, whose father served as an officer in the ARVN Marines, set herself on fire at the Vien Hoa Dao. On May 31, a seventeen-year-old girl, Nguyen Thi Van, sacrificed herself in Hue, while two more Buddhists sacrificed themselves.[87] As FitzGerald points out, "[w]ithin the week there were more suicides by fire than there had been during the entire Buddhist campaign against Diem."[88] As the Buddhist position deteriorated, the pace of immolations accelerated. On June 4, a Buddhist nun, Thich Nu Dien Dinh, immolated herself in Danang; a twenty-four-year-old nun, Thich Nu Bao Luan burnt herself; while another nun, Thich Dieu Nu Tri, sacrificed herself in Nha Trang and a novice monk destroyed himself by fire in Quang Tri.[89]

In the end, Buddhist sacrifices failed to defeat Ky. Thich Tri Quang called for a halt when he realized that Ky and Thieu meant to destroy the movement and that the United States had no intention of stopping GVN repression. As long as Ky retained U.S. backing, even self-immolations could not defeat the power of the United States and the GVN. They also failed to move American public opinion. Blaming the United States rather than the Buddhists or the NLF for the problems of South Vietnam hit too close to home for many Americans who continued to send their sons and daughters to die in Vietnam. Sensing the failure of the Buddhist campaign, many Vietnamese resigned themselves to the prospect of endless warfare, since Buddhist self-sacrifice could not overcome GVN coercion and the American desire to halt the spread of Communism.

THE THIRD FORCE

Defeated at home, Buddhist leaders sent representatives outside Vietnam to argue their case in the United States and Europe, while the ultimate failure of their plan to bring popular democracy to the country led the Buddhist leadership to embrace the Third Force concept. They claimed they were neither anti-NLF nor anti–United States but pro-peace, since they wanted to ameliorate the impact of the conflict on their people.[90] Rejecting the idea that the conflict had to be settled on the battlefield, Thich Nhat Hanh saw the "third solution" as a way for the United States to withdraw from South Vietnam with its honor intact while allowing Vietnamese to determine their own fate.[91] Most of all, the monk maintained that Vietnamese needed "to be saved from the salvation" of American intervention. While acknowledging that many Americans had commendable intentions in South Vietnam, he argued that American "good will . . . is killing us."[92]

Alfred Hassler, an American peace activist who visited South Vietnam and made contact with the remnants of the Buddhist movement in 1969, claims that numerous South Vietnamese supported the notion of a Third Force to end the conflict.[93] Vietnamese scholar Duong Van Mai Elliot also contends that she, along with other Vietnamese, increasingly saw the Third Force as the solution to the war.[94] In addition, as Buddhist activist Vo Van Ai pointed out, the Third Force had "brought down Diem . . . [and] deposed General Khanh. And in 1966 it would have overthrown Marshal Ky if the Americans had not intervened with their military strength."[95]

Probably no greater proponent of the concept of a Third Force existed than Thich Nhat Hanh. Out of the country during the Buddhist effort to overthrow Diem, he returned in early 1964 at Thich Tri Quang's request to edit several Buddhist journals and spread the message of peace that became the central element of Buddhist thought during the war years. He also helped found Van Hanh University, a Buddhist school still operating in Vietnam, and the School of Youth for Social Service (SYSS).[96]

The SYSS represented the culmination of Thich Nhat Hanh's belief in the importance of socially engaged Buddhism. Disagreeing with the militancy of the followers of Thich Tri Quang, he argued for a Buddhism bereft of political action that focused on easing the suffering of the Vietnamese people caused by the war.[97] He saw the SYSS as a Third Force inside South Vietnam neither supporting nor opposing the GVN or the NLF. Despite the war going on all around them, graduates of the SYSS opened schools, built hospitals, fed the hungry, housed the homeless, cared for refugees, arranged for local truces during natural disasters, worked for peace and tried to end the suffering of the innocent victims of the war.[98]

Thich Nhat Hanh fled South Vietnam in 1966 after a failed attempt on his life. He visited nineteen countries and talked with numerous leaders, including Robert McNamara, Pope Paul VI, Martin Luther King Jr. and members of the U.S. Congress. King later nominated the monk for the Nobel Peace Prize.[99] Thich Nhat Hanh wanted to give Americans "some understanding of how the Vietnamese peasants—the voiceless people with whom he has worked much of his life—feel about the war in their homeland."[100]

In a series of interviews, lectures and seminars around the United States, Thich Nhat Hanh maintained forcefully that the creation of a Third Force not under the influence of the United States or the NLF should determine the fate of Vietnam. Only such a nonaligned entity, he believed, could successfully negotiate a truce in place and immediately end the suffering of the Vietnamese people.[101] Afterward, he claimed, the United States would be asked to leave and the new government would negotiate with the NLF to form an independent GVN based on noninterference by all foreign powers. When asked what would happen if the Communists seized control of the government after a U.S. withdrawal, the monk reminded audiences that "if a Vietnamese Communist and I stood side by side on this platform, our answer would have to be the same: It is not your affair."[102]

Thich Nhat Hanh reasoned that most Vietnamese joined the NLF not because they adhered to Communism but to resist American intrusion into their country. In fact, he maintained that both Communism and capitalism represented Western concepts not suited for Vietnam. He claimed that most Vietnamese remained ignorant of ideology but: "They do know that their country is at war and that Americans are killing Vietnamese . . . [thus] they tend to believe that the NLF is fighting for freedom and independence." He asserted that many Vietnamese backed the NLF because of its resistance to the Americans and supported the Third

Force because of its espousal of peace, while the NLF got its strength from nationalism, not from Communism.[103]

Thich Nhat Hanh constantly emphasized that the Vietnamese should be allowed to determine their own fate, regardless of the consequences. For those who worried that a Communist victory in South Vietnam would lead to retribution by the NLF, he pointed out, "We are not savages; we are a people with an ancient culture, and we are sick in our bones of war. I do not believe there would be a bloodbath, but I wonder when you ask such a question how you would describe what your military forces are doing to my people now?" He argued that many members of the NLF also wanted a neutral government free from outside interference, including that from the DRV. After the Americans left, the new government could decide whether to unify with the DRV, which in all likelihood it would, since most Vietnamese wanted to belong to one nation.[104] In time, the monk contended, the NLF would risk losing much of its popular support if it did not work to achieve peace after the American departure.[105]

Thich Nhat Hanh's efforts in the West also had an impact in South Vietnam. During the upheaval in 1966, he composed his enormously popular book *Vietnam: Lotus in a Sea of Fire.* Mainly written to influence an American audience, the book caused a sensation in South Vietnam and gained wide readership even though it was banned by the GVN. Monks, nuns, and laypeople smuggled copies of the book into every part of the country, where Vietnamese could read about the reasons for the Buddhist struggle and the destructive impact of the American intrusion into Vietnamese society.[106]

Unfortunately for Thich Nhat Hanh, he never returned to South Vietnam. The success of his book convinced his fellow Buddhists that he would be the target of another assassination attempt if he came back, so they advised him to stay out of the country.[107] In 1968, he opened an office in Paris that later became the headquarters of the Buddhist Peace Delegation to the Paris peace talks.[108]

Unlike Ngo Dinh Diem in 1963 or Nguyen Khanh in 1964, Ky understood the importance of appearing to compromise in the crisis and the need to prevent a public-relations debacle like storming the pagodas in Danang, while at the same time maintaining a firm hand against the dissidents so that his enemies would resist the temptation to remove him from power. He also brought a number of civilians into the government, a shrewd move that appeared to give legitimacy to his regime and ensured the loyalty of groups hostile to the Buddhist leadership.

Compounding Buddhist problems, Thich Tam Chau returned to Saigon and rallied moderate elements in the Vien Hoa Dao with calls for restraint, and Ky isolated the radical Buddhists politically by creating fear of Vien Hoa Dao domination of the GVN at a time when the movement had been severely wounded in I Corps. Loan also ordered the assassination of Thich Thien Minh, who was seriously injured, thus robbing the rebellious Saigon Buddhists of their leader at their most vulnerable moment, as Ky attacked the Vien Hoa Dao and broke the power of the radical wing of the UBC.

Nevertheless, Buddhist opposition to Ky had taken many forms: nonviolent resistance in Danang, denunciations of his betrayal of the American-guaranteed April agreement, significant outbursts of inchoate violence and extreme bitterness toward continued U.S. interference in the country. Efforts at conciliation with the United States, moreover, turned into fury as Buddhists realized that Washington would not halt the GVN attacks on their strongholds in Saigon, leading enraged Buddhist students to destroy two American installations in Hue. Left with few means to resist, Buddhists engaged in a series of self-immolations to call attention to their plight as others carried on the struggle outside of Vietnam.

The GVN still had to deal with the problem of the former I Corps commanders. With the collapse of resistance in Danang, Thi decided to make peace with Ky while he still had some leverage. He met Ky at the American base at Chu Lai, where Thi agreed belatedly to accept Westmoreland's offer of medical treatment in the United States.[109] Eventually, Thi went to the United States on what he thought would be a short visit. The GVN never allowed him to return to his beloved South Vietnam, while also canceling his modest pension in 1968 in retaliation for his constant criticism of the Saigon regime. When Thi attempted to return to South Vietnam in 1972, GVN officials refused to allow him to debark from the plane.[110] Ky did not feel as benevolent toward Dinh, who was imprisoned. Dinh claims he received a harsher punishment because he refused to confirm the official GVN story, which no one believed anyway, that Ky had moved forces to Danang at the request of loyal ARVN units.[111] At the end of May, Cao returned to Saigon and assumed new duties.[112] Ky also needed to find a new commander for I Corps. Finally, he chose the chief of the ARVN Second Division, General Hoang Xuan Lam, who had a reputation for sound tactical sense but more importantly, had remained loyal to the GVN during the upheaval of the previous three months.[113]

In the end, Ky's successful attack restored American confidence in his government, particularly when he promised to hold elections for a constituent assembly. American leaders agreed with Ky's actions, since he brought the conflict to an end and ensured the short-term survival of the GVN. Yet, after the establishment of the Third Force outside of South Vietnam, Buddhist self-immolations, the placing of family altars in the streets, the burning of U.S. installations in Hue and efforts to resist GVN repression in Saigon, could there be any doubt that considerable non-Communist opposition to the United States and the GVN existed in the country?

Conclusion

The Movement Defeated?

It might be of moment to western religious people, that a
religious tradition exists in the east, before whose example
their own churches are dim witness indeed.
—Daniel Berrigan

 In the end, the Vien Hoa Dao saw its three-year cam-
paign to end the war and protect the politically power-
less citizenry of South Vietnam turned back by the police
and military power of the GVN and the United States.
Despite a brief period of self-doubt on their part, U.S.
leaders soon increased American troop levels, resulting in more violence and greater distress for the Vietnamese and American people. Thus, Buddhist-inspired instability led to
greater U.S. hegemony over the GVN and to an escalation of the fighting in a way that resulted in one of the great human tragedies of the
twentieth century.

For the United States, the 1966 decision to stay the course put it on
the road to a humiliating defeat in Vietnam. While the war represented a
monumental social catastrophe for the Vietnamese, the United States
also paid a heavy price with the emergence of severe political dissension
and polarization at home, a general loss of faith in government, the breakdown of the Cold War foreign-policy consensus, a damaged economy,
the extreme disillusionment of the soldiers who fought in the war, and
close to 58,000 Americans killed.

The inability of American officials to acknowledge the presence of widespread Vietnamese nationalism as a potent recruiting tool for the NLF, and as the force behind the Buddhist movement, meant that chaos, anarchy, and war would dominate South Vietnam for years to come. Nevertheless, for a short period of time, a window of opportunity had opened for the Johnson administration to flee from its disastrous course in Vietnam. Ultimately, decision makers could not summon the will to recall U.S. forces and convince the American people of the rightness of their judgment. Instead, they stayed with what seemed the safe course, disregarding the appalling human cost of the war despite the fact that key people in the administration knew that the United States could not win and had little popular support in South Vietnam.

Johnson, moreover, ardently believed in the concept of peace through strength that had informed almost every U.S. politician of his generation. Unlike more sophisticated students of international affairs, he endorsed and supported the prevailing ideology of the Cold War, concluding that the United States had to stand against Communist expansion in Asia and elsewhere. Although Johnson had never wanted the war, when faced with the possibility of a hostile regime in Saigon, he remained unable to seize the opportunity presented to him by the Buddhists to escape from an increasingly unpopular war.

Of course, many Vietnamese did not see it that way. They viewed the American attack on the NLF as part of a larger struggle against international Communism, the need to test new weapons, or part of an American effort to colonize South Vietnam.[1] Few outside of the GVN felt a sense of gratitude toward the United States, but many understood the heavy price being paid by their own people.

Despite their enormous sacrifices, Buddhist leaders failed in their quest to motivate their fellow citizens outside of central Vietnam to topple the GVN and end the war. The leadership stumbled when they lost touch with large segments of the UBC and the society they wanted to save. In the ideological split that fatally weakened the Vien Hoa Dao, many monks, nuns, and laypeople supported Thich Tam Chau; they saw the radicalism of monks like Thich Tri Quang as dangerous because it had brought the GVN down on all Buddhists. Thich Tri Quang and the radicals, on the other hand, saw the war as the greater hazard, since they believed that the American presence in South Vietnam would eventually lead to a

Conclusion

Communist victory and the end of the UBC. The moderates, however, supported GVN and American efforts to confront the Communists on the battlefield. Thus, both factions viewed Communism as the greatest danger, but they disagreed on the best way to halt it. Other Buddhist groups and non-Buddhist organizations that had originally backed the Vien Hoa Dao drive for elections withdrew their support out of fear that the Buddhist leadership would seize control of the constituent assembly.[2] Ky capitalized on these fears to gain enough support to crush the movement.

For the people of the Struggle Movement and those living in the rural areas of South Vietnam, the conflict seemed far simpler. They wanted to end the war to stop the killing and liberate South Vietnam from the neocolonial yoke placed on it by the United States. Ironically, at a time when the United States claimed it wanted to deliver the Vietnamese people from the dangers of Communism, members of the Struggle Movement fought to liberate their country from U.S. dominance and a war imposed on them by outsiders: the United States, northerners and southerners. Even though the bulk of the fighting took place in I Corps, much of the local population neither wanted nor appreciated the wider war brought on by American intervention. Nor did they wish for a government or a war imposed on them by the DRV. They simply sought the right to live their lives in peace in a country not controlled by foreigners.

Students, monks, and nuns constituted the critical core of the Struggle Movement: religious people because they wanted to practice Buddhist compassion and peace, students because they wanted to live. Both groups deeply resented U.S. violations of Vietnamese sovereignty and independence. While the GVN exempted students from the draft, Ky understood that widespread student opposition to military conscription would have ended the war quickly, particularly if students, assisted by monks and nuns, could have persuaded peasant boys to resist conscription also.

Jerrold Schecter attributes the Buddhist failure to an overestimation of their power that led them to reach for too much.[3] While he is correct, what choice did they really have? Their history, religious and cultural orientation, and belief in their obligation to save their people left them no choice. They had to confront the GVN and the United States in an attempt to stop the killing and prevent a Communist victory. As Thich Nhat Hanh pointed out, "you cannot be silent and be a religious leader."[4]

While Buddhist leaders exhibited high levels of scholarship in terms of philosophy and textual criticism, they remained political neophytes and very immature in their thinking. Unprepared for the rough-and-tumble world of politics outside the pagoda, their capacity to solve the problems of South Vietnam did not match their ability to understand the inherent dilemma of U.S. intervention in their country. As Stanley Karnow argues, Thich Tri Quang's "zeal could not stop the American and Communist machines that were . . . tearing the country's social tapestry to shreds."[5] Thus, the hatred and desire for revenge and retribution unleashed by the war proved too powerful to be defeated by unarmed Buddhists calling for a return to traditional life in Vietnam. But their effort to stop the war and end the suffering of their people was a valid pursuit for religious figures.

Their entry into the political realm undid their movement. But how else could they stop a war that the United States, the NLF, and the GVN were determined to fight? What is amazing is how close they came to victory: bringing Ky and the GVN to the brink of extinction; leading I Corps out of the GVN orbit from March to mid-May; and forcing Washington into a painful reconsideration of its role in South Vietnam.

Ky's attack on the Buddhists demonstrated that he understood how high the stakes were in the battle with the UBC. Failure to move could have meant a Buddhist victory and peace in Vietnam. By raising the issue of peace in a society sick of conflict, Buddhists tried to save their people from a terrible, costly, and unnecessary war that the country has yet fully to recover from. As George Kahin argues, "[i]n the spring of 1966 the Struggle Movement marshaled so much popular backing that unless U.S. military power had supported Ky and Thieu against it, the Buddhists' immediate political demands would have been met." The alternative, according to Kahin, could have been the defection of central Vietnam and the loss of Danang and Hue, the former imperial capital.[6]

Never allowing the events of 1966 to fade from its consciousness, for the remainder of the war the United States worried about a repeat of 1966 and thus always emphasized stability over democracy. As a result, it tolerated the widespread, barely concealed corruption of the Ky and Thieu regimes and the state-sponsored terror of the Thieu government, since they allowed it to prosecute the war while silencing internal dissent. By doing so, however, it ensured that South Vietnam would never form an effective government capable of resisting the NLF after its departure.

Secure in the knowledge that the United States would support them as long as they prevented a resurgence of popular feeling against the war, Ky and Thieu crushed the Buddhist Struggle Movement with waves of repression. While American leaders rejoiced that the GVN had removed the local impediments to a continued and expanded war, Buddhists suffered imprisonment without trial, persecution, and political annihilation for the remainder of the war as casualties increased and the people endured unimaginable horrors at the hands of the NLF, PAVN, the GVN, and the United States.[7] In the end, the United States negotiated an exit from Vietnam in 1973 under conditions that were remarkably similar to the Buddhist position in 1966. After nine long years of war, with their country laid waste by American firepower and Agent Orange, their population ravaged and their people in the grasp of hatred and bitterness toward one another, the Buddhists had the right to ask what the previous nine years had accomplished. If the war had ended in 1964 or 1966 with a negotiated settlement, would anything have been different from 1973, except for the enormous human cost?

Most commentators agree that the GVN severely limited Buddhist political activity after 1966. Alfred Hassler asserts that the GVN arrested five thousand Duddhists after it crushed the movement in Danang and Hue. Religious historian Sallie King argues that the GVN severely curtailed Buddhist political activity until 1975, claiming that in 1968, "of 1870 prisoners in Chi Hoa Prison, Saigon, 1665 were listed on the daily census as 'Buddhists,' fifty as 'Communists.'"[8] Karnow argues that Loan locked up numerous dissidents and held them in prison for years without due process or trial, while Kahin asserts that many Buddhists remained imprisoned until the South Vietnamese collapse in 1975.[9] All the while, Vietnamese suffered through a conflict few desired, waged by a government "about whose legitimacy, honesty, or competence they had few illusions."[10] Furthermore, Ky used his conquest of the UBC to consolidate his power in the GVN by replacing cabinet members from central Vietnam with others from the south who had supported the GVN in its struggle with the UBC. Indeed, despite GVN promises to establish a more representative government, the Buddhist uprising lead ARVN generals to further suppress democracy in South Vietnam.[11]

Although the GVN announced plans to hold elections for a constituent assembly in September, Buddhist leaders proclaimed they would boycott the voting because the GVN banned peace and neutralist elements from running for office.[12] Thich Tri Quang declared that the UBC would oppose any upcoming ballots put on by Thieu and Ky, again asserting that the continuation of the U.S.-controlled Ky regime foretold more suffering for the Vietnamese people.[13] Thich Nhat Hanh later claimed that the "elections were only a means to legitimize the kind of government Washington wants and the Vietnamese do not want to accept."[14] When the elections finally took place, even though the GVN disqualified anyone who wanted to end the fighting, Thieu and Ky received only 35 percent of the vote.[15] Ky and Thieu, moreover, promulgated a fresh statute that limited the power of the new constituent assembly.[16] Thus, the legislature, like the GVN, fell far short of the democratic institutions the United States claimed to want to bring to South Vietnam.

Washington also took steps to ensure that no additional displays of public opinion occurred in South Vietnam. Karnow argues that after the events of 1966, the U.S. government exercised a tighter grip on the GVN, so that it would allow the United States to carry on the war unimpeded by people calling for peace. As historian Jeffrey Clarke points out, the "crisis also marked the last stand of the Buddhists as an intermediate political force, leaving the Vietnamese people little choice between the Saigon generals on one end of the political spectrum and the Viet Cong on the other."[17]

Yet it does not end there. The long-term damage of the Buddhist crisis can hardly be overestimated, since "the world had watched the ludicrous spectacle of the largest power on earth occupying one of the smallest and helplessly trying to unknot a civil war inside a revolution." Buddhist leaders had exposed the narrow political base of the GVN and the American commitment to any regime that would continue the war, regardless of whether it had political support or not, while increasing the growing doubts in the United States over the war.[18]

The Buddhist Movement, however, had not totally collapsed. Seemingly defeated in openly defying the GVN, they moved their organization underground. Kahin visited South Vietnam at the end of 1966 as part of a U.S. government effort to get antiwar intellectuals on board. Instead, he traveled around the country interviewing Buddhist activists and discovered a dynamic underground network still trying to bring peace to the country and open talks with the NLF. Understanding the need for the American people to hear the voices of the Vietnamese people, Kahin was instrumental in bringing South Vietnamese like Thich Nhat Hanh and Cao Ngoc Phuong to Cornell University to give the other side of the story.[19]

A beautiful young Vietnamese woman, Nhat Chi Mai, perhaps best expressed the continuing anguish felt by many Buddhists over the war when she immolated herself for the cause of peace in May 1967. Before her death, she penned a letter to President Johnson in which she pleaded for an end to the war that could destroy her country. At one point, she wondered, "Do you realize that most Vietnamese in the bottom of our heart feel hatred towards those Americans who have brought the sufferings of the war to our country?" She declared, "I want to use my body as a torch . . . to dissipate the darkness . . . and to bring Peace to Vietnam." Despite brutal GVN suppression of the UBC after 1966, about fifty thousand Vietnamese marched in her funeral procession.[20]

Although demoralized by GVN constraints, Buddhist peace advocates gained new life from the self-immolation of Nhat Chi Mai. Ignoring harsh GVN repression of adherents of reconciliation, a week later, the Vien Hoa Dao appealed for "a cease-fire and a week of prayer for peace," pointing out that a recent CBS poll had discovered that "81% of people interviewed in areas controlled by the Saigon government want peace above all."[21]

In 1968, sensing the deep antagonism toward the GVN, the NLF launched the Tet Offensive, hoping to spark an urban uprising against the GVN. Instead, U.S. and ARVN forces defeated the Communists through the use of unprecedented amounts of firepower in the urban areas. After driving the NLF out of the cities, the GVN came down hard on Buddhist peace elements who had responded to the bloodletting with renewed pleas for an end to the fighting, incarcerating thousands of suspects. The GVN also attacked members of a new group called the Alliance of National, Democratic and Peace Forces, for appealing for reconciliation in the wake of the Tet Offensive.[22]

Still trying to raise international awareness for the need for a cease-fire in their country, the UBC established the Buddhist Peace delegation to the Paris Peace Talks in 1969, with Thich Nhat Hanh as the chief delegate. He used his position to launch repeated appeals for peace in Vietnam while also trying to build support outside the country for an immediate stand-down. Ironically, after some antiwar groups accused the UBC of being under the influence of the CIA, Buddhist peace activists were prevented from participating in some international peace conferences.[23]

As the war increased in intensity, the UBC exerted greater efforts to bring it to an end. In February 1969, Thich Thien Minh and a group of his followers who had been advising young Vietnamese men in ways to avoid the draft received extended prison terms for their antiwar efforts. In 1970 the UBC started a Hoa Binh (peace) campaign that was ruthlessly attacked by GVN security forces. A few months later, a UBC-supported Lotus Blossom political party received the highest vote total in a South Vietnamese election, the result of the Vien Hoa Dao's stated desire for an American departure and the formation of a regime dedicated to peace. In January 1971, some 150,000 Vietnamese held a rally at the An Quang pagoda, calling for peace and an immediate cease-fire with no preconditions. In May 1971, approximately 50,000 people marched in Saigon to commemorate the immolation of Nhat Chi Mai. In August 1974, the UBC inaugurated a "Do Not Shoot Your Brother" campaign that encouraged combatants on both sides to refrain from killing each other. All the while, Buddhist monks and nuns continued to immolate themselves to call the world's attention to their people's suffering. Finally, Thich Tri Quang helped arrange for Duong Van Minh to take power in the waning days of the conflict, ensuring that a "long and hideous war was finished."[24]

The UBC had little time to celebrate, however. Their new Communist overlords, fearing the UBC's broad appeal, gradually attacked them and other religious organizations with the same vigor they had utilized against the GVN and the United States. In time, security forces raided pagodas, closed down orphanages, disbanded religious organizations, and placed prominent Buddhist leaders like Thich Tri Quang under house arrest or imprisonment in remote locations. Worst of all, from the UBC standpoint, the new regime eventually established a government-sponsored and -controlled Buddhist church that became the only recognized Buddhist religious association in the country.[25]

Perhaps the greatest irony of all is that at the dawn of the twenty-first century, South Vietnam no longer exists and the United States has little interest in Vietnam. Yet the UBC still opposes the Communist government. How, then, should the UBC be judged? As a political movement, it failed; the war continued for another nine years after the defeat of the Struggle Movement. Yet, as Sallie King argues, it represented more than that. "Of the Unified Buddhist Church and the Buddhist Struggle Movement it can only be said that theirs is one of the great examples of courage, altruism, and activist spirituality of all time," she writes. "The Buddhists who participated in the Struggle Movement, who worked in the countryside to help peasants survive, who immolated themselves for peace—these people were moved, in fact, by the ideals of their Buddhist faith."[26]

Alas, wartime "Vietnam was not a land for pacifists."[27]

Notes

PREFACE

Epigraph: The reflections of a former North Vietnamese solider, Bao Ninh, author of the poignant antiwar novel *The Sorrow of War.* Bao Ninh, *The Sorrow of War* (Hanoi, 1993), 193.

1. Standard Vietnam War historiography generally divides historians into three groups. As Robert Divine points out, historical interpretation immediately after an American war normally emphasizes the positive aspects of the war and its widespread support. In time, revisionists challenge many of the orthodox assumptions. Then comes a post-revisionist stage where various aspects of the earlier interpretations are combined to achieve a crude consensus. In the case of the Vietnam War, however, the initial works emphasized the inability of the United States to prevail in the quagmire or stalemate of Vietnam and concluded that the war was unwinnable. Later, with the emergence of neo-conservatism in the 1980s, a new group of historians, some of whom had participated as military officers and civilian officials in the war, offered new interpretations. Many of them argued that the war had been winnable and that the failure to persevere to victory constituted a political and moral failing on the part of the civilian leadership of the United States. Others claimed that the U.S. military blundered in Vietnam due to its inability to comprehend the political dimensions of the struggle and tailor a strategy to support the political goals. Still others scored the strategy and tactics chosen by General William C. Westmoreland, some criticized organizational and structural changes in the U.S. Army implemented during the 1950s, while another group argued that excessive civilian control and interference led to defeat. Recently, the historiography has begun to enter the post-revisionist stage, highlighted by the work of scholars attempting to assess the war by examining internal, indigenous factors in Vietnam. See Divine, "Vietnam Reconsidered."

2. "Vietnam Shifts Since '63," *New York Times* (June 13, 1965): 7.

3. George Kahin, interview by the author, Ithaca, New York, September 1996. Notes from this and all of the interviews conducted for this work remain on file in the author's office at Eastern Kentucky University.

4. Herring, *America's Longest War,* 157.

5. Charles Mohr, "Buddhists Insist Ky Junta Must Go," *New York Times* (May 28, 1966): 1.

6. Charles Mohr, "Questions in Vietnam," *New York Times* (May 31, 1966): 10.

7. For a discussion of this, see Herring, "Peoples Quite Apart."

8. Mole, *Vietnamese Buddhism*; and "Buddhism and the Buddhist Programming of the Asia Foundation in Asia," *The Asia Foundation* (San Francisco, 1968), 17–20.

INTRODUCTION

Epigraph: Thich Nhat Hanh, address to Kyoto Conference on Religion and Peace, October 16–21, 1970.

1. Mole, *Vietnamese Buddhism*; and "Buddhism and the Buddhist Programming of the Asia Foundation in Asia," *The Asia Foundation* (San Francisco, 1968), 17–20, 110–20.

2. David Halberstam, "Buddhists Mourn Vietnam Victims," *New York Times* (May 29, 1963): 5.

3. Buddhists in Saigon Mark May 8 Clash with Regime, *New York Times* (May 22, 1963): 3; and Saigon Replaces Three in Dispute, *New York Times* (June 2, 1963): 2.

4. Thich Thien-An, *Buddhism and Zen in Vietnam*; and David Halberstam, "Diem Asks Peace in Religious Crisis," *New York Times* (June 12, 1963): 7. See chapter five for a more detailed discussion of self-immolation.

5. "Telegram from the Department of State to the Embassy in Vietnam," July 2, 1963, U.S. Department of State, *Foreign Relations of the United States: Vietnam, 1961–63,* volume 4, Aug.–Dec. 1963, (Washington, 1991), 443–44 (hereafter cited as *FRUS: Vietnam*); David Halberstam, "Diem Regime under Fire," *New York Times* (July 7, 1963), 4:5; and "Telegram from the Embassy in Vietnam to the Department of State," August 14, 1963, *FRUS: Vietnam, 1963,* vol. 4, 565–67.

6. "Buddhists Seized," *New York Times* (August 21, 1963): 1.

7. Hammer, *Death in November*, 168-98; and Rusk, *As I Saw It,* 440.

8. David Halberstam, "Ranking Saigon Buddhist and 2 Aides Flee into American Embassy," *New York Times* (September 2, 1963): 1; "Telegram from the Embassy in Vietnam to the Department of State," September 9, 1963, *FRUS: Vietnam, 1963,* vol. 4, 136–37; and "U.S. to Refuse Saigon Plea," *New York Times* (September 3, 1963), 3.

9. "Memorandum of a Conversation, White House, Washington," (September 11, 1963), *FRUS: Vietnam, 1963,* vol. 4, 188–90; and Hammer, *Death in November,* 280–311.

10. "Telegram from the Embassy in Vietnam to the Department of State," November 3, 1963, *FRUS: Vietnam, 1963,* vol. 4, 548, and Karnow, *Vietnam: A History,* 339, 379, 380, 445–50.

11. For an excellent explanation of the importance that Buddhist monks and nuns attach to their relationship to the people, see Minh Chi, Ha Van Tan and Nguyen Tai Thu, *Buddhism in Vietnam*; and Minh Chi, "A Survey of Vietnamese Buddhism: Past and Present." The author discussed this during interviews with Professor Minh Chi in Vietnam in 1996, 1999, and 2000.

12. Thich Nhat Hanh, *Love in Action,* 1–13.

13. Douglas Pike, interview by the author, July 1996. Pike, who served as a U.S. foreign service officer in South Vietnam from 1960 to 1975, believes this contemptuous attitude may have contributed to the NLF decision to slaughter over two thousand mainly Buddhist civilians during the occupation of Hue in 1968. Also see Topmiller, "Buddhist Crisis of 1963," 14; and Benz, *Buddhism or Communism,* 97, 229; and Kahin interview, October 1996.

14. While in Ho Chi Minh City during March 1997, the author sought out Vietnamese religious figures who belonged to sects that did not align with the UBC. Thich Thien Minh (not the same monk as the one mentioned in this work), a Vietnamese Theravada monk, claimed that while two Vietnamese Theravada monks, Thich Ho Giac and Thich Phap Tri, held leadership positions in the UBC, most of the monks in this sect stayed out of the struggle with the GVN but still agreed with Buddhist efforts to end the war. Some monks formed a different organization but, within a year, joined the UBC. During the same trip, the author visited a Khmer Theravada pagoda in Ho Chi Minh City, where two monks and a layperson told him that while most members of their sect avoided joining the UBC, they also supported the Buddhist mission of ending the war. They argued that most Khmer monks opposed U.S. intervention in South Vietnam because of the high rate of civilian casualties from American operations. In addition, they claimed that most Vietnamese did not accept the presence of foreign soldiers in their country and that many monks responded to this feeling by opposing the war (Thich Thien Minh, Eka Suvanna, Phala Suvanna, and Nguyen Huu Nghiep, interviews by the author, Ho Chi Minh City, Vietnam, March 1997).

15. Hedrick Smith, "Buddhists Unify Vietnam Church," *New York Times* (January 4, 1964): 5. Like Vietnamese Buddhism itself, the Unified Buddhist Church of Vietnam has demonstrated an astonishing resiliency in the face of continued repression and persecution. In 1995, the UBC continued the cause of religious freedom in Vietnam by challenging the Communist government to allow true religious freedom in Vietnam. See "Vietnam: The Suppression of the Unified Buddhist Church," 1–16.

16. Bureau of Naval Personnel, *The Religions of South Vietnam,* 20–21. Although many Westerners consider the Cao Dai sect in Vietnam to be an offshoot of Buddhism, they regard themselves as the culmination of Buddhism, Catholicism, and all other religions. Their fervent anti-Communism and sense of religious uniqueness prevented them from joining with the UBC (Hum Dac Bui, letters to author, 1993). Thanks to Thich Tam Thien for trying to clear up the author's confusion about the difference between Vietnamese Hinayana and Theravada sects (Thich Tam Thien, interview by the author, Ho Chi Minh City, Vietnam, March 1997).

17. Nguyen Tai Thu, ed., *History of Buddhism in Vietnam,* 369–70.

18. Le Van Hoa, "Correlates of the Politically Radical-Conservative Attitudes," 1–53.

19. Chan Khong, *Learning True Love,* 49; and Peter Grose, "The War in South Vietnam: Even the Optimist Is Gloomy," *New York Times* (May 31, 1964): 1.

20. Vo Van Ai, who was sent by the Buddhist organization to Paris in 1965 to establish an overseas branch of the Buddhist movement, claims that most of the leadership in the 1960s studied together in the 1930s, as part of the resurgence of

Buddhism in Vietnam, and were infused with the idea of bringing social justice to Vietnam. Also see Batchelor, *Awakening of the West,* 360–61.

21. Warner, "Vietnam's Militant Buddhists," 29; and Topmiller, "The 1963 Buddhist Crisis in South Vietnam," 96.

22. Thich Quang Lien, an important Buddhist leader in his own right, told the author that he thought Thich Tri Quang was a Communist, until he was placed under house arrest by the Communists in 1975. He remains under house arrest today at the An Quang pagoda in Ho Chi Minh City. The author made four attempts to visit him during the summer of 1996 and another in March 1997, but he refuses to talk to foreigners (Thich Quang Lien, interview by the author, Ho Chi Minh City, Vietnam, July 1996).

23. Schecter, *New Face of Buddha,* 162. During a telephone conversation in November 1994, Dr. Kahin told the author that it was commonly believed in Saigon at that time that Thich Tam Chau might have received indirect support from the American embassy. In an interview in Seattle during the summer of 1996, Thich Minh Chieu, a close associate of Thich Tam Chau, told the author that Thich Tam Chau did not take money from the United States but was intimidated by U.S. efforts to control the internal affairs of South Vietnam, which rendered him susceptible to U.S. pressure.

24. Schecter, *New Face of Buddha,* 162–63.

25. Hope, "Vietnam Perspectives," 16.

26. Wyatt, *Paper Soldiers,* 150–66.

27. Batchelor, *Awakening of the West,* 361.

28. Luce and Sommer, *Vietnam: The Unheard Voices,* 113.

29. Huyen, "Literature and the Vietnamese," 37–48.

30. Suzuki, *Introduction to Zen Buddhism,* 64–65.

31. Creel, *Chinese Thought.*

32. Suzuki, *Introduction to Zen Buddhism,* passim.

33. Thich Tam Thien, interview by the author, Ho Chi Minh City, Vietnam, March 1997.

34. Ling, *Buddha, Marx and God.*

35. Thich Nhat Hanh, *Heart of Understanding.*

36. Suzuki, *Introduction to Zen;* Wu, *Golden Age of Zen;* and Thich Nhat Hanh, *Zen Keys.*

37. Minh, *Buddhism in Vietnam.*

38. Hue-Tam, *Millenarianism and Peasant Politics.*

39. Diem, *In the Jaws of History,* 106–12.

40. Kolko, *Anatomy of a War,* 152–60.

41. Ibid., 154.

42. Kahin, *Intervention,* 182–201. Kahin has the most complete account of the Pentagon coup and, in addition, claims that the generals who were deposed by Khanh in January 1964 later admitted that they were planning to install a neutralist government. In a conversation with the author during the summer of 1996, Khanh confirmed that he received the green light from the U.S. embassy to carry out the coup.

43. Thich Nhat Hanh, *Vietnam: Lotus in a Sea of Fire,* 90. Also see Tran Van

Don, *Our Endless War,* 122, 134–35. Don claims that Khanh misrepresented a number of innocent actions by the generals, such as allowing exiled anti-Diem activists to return home, to convince the Americans that the generals were moving to a neutral government. Maxwell Taylor confirms Don's statements (Taylor, *Swords and Plowshares,* 308). Khanh claims that Don worked for French intelligence.

44. Taylor, *Swords and Plowshares,* 309–10, and Kahin, *Intervention,* 203–4.

45. Le Van Hoa, "Correlates," 50, and Taylor, *Swords and Plowshares,* 312. Kahin points out, however, that Catholics were not as monolithic as usually described. Many also wanted the fighting to end.

46. Peter Grose, "Buddhist Unrest Troubles Khanh," *New York Times* (May 9, 1964): 4; Le Van Hoa, "Correlates," 50; and "Summary Record of a Meeting, Honolulu, June 1, 1964, 8:30 a.m.–4:30 p.m.," *FRUS: Vietnam, 1963–1968,* vol. 1, 1964: 414.

47. Peter Grose, "Third Ngo Brother Executed in Saigon with 300 Observing," *New York Times* (May 10, 1964): 1.

48. "Top Buddhist Joins Protest to Saigon," *New York Times* (May 14, 1964): 6; *The LBJ National Security Files* (University Publications of America), Reel 19; "Telegram from the Embassy in Vietnam to the Department of State, May 14, 1964," 321; "Telegram from the Embassy in Vietnam to the Department of State, May 14, 1964," *FRUS: Vietnam,* vol. 1, 1964: 316; and "Buddhists Raise Status in Saigon," *New York Times* (May 16, 1964): 2.

49. Peter Grose, "Catholics Rally in Saigon, Charging Bias by Regime," *New York Times* (June 8, 1964): 1.

50. Tran Van Don, *Our Endless War,* 128–29; Fulham, "Vietnamese Sand Castle," 13; and "Telegram from the Embassy in Vietnam to the Department of State, August 22, 1964," *FRUS: Vietnam,* vol. 1, 1964: 696.

51. "Nation Declared under State of Emergency," *Saigon Post* (August 8, 1964): 1.

52. "General Khanh, President of the Republic," *Saigon Post* (August 17, 1964): 1.

53. "Saigon Students Score Army Rule," *New York Times* (August 22, 1964): 2; "Students Burn Charter Copy," *New York Times* (August 23, 1964): 3; Peter Grose, "Khanh Responds to Young Critics," *New York Times* (August 23, 1964): 3; "Students Attack National Radio Station," *Saigon Post* (August 24, 1963): 1; "Ministry Office Sacked," *New York Times* (August 24, 1964): 3; "U.S. Army Billet Stoned," *New York Times* (August 24, 1964): 3; "Struggle Continues, Buddhists Told," *Saigon Daily News* (August 19, 1964): 2; and "Students Honor Youthful Martyr," *Saigon Post* (August 26, 1964): 1.

54. Peter Grose, "Violence Widespread," *New York Times* (August 25, 1964): 10; Peter Grose, "Riots Continuing," *New York Times* (August 26, 1964): 1; "Anarchy and Agony," *Time* (September 4, 1964): 33; Peter Grose, "Rulers in Saigon Unable to Agree on a New Regime," *New York Times* (August 27, 1964): 1; and "Danang Rioters Hit U.S. Run Hospital," *New York Times* (August 27, 1964): 3.

55. "Telegram from the Embassy in Vietnam to the Department of State, August 25, 1964," *FRUS: Vietnam,* vol. 1, 1964: 702.

56. Josef Reisinger, "Vietnam's Schizophrenia," *Far Eastern Economic Review* 47 (October 29, 1964): 265–67.

57. Peter Grose, "Khanh Quitting but May Return Under Code," *New York Times* (August 26, 1964): 1; "Drastic Changes Urged by Buddhist Leaders," *Saigon Post* (August 26, 1964): 1; and "General Khanh Resigns as President," *Saigon Daily News* (August 26, 1964): 1.

58. Kahin, *Intervention,* 228, and "Telegram from the Central Intelligence Agency Station in Saigon to the Agency, August 25, 1964," *FRUS: Vietnam,* vol. 1, 1964: 658.

59. "Triumvirate Named: Khanh Heads Caretaker Government," *Saigon Post* (August 28, 1964): 1.

60. "Telegram from the Embassy in Vietnam to the Department of State, August 26, 1964," *FRUS: Vietnam,* vol. 1, 1964: 708.

61. Kahin, *Intervention,* 230.

62. "Saigon Regime Names Civilian Acting Premier," *New York Times* (August 29, 1964): 1.

63. Tad Szulc, "Backing of Khanh Affirmed by U.S.," *New York Times* (August 24, 1964): 10; and Diem, *In the Jaws of History,* 120–21.

64. Maruyama, "America's Logic and Vietnam's Logic," 205–13.

65. Thich Nhat Hanh, *Vietnam: Lotus in a Sea of Fire,* 82.

66. Kahin, *Intervention,* 234.

67. "Telegram from the Embassy in Vietnam to the Department of State, August 27, 1964," *FRUS: Vietnam,* vol. 1, 1964: 713.

68. Westmoreland, *A Soldier Reports,* 66–71; and Taylor, *Swords and Plowshares,* 308–28.

69. "Notes Prepared by the Secretary of Defense (McNamara), May 14, 1964," *FRUS: Vietnam,* vol. 1, 1964: 324.

70. "Again, the Buddhists in South Vietnam," 27–28.

71. "Anarchy and Agony," 33–34.

72. Higgins, "Ugly Americans of Vietnam," 377.

73. Peter Grose, "Diplomats Weigh Future of Khanh," *New York Times* (August 31, 1964): 3.

74. "Anarchy and Agony," 33.

75. "Dissatisfied Buddhists," 34.

76. "Telegram from the Embassy in Vietnam to the Department of State, September 6, 1964," *FRUS: Vietnam,* vol. 1, 1964: 733–35.

77. "Troops Occupy Public Offices," *Saigon Daily News* (September 14, 1964): 1; "24-Hour Military Revolt Smashed," *Saigon Daily News* (September 15, 1964): 1; and Peter Grose, "Khanh Is Pressing Wide Army Shifts," *New York Times* (September 17, 1964): 11.

78. "Delta Troops Stage Coup," *Saigon Post* (September, 14, 1964): 1; and "Compromise Ends Coup," *Saigon Post* (September 14, 1964): 1.

79. "Too Little, Too Late," 543.

80. Young, *The Vietnam Wars,* 126.

81. "Phan Khac Suu Chief of State," *Saigon Post* (October 26, 1964): 1.

82. Forest, *Unified Buddhist Church of Vietnam,* 6, 31.

83. Taylor, *Swords and Plowshares,* 323–25.

84. FitzGerald, *Fire in the Lake,* 343.

85. Peter Grose, "Regime's Foes Riot in Streets of Saigon," *New York Times* (November 23, 1964): 1.

86. "Huong Blames Riots on 'Politicians,'" *Saigon Post* (November 24, 1964): 1; Kahin Files, *Dalat Generals,* 1–6; "Troops Disperse Demonstrations," *Saigon Post* (November 23, 1964): 1; and "Huong Government Faces Crucial Test," *Saigon Post* (November 25, 1964): 1.

87. "Huong Blasts Troublemakers," *Saigon Post* (November 27, 1964): 1.

88. "Saigon under Martial Law," *Saigon Post* (November 28, 1964): 1; "Martial Law Clapped on Saigon, Gia Dinh," *Saigon Daily News* (November 28, 1964): 1; and "Buddhists Deny Demonstrations Started from Buddhist Center," *Saigon Daily News* (November 28, 1964): 1.

89. "Procession Turns into Demonstration," *Saigon Post* (November 30, 1964): 1.

90. "Buddhist Institute Reopened to Public," *Saigon Post* (December 12, 1964): 1; Peter Grose, "Buddhist Leaders Open Fast in Fight on Saigon Regime," *New York Times* (December 13, 1964): 1; and "500 Buddhists Fast in Saigon Protest," *New York Times* (December 16, 1964): 3.

91. "Message from the Ambassador in Vietnam [Taylor] to the President, December 16, 1964," *FRUS: Vietnam,* vol. 1, 1964: 998–1000.

92. Diem, *In the Jaws of History,* 122; and "Generals' Purge Illegal but Unavoidable: Ky," *Saigon Post* (December 22, 1964): 1.

93. Three of the officers present, Ky, Thieu and Thi, were destined to clash in 1966 in the most serious Buddhist disturbance of the Vietnam War (Taylor, *Swords and Plowshares,* 330–31).

94. While Khanh was telling the author this story, he turned to his friend Tran Bang Tam and said to her in Vietnamese, "[H]e dared to speak to me that way." Khanh saw this as a continuation of Taylor's arrogant, haughty attitude toward members of the Vietnamese military and government and further proof that the GVN should move towards a negotiated settlement. (Nguyen Khanh, interview by the author, Fremont, Calif., July 1996). Also see Shaplen, *Lost Revolution,* 296.

95. Young, *Vietnam Wars,* 133.

96. "Message from the Ambassador in Vietnam [Taylor] to the President, December 23, 1964," *FRUS: Vietnam,* vol. 1, 1964: 1031–32.

97. Khanh was adamant about this in an interview with the author. He felt then, and feels now, that too many lives had been lost and that it was time to bring the war to a conclusion (Khanh interview, July 1996).

98. Diem, *In the Jaws of History,* 121.

99. McNamara, *In Retrospect,* 164.

100. Kaiser, *American Tragedy,* 394–95.

101. Bui Diem, Quat's closest advisor, reports that the United States did not even consult the GVN before landing marines at Danang in 1965 (Diem, *In the Jaws of History,* 130).

102. Forest, *Unified Buddhist Church of Vietnam,* 6.

103. "Thich Quang Lien's Peace Movement," Kahin Files, 7. The author interviewed Thich Quang Lien, who founded one of the peace efforts in 1965, during a

visit to the Thich Quang Duc Pagoda in July 1996. The monk claimed that he did not oppose U.S. intervention but wanted to end the killing, which he felt was destroying his country. After 1966, he retired to head a monastery dedicated to the study of peace. Still a man of principle, he was very outspoken in his condemnation of recent religious repression by the Communist government of Vietnam (Thich Quang Lien, interview by the author, Ho Chi Minh City, Vietnam, July 1996).

104. Forest, *Unified Buddhist Church of Vietnam,* 6.

105. Forest, *Unified Buddhist Church of Vietnam,* 7.

106. Memo, Thompson and Ropa to Bundy, 1-7-66, Vietnam vol. 45, VCF; Cable, CIA Intelligence Information Cable, 2-7-66, "Comments and Observations Concerning the 3 February Directorate Meeting," Vietnam vol. 47, VCF.

107. One of his more famous statements concerned the need for a Hitler-like ruler to confront the problems of South Vietnam. See "Pilot with a Mission," 26. In later years, Ky was accused of involvement in the heroin trade, gambling, and rackets in Vietnam and of control over a network of Asian gangs in the United States after 1975 (Indochina Archive, Nguyen Cao Ky: Biography File).

108. "War Gov't Takes Tough Measures," *Saigon Post* (June 22, 1965): 1.

109. Colby, *Lost Victory,* 176–80.

110. Herring, *America's Longest War,* 128–44. For an excellent discussion of U.S. peace moves during the war, see Herring, *LBJ and Vietnam.*

111. Vo Van Ai, e-mail to author, 5-31-96.

1. Origins of the Buddhist Crisis of 1966

Epigraph: Embtel 3817 (Saigon), Lodge to Rusk, 4-8-66, Vietnam vol. 50, Vietnam Country File, NSF LBJ Library (hereafter cited as VCF).

1. Kahin, *Intervention,* 417; Vo Van Ai, e-mail to author, 5–23–96; and Charles Mohr, "Behind Saigon's Purge: Honolulu Talks with Johnson Gave Ky Confidence to Move against His Rival," *New York Times* (March 14, 1966): 2.

2. Kahin interview, October 1996.

3. Pike, interview by the author, Berkeley, Calif., July 1996.

4. Karnow, *Vietnam: A History,* 444, and Westmoreland, *A Soldier Reports,* 169–70.

5. Diem, *In the Jaws of History,* 165–66.

6. "Pilot with a Mission," 26.

7. Cable, CIA Intelligence Information Cable, "Prime Minister Ky's View That General Thi May Have Lost Support of the Populace and May Be Engaged in Political Moves against the Government," 4-4-66, Vietnam vol. 48, VCF.

8. Ky, *How We Lost the Vietnam War,* 89.

9. Report, CIA Weekly Report: "The Situation in South Vietnam, 1-5-66," Vietnam vol. 45, VCF; and Vo Van Ai, e-mail to author, 5-23-96.

10. Nguyen Chanh Thi, interview by the author, Lancaster, Pa., April 1997.

11. Embtel 3265 (Saigon), Lodge to Rusk, 3-9-66, Vietnam vol. 48, VCF.

12. Donnell and Joiner, "South Vietnam," 54; and Thi interview, April 1997. Every time the author mentioned to Thi that he had been fired or dismissed, he

would grab his sleeve and exclaim, "No, no, no!" Although he argues that he was so fed up that he was ready to leave office anyway, it is obvious that his vote was a face-saving gesture in a society where face is very important.

13. Rose Kushner, Indochina Archive, Nguyen Chanh Thi: Biography File; and Thi interview, April 1997.

14. Cables, CIA to White House Situation Room, 3-11-66 and 3-10-66, Vietnam vol. 48, VCF.

15. "NLC Confirms Confidence in PM Ky, Grants Gen. Thi Request for Leave," *Saigon Daily News* (March 12, 1966): 1; and "Gen. Thi on 'Leave'; Successor Named," *Saigon Post* (March 12, 1966): 1.

16. Cable, CIA Intelligence Information Cable, "Possibility of Student Demonstrations in Danang against Inflation and Deputy Prime Minister Nguyen Huu Co," 2-10-66, Vietnam vol. 47, VCF.

17. FitzGerald, *Fire in the Lake,* 372–73.

18. Report, CIA Weekly Report: "The Situation in South Vietnam, 3-2-66," Vietnam vol. 48, VCF.

19. Despite the ongoing problem of corruption, the United States remained committed to the military junta because it seemed to be the only force capable of carrying on the war. See Kolko, *Anatomy of a War,* for an excellent discussion of the problem of corruption in South Vietnam and the American role in perpetuating it.

20. While the author thoroughly enjoyed meeting all of the people interviewed for this work, Thi made the greatest impression on him. He is a person who radiates honesty, commitment, passion, integrity and a deep love for Vietnam. Tragically, he was never allowed to return to Vietnam after he left in 1966 for what he thought was a temporary sojourn.

21. During his visit to central Vietnam in March 1997, the author was constantly amazed at the level of good feeling toward Thi that still exists in the region. When the author told people he planned to interview Thi after his return to the United States, they always asked the author to tell Thi how popular he still is in Hue and Danang. At one point, while drinking beer at the DMZ bar in Hue, the author mentioned Thi's name to the manager, who quickly pointed out that the house next door had previously belonged to Thi's uncle.

22. *Time,* 2-18-66, 28; Don, *Our Endless War,* 172; Luce, *Unheard Voices,* 125; and Diem, *In the Jaws of History,* 165.

23. Rowland Evans and Robert Novak, Indochina Archive, Nguyen Chanh Thi: Biography File.

24. Letter, "Colonel Howard B. St. Clair to Bromley Smith," 4-8-66, Vietnam vol. 51, VCF.

25. Charles Mohr, "Ky Rival's Ouster Sets Off Protest," *New York Times* (March 12, 1966): 3. Westmoreland and Lodge cooked up a scheme to invite Thi to the United States to secure treatment for a sinus condition. This led Thi to allude to the odors emanating from Saigon when he greeted welcoming crowds in I Corps (Embtel 3288 [Saigon], Lodge to Rusk, 4-10-66, Vietnam vol. 48, VCF); Luce, *Unheard Voices,* 126; Robert Shaplen, "Letter from South Vietnam," 148; Diem, *In the Jaws of History,* 166; and Westmoreland, *A Soldier Reports,* 169.

26. Charles Mohr, "Buddhists Criticize Ky Regime; Protests on Ouster of Thi Grow," *New York Times* (March 13, 1966): 1.

27. Neil Sheehan, "Shops in Danang Shut in Protest," *New York Times* (March 14, 1966): 1.

28. Robert Shaplen, "Letter From South Vietnam," 142.

29. Neil Sheehan, "Students Assail Clique," *New York Times* (March 16, 1966): 2.

30. Cable, CIA Intelligence Information Cable, "Reason for Decision to Permit General Thi to Visit Danang," 3-16-66, Vietnam vol. 48, VCF.

31. Neil Sheehan, "Thi Urges Calm in Danang," *New York Times* (March 17, 1966): 5.

32. "Can Ky Hang on in Vietnam?" *New York Times* (March 20, 1966): IV: 1; and Neil Sheehan, "Hue Hails Gen. Thi; Dissension Grows," *New York Times* (March 18, 1966): 1.

33. Charles Mohr, "Buddhists Denounce 'Rotten' Rule by Ky," *New York Times* (March 16, 1966): 1; Cable, CIA to White House Situation Room, 3-21-66, Vietnam vol. 49, VCF; and CIA memo, "Struggle Groups in I Corps," 4-1-66, Vietnam vol. 50, VCF.

34. Charles Mohr, "Anti-Ky Protests by Saigon Monk Draws Thousands," *New York Times* (March 17, 1966): 1; "Anti-Ky Rallies Erupt in Saigon," *New York Times* (March 27, 1966): 1; R.W. Apple Jr., "Protest March in Nha Trang," *New York Times* (March 26, 1966): 2; and FitzGerald, *Fire in the Lake,* 374.

35. CIA memo, "The Political Situation in South Vietnam: The Current Crisis, Possible Future Developments, U.S. Options," 4-2-66, Vietnam vol. 50, VCF.

36. FitzGerald, *Fire in the Lake,* 374–75; and Herring, *America's Longest War,* 156–57.

37. Embtel 3621 (Saigon), Lodge to Rusk, 3-31-66, Vietnam vol. 49, VCF.

38. "Hue Demonstrators Bar Junta General from Leaving City," *New York Times* (April 1, 1966): 3; and Embtel 3642 (Saigon), Lodge to Rusk, 4-1-66, Vietnam vol. 50, VCF.

39. "General Chieu Back in Saigon," *Saigon Daily News* (April 4, 1966): 1.

40. Cable, CIA to White House Situation Room, "Political Agitation," 4-1-66, Vietnam vol. 50, VCF.

41. Charles Mohr, "3000 Troops Lead Vietnam Protest against Regime," *New York Times* (April 3, 1966): 1; and Kahin File, "Trial Transcript and *Hoa Binh* Commentary," 1–32.

42. R.W. Apple Jr., "Saigon Refuses to Yield to Pressure by Buddhists," *New York Times* (March 19, 1966): 1.

43. Kahin claims that Lodge urged Ky to renege on his agreement with the Buddhists (Kahin, *Intervention,* 420); Embtel 3408 (Saigon), Lodge to Rusk, 3-19-66, Vietnam vol. 49, VCF.

44. Charles Mohr, "Buddhists Irked by Ky Criticism," *New York Times* (March 22, 1966): 4; and R.W. Apple Jr., "Buddhists Assail Ky Regime and U.S. at Rally in Saigon," *New York Times* (March 31, 1966): 1.

45. Embtel 3382 (Saigon), Lodge to Rusk, 3-17-66, Vietnam vol. 49, VCF.

46. Embtel 3336 (Saigon), Lodge to Rusk, 3-16-66, and Embtel 3408 (Saigon), Lodge to Rusk, 3-19-66, Vietnam vol. 49, VCF.

47. "Gov't's and People's Viewpoints Not Different, P.M. Ky Says," *Saigon Daily News* (March 28, 1966): 1.

48. "PM Says Gen. Thi Will Be Given New Assignment," *Saigon Daily News* (March 30, 1966): 1.

49. Embtel 3577 (Saigon), Lodge to Rusk, 3-29-66, Vietnam vol. 49, VCF.

50. Pike interview, July 1996.

51. Kahin, *Intervention,* 420.

52. Embtel 3540 (Saigon), Lodge to Rusk, 3-27-66, Vietnam vol. 49, VCF.

53. Embtel 3604 (Saigon), Lodge to Rusk, 3-31-66, Vietnam vol. 49, VCF; and Embtel 3614 (Saigon), Lodge to Rusk, 3-31-66, Vietnam vol. 49, VCF.

54. Charles Mohr, "Ky Moves up Date for Constitution," *New York Times* (March 26, 1966): 1.

55. "N.L.C. Announces Early Formation of Political Congress, Firm Measures," *Saigon Daily News* (April 4, 1966): 1.

56. "Premier Ky Warns Public Servants against Undiscipline," *Saigon Daily News* (April 1, 1966): 1; and "Civil Servants, Military Involved in Subversive Activities to Be Severely Punished," *Saigon Daily News* (April 1, 1966): 2.

57. This is a further indication of the American tendency to disregard the wishes of the Vietnamese people in its campaign to confront the NLF in Vietnam. As Vo Van Ai points out, many Vietnamese welcomed American assistance against the Communists, but the clumsiness of the American effort alienated the population and strengthened the NLF (Vo Van Ai, e-mails to author, 5-23-96 and 5-31-96).

58. Charles Mohr, "Ky Says Troops Will Go to Danang to Restore Order," *New York Times* (April 4, 1966): 1.

59. Embtel 3577 (Saigon), Lodge to Rusk, 3-29-66, Vietnam vol. 49, VCF.

60. Kahin, *Intervention,* 421; and Memo, Consul General in Hue to Lodge, 4-3-66, "Reaction to Ky's April 3 Press Conference," Vietnam vol. 50, VCF.

61. "Prime Minister Ky Moves against Demonstrations," *Saigon Daily News* (April 4, 1966): 1.

62. Kahin, *Intervention,* 420–21; and Kahin interview, September 1996.

63. Kahin, *Intervention,* 403. Much of the problem, according to Thich Minh Chieu, a close associate of Thich Tam Chau, was the American tendency to demand control over every facet of Vietnamese life, further alienating many Vietnamese (Thich Minh Chieu, interview by the author, Seattle, Washington, July 1996).

64. Westmoreland, *A Soldier Reports,* 168.

65. Embtel 2854, Porter to Rusk, 2-7-66, Vietnam vol. 47, VCF.

66. Nor were these conditions confined to central Vietnam. During an interview with Phala Suvanna and Eka Suvanna, two Cambodian Theravada monks, both assured the author that most of their fellow monks opposed U.S. intervention in the country due to the heavy civilian casualties caused by American operations. Even though they were not part of the UBC, they claimed that Buddhist compassion led them to oppose the war and protect the people. In addition, they argued that

most Vietnamese opposed the presence of the Americans in South Vietnam. (Interview by the author, Candransi Pagoda, Ho Chi Minh City, Vietnam, March 1997.)

67. Woodside, "Some Southern Vietnamese Writers," 53–58.

68. Kahin, *Intervention,* 404–9; and Kahin interview, September 1996. Kahin discusses the horrible effects of these weapons on the civilian populace the United States had supposedly entered Vietnam to protect. Buddhist activists smuggled him into a hospital full of wounded civilians on Christmas Day 1966, while most of the senior staff had the day off. He had nightmares about the condition of the people he saw that day for a long time afterward. As a former hospital corpsman with the U.S. Marines, the author can attest to the gruesome nature of the wounds caused by these weapons. While in Ho Chi Minh City in July 1996, the author visited the American War Crimes Museum, which has numerous graphic displays of the effects of American firepower during the war. One room, dedicated to the impact of Agent Orange, had a number of containers holding deformed fetuses that resulted from the use of defoliants in South Vietnam. Recently, Vietnam claimed that 75,000 babies with birth defects were born after the war. One of the people the author interviewed for this work, Father Josephus Le Van Phuc, sent the author a picture of disabled children who have been born in the last ten years in central Vietnam, along with a plea for help.

69. Woodside, "Some Southern Vietnamese Writers," 53–58.

70. Luce, *The Unheard Voices,* 121–23.

71. As a young American serviceman in Danang during 1968, the author was shocked by the level of anti-Americanism in the city. He recalls being taunted by school girls on a city bus, who expressed their preference for Ho Chi Minh, whom they considered "number 1," as opposed to U.S. Marines, who were "number 10."

72. Memo, Habib to Lodge, 2-17-66, "Conversation with Tri Quang," Vietnam vol. 47, VCF.

73. Thich Nguyen An, interview by the author, July 1996; Kahin file, "Letter from Thich Tri Quang to Thich Nhat Hanh."

74. Thich Nguyen An, interview, July 1996.

75. Vo Van Ai, e-mail to author, 5-23-96.

76. Tran Hong Lien, interview by the author, Ho Chi Minh City, Vietnam, August 1996; Thich Quang Lien, interview by the author, Ho Chi Minh City, Vietnam, August 1996; and Ban Hoang, interview by the author, Seattle, Washington, July 1996.

77. Thich Nhat Hanh, *Love in Action,* 4.

78. Pike interview, July 1996. Also see Suzuki, *Introduction to Zen,* 99–117.

79. Kahin interview, September 1996.

80. CIA memo, "The Political Situation in South Vietnam: The Current Crisis, Possible Future Developments, U.S. Options," 4-2-66, Vietnam vol. 50, VCF.

81. Vo Van Ai, e-mail to author, 5-23-96.

82. Thich Minh Chau, interview by the author, Vanh Hanh Institute, Ho Chi Minh City, Vietnam, August 1996. The An Quang pagoda is still the center of Buddhist radicalism in Vietnam. When the author visited there in 1996 and 1997, he was struck by its immaculate appearance, its sense of order and discipline in com-

parison to other pagodas in the country that had a run-down, decrepit appearance. Even the repression of the Communists has failed to blunt the spirit of the An Quang. The first time the author visited the pagoda, he walked upstairs to the worship area while a number of monks and nuns chanted in front of the altar. As he sat there in a lotus position, a young woman approached him and handed him a hymnal so he could follow along. Suddenly, the author observed an older monk walk into the room and sit next to another elderly monk. Because he was sitting on the floor, the author could see the first monk slip a piece of paper from beneath his robes to the other monk. Just then, the author looked up and could see one of the ubiquitous informers the government uses to spy on religious sites leaning over a rail and straining to see what the one monk had passed to the other. Unfortunately, the author did not see the end of the story. He decided to leave rather than get caught up in a police raid, since he was conducting research on a tourist visa, a criminal offense in Communist Vietnam.

83. Vo Van Ai, e-mail to author, 5-23-96. Buddhism describes itself as the middle way, since the Buddha founded it as a middle path between hedonism and extreme asceticism.

84. Pike interview, July 1996; and Kahin interview, September 1996.

85. Thich Dui Tri, interview by the author, Danang, Vietnam, March 1997.

86. Young, *Vietnam Wars,* 167; and Luce, *Unheard Voices,* 120–23.

87. Thich Nguyen An interview, July 1996.

88. The inclusion of Thich Minh Chau in this group is particularly noteworthy, since he consistently opposed Buddhist political activity and emphasized that Buddhists should focus on education and cultural projects. He is still the rector of the Vanh Hanh Institute in Ho Chi Minh City, an educational facility dedicated to training Buddhist monks and nuns. During our interview, he told the author that the institute received major financial support from the Asia Foundation before 1975. The author suspects that the Asia Foundation was used to channel CIA money to friendly groups. When the author mentioned this to Kahin, he also thought it could be true (Thich Minh Chau interview, July 1996; and "Buddhist Leaders Raise Voice," *Saigon Daily News* [March 14, 1966]: 1). Actually, Thich Tri Quang first laid out these ideas in a meeting with Philip Habib on February 14, 1966. See "Memorandum of Conversation with Thich Tri Quang," Habib to Lodge, 2-17-66, Vietnam vol. 47, VCF.

89. "Buddhist Deputy Chaplain Elaborates on 4–Point Communiqué during Mammoth Meeting at V.H.D." *Saigon Daily News* (March 18, 1996): 1. Lodge and Ky thought the call for popular elections constituted a "reckless" suggestion. See Embtel 3361 (Saigon), Lodge to Rusk, 3-16-66, Vietnam vol. 48, VCF.

90. Sacks, "Restructuring Government in South Vietnam," 525.

91. Cable, CIA Intelligence Information Cable, "Buddhist Political Plans and Discussions with Government Leaders," 3-16-66, Vietnam vol. 48, VCF.

92. "Ven. Thien Minh Clarifies Buddhist Position," *Saigon Daily News* (March 28, 1966): 1.

93. Bennett, "Political Implications of Economic Change," 581–91; and Kahin, *Intervention,* 411.

94. Kahin, *Intervention,* 410.

95. "Pilot with a Mission," 26.

96. Kahin, *Intervention,* 415.

97. Kahin interview, September 1996.

98. Vo Van Ai, e-mail to author, 5-23-96; and Kahin, *Intervention,* 414.

99. Forest, *Unified Buddhist Church of Vietnam,* 4.

100. Shaplen, "Letter from South Vietnam," 142; Herring, *America's Longest War,* 157; and Westmoreland, *A Soldier Reports,* 168.

101. Donnell and Joiner, "South Vietnam: 'Struggle' Politics," 55.

102. "Taylor Resigns; Lodge Returns," *Saigon Post* (July 10, 1965): 1; and Embtel 2343 (Saigon), Lodge to Rusk, 1-3-66, Vietnam vol. 45, VCF.

2. Conservative Backlash

Epigraph: Memo, Rostow to the President, 4-5-66, Vietnam vol. 50, VCF.

1. (No article title—blanked out by Vietnamese censors), *Saigon Daily News* (April 7, 1966): 1.

2. "Gen. Ky Flies to Danang to Try Solve Crisis," *Saigon Daily News* (April 6, 1966): 1; and Charles Mohr, "Ky Goes to Danang with a Regiment to Reassert Rule," *New York Times* (April 5, 1966): 1.

3. "Ky Heads Troops To Danang," *Saigon Post* (April 6, 1966): 1.

4. FitzGerald, *Fire in the Lake,* 376.

5. Charles Mohr, "Ky Stays Hand at Danang and Recants Red Charge; Buddhist Press Demand," *New York Times* (April 6, 1966): 1.

6. Charles Mohr, "Junta in Vietnam Appears Divided," *New York Times* (April 8, 1966): 1.

7. "General Co Presses for Danang Solution," *Saigon Post* (April 8, 1966): 1.

8. "Gov't, Buddhists Agree on Polls," *Saigon Post* (April 7, 1966): 1.

9. "NLC Agrees on Constituent Assembly without Delay," *Saigon Daily News* (April 8, 1966): 1.

10. Cable, CIA to White House Situation Room, 4-11-66, Vietnam vol. 51, VCF.

11. State 2995, Rusk to Lodge, 4-6-66, Vietnam vol. 50, VCF.

12. "Buddhist Leaders to Start Open Struggle," *Saigon Daily News* (April 11, 1966): 1; and "Buddhists to Boycott Nat'l Political Congress," *Saigon Post* (April 11, 1966): 1.

13. "Buddhist Warn Regime in Saigon Civil War Is Near," *New York Times* (April 11, 1966): 1.

14. Charles Mohr, "Saigon Leader Says Junta Is Eager to Give Up Power," *New York Times* (April 12, 1966): 1.

15. "Directory Chairman Signs Decree-Law on Constituent Assembly Election," *Saigon Daily News* (April 15, 1966): 1.

16. "Gov't Makes Concessions to VHD," *Saigon Daily News* (April 16, 1966): 1; and Kahin, *Intervention,* 424.

17. "Hue Students Continue to Demand Resignation of Gov't," *Saigon Daily News* (April 16, 1966): 1.

18. "Vien Hoa Dao Orders Suspension of Struggle," *Saigon Daily News* (April 18, 1966): 1; and Kahin, *Intervention,* 426.

19. "Ven. Tri Quang Calls Off Struggle in Northern Provinces," *Saigon Daily News* (April 19, 1966): 1; and "Ky Stays till after Elections," *Saigon Post* (April 19, 1966): 1.

20. Embtel 4057 (Saigon), Lodge to Rusk, "Tri Quang's Speech," 4-18-66, Vietnam vol. 51, VCF.

21. "Notes from *Hoa Binh,*" Kahin File (September 13, 1976): 1.

22. "Tri-Quang Denies Being Anti-American, Pro-Communist," *Saigon Daily News* (April 12, 1966): 1.

23. "Powerful Buddhist: Tri Quang," *New York Times* (April 20, 1966): 2.

24. Charles Mohr, "Tri Quang Assails Both Reds and U.S.," *New York Times* (April 20, 1966): 1.

25. Colonel Tran Huu Phuoc, political officer for the ARVN Second Division during this period, claims that most of the people did not understand the danger of Communism and thus were vulnerable to Buddhist calls for peace. He is convinced that the Buddhists would have negotiated with the NLF (Tran Huu Phuoc, interview by the author, Lexington, Ky., December 1996).

26. "Quang Admits VN Needs U.S.," *Saigon Post* (April 20, 1966): 1.

27. Memo, CIA Intelligence Memorandum, "Thich Tri Quang and Buddhist Political Objectives in South Vietnam," 4-20-66, Vietnam vol. 51, VCF.

28. Neil Sheehan, "Buddhists' Key: Student Leaders," *New York Times* (April 17, 1966): 5.

29. "Buddhist Leaders to Ceylon Talks," *Saigon Post* (May 3, 1966): 1.

30. Thich Minh Chieu argues that Thich Tri Quang wanted Thich Tam Chau's support in the campaign against Ky and would have succeeded if the moderate monks had joined him. Thich Tam Chau, however, refusing to turn against Ky, left the country instead. In addition, Kahin told the author that suspicion between the radicals and moderates in the Vien Hoa Dao remained very high, augmented by the lingering rumors that Thich Tam Chau was an informant for the Americans (Thich Minh Chieu interview, July 1996; and Kahin interview, September 1996).

31. "Gen. Dinh New I Corps Commander," *Saigon Post* (April 10, 1966): 1; and Topmiller, "Buddhist Crisis of 1963," 47, 52.

32. "Central VN Situation Stabilized: Gen. Dinh," *Saigon Post* (April 24, 1966): 1; and Embtel 4171 (Saigon), Lodge to Rusk, 4-24-66, Vietnam vol. 51, VCF.

33. FitzGerald, *Fire in the Lake,* 377.

34. "Trial Transcript and *Hao Binh* Commentary," Kahin File (November 15, 1976): 10.

35. "Col. Lieu No Longer Director of Nat. Police," *Saigon Daily News* (April 23, 1966): 1.

36. Embtel 3761 (Saigon), Lodge to Rusk, 4-6-66, and CIA Intelligence Information Cable, "A General Officer's Assessment of Groups Forming in the Military with the Aim of Making Demands on the Government," 4-25-66, Vietnam vol. 50,

VCF; and Karnow, *Vietnam: A History,* 447. Thi claims he had a confrontation with Loan after the war over his actions in 1968. Thi argues that Loan still does not realize the enormous damage he did to the U.S. effort in South Vietnam by his summary execution of the NLF operative, which was recorded for posterity by a Western television crew (Thi interview, April 1997).

37. Truong Nhu Tang, *Vietcong Memoir*, 90–95.

38. Robert Shaplen, *Lost Revolution*, 248. Douglas Pike told the author that he spent eighteen months after the Buddhist Crisis of 1963 questioning NLF prisoners in a failed attempt to prove Communist complicity in the overthrow of Diem (Pike interview, July 1996).

39. Kolko, *Anatomy of a War,* 205. The author was able to find a number of NLF documents confirming this point at the Indochina Archive, University of California, Berkeley, including: "The Processes of Revolution and the General Uprising," *Vietnam Documents and Research Notes* (October 1968): 11–13; "COSVN Resolution on Mission in the South," (January 1965): 4–9; and "Le Duan Letter to the Saigon Party Committee—Issued between Mid-1966 and Mid-1967," 6–10.

40. Shaplen, *Lost Revolution,* 272–73.

41. Kolko, *Anatomy of a War,* 205. At times, local NLF cadres received criticism from higher authorities for failing to tap into the Buddhist movement. See, from the Indochina Archive, "COSVN Resolution 2, Late 1963 or Early 1964," 4–12.

42. Schecter, *New Face of Buddha,* 157.

43. Buddhist fears in this regard were well founded. After their victory over South Vietnam, the Communists set up a puppet Buddhist organization supported by the state while they severely repressed the UBC and other religious groups that sought to carry their message to the people without state sanction. See Robert Topmiller, "Tu Do Ton Giao Tai Viet Nam?" 75–80.

44. Much of the material Dr. Kahin graciously shared with the author included transcripts from a Vietnamese Catholic journal, *Hoa Binh* (Peace), established by Catholics to press the cause of peace.

45. "Buddhists to Boycott Nat'l Political Congress," *Saigon Post* (April 11, 1966): 1; and Neil Sheehan, "Catholics in Bien Hoa Demand That Ky Act against Buddhists," *New York Times* (April 18, 1966): 1.

46. "Catholic Bloc Organized," *Saigon Post* (April 15, 1966): 1.

47. "Bien Hoa Catholics Hold Demonstrations," *Saigon Daily News* (April 18, 1966): 1.

48. "Saigon Catholics March," *Saigon Daily News* (April 25, 1966): 1.

49. "Catholics Stage Anti-Lodge Rally," *Saigon Daily News* (May 3, 1966): 1.

50. "Economic Crisis Marks 'May Day' March," *Saigon Post* (May 3, 1966): 1; and "5000 in Saigon March on U.S. Offices," *New York Times* (May 1, 1966): 2.

51. "Trial Transcript and *Hoa Binh* Commentary," 10, 13. In March 1997, the author visited Phu Cam village, a Catholic enclave in Hue only about 1,000 meters from the Tu Dam Pagoda, the headquarters of Thich Tri Quang in 1966. The most striking part of the village is the enormous Phu Cam Cathedral, founded in 1624, which sits on a hill overlooking the village. Inside is a monument to all of the former bishops of Hue, including Ngo Dinh Thuc, Diem's brother and the man who

sparked the Buddhist Crisis of 1963. While the author walked around inside the church, a young man who he assumed was a government informant followed him. According to Truong Van Loc, the NLF could never make any inroads into the Phu Cam community during the war because of its Catholic population. The author also interviewed a Catholic priest in Hue, Father Josephus Le Van Phuc, who was in Hue during 1966. He confirmed that many Catholics in the city were afraid of the radical Buddhists and did suffer persecution at their hands during the agitation of 1966. The author tried to interview other Catholic clergy in Hue and Danang, but they were extremely hesitant to talk. In fact, a nun in Danang refused to give her name until the interview was complete, even though she was not very forthcoming. The author attributed their reluctance to talk to fear of more persecution from the Communists (Interviews, Truong Van Loc and Josephus Le Van Phuc, Hue, Vietnam, March 1997).

52. "Pro-Gov't Demonstrations Set by Youths, NVN Refugees," *Saigon Post* (April 24, 1966): 1.

53. "New Front Urges 3–Year Postponement of Elections," *Saigon Post* (May 9, 1966): 1.

54. The author was able to verify this during a series of interviews with former Cao Dai and Hoa Hao leaders in Ho Chi Minh City, Tay Ninh and An Giang province during December 2000.

55. Embtel 3713 (Saigon), Lodge to Rusk, 4-4-66, Vietnam vol. 50, VCF.

56. Embtel 4096 (Saigon), Lodge to Rusk, 4-20-66, Vietnam vol. 51, VCF.

57. "Tension Mounting Again in Both Danang & Saigon," *Saigon Daily News* (April 23, 1966): 1.

58. Embtel 4140 (Saigon), Lodge to Rusk, 4-22-66, Vietnam vol. 51, VCF.

59. Embtel 4394 (Saigon), Lodge to Rusk, 5-5-66, Vietnam vol. 52, VCF.

60. Interview, Hue, Vietnam, March 1997. This former ARVN paratrooper, who asked not to be identified because of the heavy persecution he has received from the Communists since the war ended, told the author that as a Buddhist he had to follow the instructions of the monks because "they came from the gods." Yet he was part of the force that attacked the Struggle Movement in Hue and Danang. His ability to balance both ideas is very typical of the Asian capacity to accept ambiguity without the discomfort usually felt by Westerners.

61. The author attributes this insight to Thich Tam Thien. During two research trips to Vietnam, the author interviewed his teacher, Thich Tri Quang (a different monk from the one in this work). When the author complained that he was frustrated that he could not get his master to talk about politics or history, Thich Tam Thien replied, "That is why he is the most influential monk in Vietnam, today." He explained that since he avoids political involvement, his master's prestige as a religious figure is enhanced and the people and the government respond to his leadership on social justice issues (Thich Tam Thien, interview by the author, March 1997).

Father Josephus Le Van Phuc was the only Catholic prelate who would talk about the Struggle Movement in central Vietnam in 1997. He told the author that the Buddhists committed a grave error in 1966 when they became involved in political activity. Like many Catholics, he believes their efforts should have been directed at defeating the Communists (Father Josephus Le Van Phuc, interview by the author, March 1997).

62. La Thanh Ty, interview by the author, March 1997. During an interview at the Tinh Hoi pagoda in Danang, Ty argued that many people in central Vietnam were fed up with atrocities committed by South Korean soldiers and the irresponsible use of firepower by the United States that killed many civilians. He claimed most ARVN soldiers did not want to fight the war and that the Buddhists knew that many American soldiers also did not want to fight. Ty spent three years in jail for his participation in the Struggle Movement. He agrees that the Buddhists could have prevented a Communist victory.

63. Kamm, *Dragon Ascending,* 173. The author has confirmed this in numerous conversations with Vietnamese who expressed fear of and contempt for the Communists. In some ways, the insurgents had an almost mystical quality, in that many people were convinced they could go anywhere or do anything they wanted.

64. "South Viet Nam, The Light That Failed," 39.

65. Oral Interview with the Nguyen family, April 1997.

66. Jamieson, *Understanding Vietnam,* 40.

67. Oka, "Buddhism as a Political Force," 9–10.

68. Oral interview, Kieu Huu Tu, La Thanh Ty, Thich Thien Chieu, Tin Hap, Thich Giac Vien, and Thich Dui Tri, March 1997, and Thi interview, April 1997. During the author's interviews in central Vietnam with former members of the Struggle Movement, every monk and layperson interviewed responded with Hoa Binh (peace) and Doc Lap (independence) when asked what the goal of their movement had been in 1966. By "independence," they meant escaping American domination of their country. Thich Thien Chieu told the author that most Buddhists "wanted peace most of all" and were willing to talk to the NLF, if necessary, to end the fighting.

69. "Troops Clear Demonstrators from Information Office," *Saigon Post* (April 6, 1966): 1; and "Youths Defy Buddhist Elders," *Saigon Post* (April 8, 1966): 1.

70. "Lodge Sees Red Hand in VN Politics," *Saigon Post* (April 23, 1966): 1.

71. Cable, CIA to White House Situation Room, 4-16-66, "Indications of Deteriorating Situation in I Corps Area," Vietnam vol. 51, VCF.

72. "Trial Transcript and *Hoa Binh* Commentary," 7.

73. Embtel 4401 (Saigon), Porter to Rusk, 5-6-66, Vietnam vol. 52, VCF.

74. R.W. Apple Jr., "Saigon Striving for Compromise with Buddhists," *New York Times* (April 7, 1966): 1.

75. "P.M. Ky Says He May Stay Another Year," *Saigon Daily News* (May 9, 1966): 1.

76. "Military Gov't Stays: Ky," *Saigon Post* (May 8, 1966): 1; and Neil Sheehan, "Election Talks in Vietnam Go on after Compromise," *New York Times* (May 6, 1966): 1.

77. "Ven. Tri Quang Asked to Come to Saigon," *Saigon Daily News* (May 10, 1966): 1.

78. "Danang Mayor Sees Bad Time," *New York Times* (May 8, 1966): 3.

79. "Secretary Rusk Says Gen. Ky Was Misquoted," *Saigon Daily News* (May 10, 1966): 1.

80. State 3343, Rusk to Lodge, 5-7-66, and State 3348, Rusk to Lodge, 5-7-66, Vietnam vol. 52, VCF.

81. "Notes from *Hoa Binh,*" Kahin File (September 13, 1976): 1.

82. FitzGerald, *Fire in the Lake,* 376.

83. According to Thich Nguyen An, Buddhist monks "talked about the people's problems" with the war, not about the larger strategic interests of the United States or GVN (Thich Nguyen An, interview by the author, Seattle, Washington, July 1996; and Charles Mohr, "Ky Says Troops Will Go to Danang to Restore Order," *New York Times* (April 4, 1966): 1.

84. Forest, *Unified Buddhist Church of Vietnam,* 7.

85. FitzGerald, *Fire in the Lake,* 377–78.

3. CONFRONTATION IN DANANG

Epigraph: "The Buddhist Crisis of 1966, *Hoa Binh* Interview with General Ton That Dinh," Kahin File (March 1972): 7.

1. Krulak, *First to Fight,* 205–16; and Asprey, *War in the Shadows,* 1274–95.

2. Westmoreland, Oral History Interview 2, 9-21-86, 7, LBJ Library.

3. Walt, Oral History Interview, 1-24-69, 5–7, LBJ Library. Certainly, Walt overstates his case here. In 1968, the author watched the airstrip at Danang suffer intensive shelling from the countryside Walt claims was pacified.

4. Edwin Simmons, interview by the author, January 1997. Simmons was Walt's G-3 at the beginning of the Buddhist Crisis and later commanded the Ninth Marines.

5. Ibid. General Simmons attributed many of Walt's actions to the first signs of his later mental illness. When the author asked him about Westmoreland, Simmons leapt out of his chair and paced furiously around the room while pouring out his frustrations with the U.S. commander.

6. Ibid.

7. Shulimson, *U.S. Marines in Vietnam,* 81; and Message, 3-26-66, III MAF Journal and File, USMC Archives (hereafter cited III MAF Journal).

8. Embtel 3523 (Saigon), Lodge to Rusk, 3-26-66, Vietnam vol. 49, VCF.

9. Shulimson, *U.S. Marines in Vietnam,* 81; MACV to NMCC [National Military Command Center], 4-26-66, III MAF Journal; and General Westmoreland Historical Briefing, 3-27-66, Westmoreland Papers, LBJ Library. Buu Ton's family name, which means "precious," indicates that he was related to the royal family of Vietnam. Many thanks to Truong Van Loc for pointing this out to the author (Truong Van Loc interview, Hue, Vietnam, March 1997).

10. Walt, *Strange War, Strange Strategy,* 115–18.

11. Clarke, *United States Army in Vietnam,* 130–32.

12. III MAF to MACV, 4-3-66, III MAF Journal.

13. III MAF to MACV, 4-5-66, "Resume of Alert Actions as of 050800H," III MAF Journal.

14. Spot Report, 4-5-66, III MAF Journal.

15. *Operations of the III Marine Amphibious Force: Vietnam* (January 1967): 32, U.S. Marine Corps Historical Center.

16. Walt, *Strange War, Strange Strategy,* 120–21.

17. Simmons, *The Marines in Vietnam,* 63; and Shulimson, *U.S. Marines in Vietnam,* 83.

18. Westmoreland, *A Soldier Reports,* 171.

19. Memo, "Current Situation in Danang," Memo for the Record, 4-9-66, Westmoreland Papers.

20. *Operations, III MAF,* 33.

21. *Operations, III MAF,* 33.

22. Shulimson, *U.S. Marines in Vietnam,* 80.

23. Nguyen Cao Ky, *How We Lost the Vietnam War* (New York, 1976), 94. It is very difficult to rely on Ky's memoirs, since he insists on magnifying his role totally out of proportion while playing down the actions of others. Where other documentation exists, it usually calls Ky's account into question.

24. Clarke, *United States Army in Vietnam,* 131.

25. Shulimson, *U.S. Marines in Vietnam,* 84; and Simmons, *Marines in Vietnam,* 63.

26. "Significant Events-15 May," 5-15-66, and Cable, First MarDiv [First Marine Division] to III MAF, 5-16-66, III MAF Journal; and Simmons, *Marines in Vietnam,* 63.

27. Shulimson, *U.S. Marines in Vietnam,* 84.

28. Ibid.

29. Report, General Walt to the National Military Command Center, 5-15-66, Vietnam vol. 53, VCF.

30. Walt, *Strange War, Strange Strategy,* 132.

31. Shulimson, *U.S. Marines in Vietnam,* 84–85; and Embtel 4627 (Saigon), Porter to Rusk, 5-16-66, Vietnam vol. 53, VCF.

32. Spot Report, 5-16-66, III MAF Journal.

33. Swain 3 to Parchment 3, 5-17-66, III MAF Journal.

34. Shulimson, *U.S. Marines in Vietnam,* 85–86; Westmoreland, *A Soldier Reports,* 173; Schecter, *New Face of Buddha,* 229–30; and Richard Stevenson, interview by the author, Lexington, Ky., May 2001. Westmoreland claims that Hamblen gave the door gunner instructions to fire at the ARVN officer, who Westmoreland says was the only casualty. In addition, he argues that the helicopter sustained so much damage that it had to land shortly afterward and transfer the passengers to another helicopter. Schecter claims that the gunner reacted automatically, wounding six and killing the officer who fired the shots, a more plausible story than Westmoreland's. Stevenson, who witnessed the shooting, asserts that the gunner was instructed to open fire and that more than one person was wounded in the incident.

35. Shulimson, *U.S. Marines in Vietnam,* 86.

36. The author visited this bridge during his stay in Danang during March 1997. The river, now called the Han, is very wide at this point, and only a pair of bridges connects the two sections of the city. Although the author could appreciate

the strategic importance of the structure, he was struck by the courage of the young Marines who sprinted across its wide span under the guns of ARVN dissidents.

37. Shulimson, *U.S. Marines in Vietnam,* 86–87; Westmoreland, *A Soldier Reports,* 173; and Walt, *Strange War, Strange Strategy,* 126–41.

38. Letter, "Walt to Simmons," USMC Archives (May 23, 1978): 2–3.

39. Walt, *Strange War, Strange Strategy,* 129.

40. Clarke, *United States Army in Vietnam,* 138; and Memo, Rostow to the President, 5-21-66, Vietnam vol. 53, VCF.

41. Message, III MAF to Third MarDiv (Third Marine Division), 5-19-66, III MAF Journal.

42. III MAF to MACV, 5-19-66, III MAF Journal.

43. Third MarDiv to III MAF, 5-19-66, III MAF Journal.

44. III MAF to First MarDiv (First Marine Division), 5-20-66, III MAF Journal.

45. Shulimson, *U.S. Marines in Vietnam,* 87–88; Simmons, *The Marines in Vietnam,* 64; and Westmoreland, *A Soldier Reports,* 174.

46. Kahin, *Intervention,* 428–29.

47. Letter, "Walt to Simmons" (May 23, 1966): 3, USMC Archives.

48. Shulimson, *U.S. Marines in Vietnam,* 87; and Westmoreland, *A Soldier Reports,* 174.

49. Report, "Significant Events, 21 May, 5-22-66," III MAF Journal.

50. Memo, Memorandum for the President, "South Vietnam," 5-21-66, Vietnam vol. 53, VCF.

51. Shulimson, *U.S. Marines in Vietnam,* 88.

52. Memo, Heintges to Westmoreland, 3-24-66, Westmoreland Papers.

53. Memo, "Meeting at Chu Lai on 24 March 1966," 3-24-66, Westmoreland Papers.

54. General Westmoreland's Historical Briefing, 3-27-66, Westmoreland Papers.

55. Westmoreland, *A Soldier Reports,* 170.

56. Cable (MAC 2650), Westmoreland to Walt, 4-3-66, Westmoreland Papers.

57. General Westmoreland's Historical Briefing, 4-9-66, Westmoreland Papers.

58. Ibid.

59. Memo, "Telephone Conversation with Mr. Habib," Memorandum for the Record, 5-22-66, Westmoreland Papers.

60. Westmoreland, *A Soldier Reports,* 176.

61. Shulimson, *U.S. Marines in Vietnam,* 85; and Schecter, *New Face of Buddha,* 228.

62. Westmoreland, *A Soldier Reports,* 172.

63. Clarke, *United States Army in Vietnam,* 134.

64. "The Buddhist Crisis of 1966," *Hoa Binh* interview with General Ton That Dinh, Kahin File, (March, 1972): 9.

65. Ibid.

66. *Hoa Binh* interview with General Ton That Dinh, Kahin File, (March, 1972): 12.

67. Memo, "Fonecon, Lt. Gen. Nguyen Huu Co and Lt. Gen. John A. Heintges," 5-16-66, Memorandum for the Record, Westmoreland Papers.

68. *Hoa Binh* interview with General Ton That Dinh, Kahin File, (March, 1972): 5.

69. Ibid.

70. *Hoa Binh* interview with General Ton That Dinh, Kahin File, (March, 1972): 8.

71. *Hoa Binh* interview with General Ton That Dinh, Kahin File, (March, 1972): 5–6. It is very telling that the GVN, which routinely exercised news censorship, allowed this account to be published in 1972. Perhaps Ky and Thieu wanted others to know they had not thought up the operation against Danang by themselves.

72. *Hoa Binh* interview with General Ton That Dinh, Kahin File, (March, 1972): 1–2. During a July 1966 interview with General Nguyen Khanh, prime minister of South Vietnam for most of 1964, he told the author that one of the problems Americans had in Vietnam was not understanding the complexity of the long-standing relationships among many of the generals in ARVN. Thus, an event that had happened years before could be the reason for political positions taken years later. After reading Dinh's account of the conflict between Walt and Westmoreland, the author realized that ARVN generals understood and tried to make allowances for long-standing animosity among U.S. commanders, which they accepted with an almost casual air (General Nguyen Khanh, interview by the author, Fremont, Calif. July 1966).

73. Walt, *Strange War, Strange Strategy,* 122; and Dinh interview with *Hoa Binh.* Dinh claims that the tanks used in this operation, M-41's, were new to the area, having been landed the night before. He also argues he had reports that Americans drove the tanks and participated in the suppression of the Buddhists. His assertion receives support from General Edward Lansdale, who reported in 1981 that during a conversation with Lodge in the spring of 1966, the U.S. ambassador told him, "Well, Westy and I have sent some troops and armor up to the area." Unfortunately, Lansdale could not remember exactly where the troops were sent. He did point out, however, that "both [Westmoreland and Lodge] were very proud" of the actions they had taken in Danang (Edward G. Lansdale, Oral History, 9-15-81, pages 55–57, LBJ Library).

74. Cable, MACVCC [MACV Command Center] to NMCC [National Military Command Center], 5-15-66, Vietnam vol. 53, VCF.

75. FitzGerald, *Fire in the Lake,* 384; and Clarke, *United States Army in Vietnam,* 136. Thi claims he called Walt and arranged for Dinh's escape from Danang. Thi also told the author that the United States put Ky in office because U.S. officials knew he would follow their orders (General Nguyen Chanh Thi, interview by the author, Lancaster, Pa., April 1997).

76. *Hoa Binh* interview with General Ton That Dinh, Kahin File, (March, 1972): 7.

77. Karnow, *Vietnam: A History,* 447.

78. Westmoreland, *A Soldier Reports,* 172–73; FitzGerald, *Fire in the Lake,* 385; *Hoa Binh,* 17; and Embtel 4790 (Saigon), Lodge to Rusk, 5-20-66, Vietnam vol. 53, VCF.

79. Clarke, *United States Army in Vietnam,* 138; and Cable, MACVCC to NMCC, 5-18-66, Vietnam vol. 53, VCF.

80. Embtel 4733 (Saigon), Porter to Rusk, 5-18-66, Vietnam vol. 53, VCF.

81. "Trial Transcript and *Hoa Binh* Commentary," 17.

82. Simmons, *Marines in Vietnam*, 64.

83. Shulimson, *U.S. Marines in Vietnam*, 92.

84. Simmons interview, January 1997; and Schecter, *New Face of Buddha*, 231.

85. Caputo, *Rumor of War*, 317.

86. U.S. Department of State, "Telegram From the Chairman, Joints Chiefs of Staff (Wheeler) to the Commander, Military Assistance Command, Vietnam (Westmoreland)," May 20, 1966, *Foreign Relations of the United States:* Vietnam vol. 4, 1966, 394–96.

87. Clarke, *United States Army in Vietnam*, 130; *Operations, III MAF*, 3; and Simmons interview, January 1997. While most of this account contains the usual optimistic jargon found in American military reports from Vietnam, the appearance of this statement is very telling. As General Simmons pointed out in our interview, the constant demands from higher authorities for indications of measurable improvement in the war led most commanders to "cook the books" to indicate progress.

88. *III MAF Command Chronology* (May 1966): 23, USMC Archives.

89. Westmoreland, *A Soldier Reports*, 170.

90. Takashi Oka, "Letter to R.H. Nolte," Kahin Files.

91. Embtel 5684 (Saigon), Lodge to the President, 6-22-66, Vietnam vol. 55, VCF.

4. American Reassessment of Its Role in South Vietnam

Epigraph: Lyndon Johnson, explaining his reluctance to commit American forces to Vietnam in 1964. Telephone conversation, President Lyndon Johnson and McGeorge Bundy, 5-27-64, in Beschloss, *Taking Charge*, 372.

1. Young, *Vietnam Wars*, 167; and State 2735, Rusk to Lodge, 3-16-66, Vietnam vol. 48, VCF.

2. Ky, *How We Lost the Vietnam War*, 91; and Westmoreland, *A Soldier Reports*, 169.

3. Cable, CIA to White House Situation Room, 3-31-66, Vietnam vol. 49, VCF. Pike claims that the embassy constantly measured Vietnamese attitudes toward Americans and discovered that anti-Americanism grew in direct proportion to the number of Americans in the country (Pike interview, July 1996).

4. Young, *Vietnam Wars*, 168.

5. Embtel 3672 (Saigon), Lodge to Rusk, 4-2-66, Vietnam vol. 50, VCF; and State 2884, Rusk to Lodge, 3-30-66, Vietnam vol. 49, VCF.

6. Gardner, *Pay Any Price*, 272.

7. Karnow, *Vietnam: A History*, 444–46.

8. Memo, McCaffery to Komer, 3-24-66, Vietnam vol. 49, VCF.

9. State 2736, Rusk to Lodge, 3-16-66, Vietnam vol. 48, VCF.

10. Charles Mohr, "Ky Says Troops Will Go to Danang," 1; and "Ky Heads Troops to Danang," *Saigon Post* (April 6, 1966): 1.

11. Kahin, *Intervention*, 423.

12. State 2965, Rusk to Lodge, 4-5-66, Vietnam vol. 50, VCF.

13. Embtel 4128 (Saigon), Lodge to Rusk, 4-21-66, Vietnam vol. 51, VCF.

14. Max Frankel, "U.S. Aides Assail Buddhist Leader in Saigon Dispute," *New York Times* (April 9, 1966): 1.

15. Memo, Rostow to McNamara and Rusk, "Breaking Tri Quang's Momentum," 4-9-66, Vietnam vol. 51, VCF. One White House official used the Russian Revolution comparison to describe Rostow as Johnson's Rasputin, a far more accurate parallel (Young, *Vietnam Wars,* 169).

16. Memo, "Comments on the Present Situation in South Viet-Nam," 4-4-66, Vietnam vol. 50, VCF.

17. Memo, Taylor to the President, "Current Situation in South Vietnam," 4-12-66, Vietnam vol. 51, VCF.

18. Memo, "Telephone Message from the President," 4-13-66, Vietnam vol. 51, VCF.

19. State 3023, Rusk to Lodge, 4-8-66, Vietnam vol. 51, VCF.

20. Embtel 3817 (Saigon), Lodge to Rusk, 4-8-66, Vietnam vol. 50, VCF.

21. "U.S. Wants Saigon to Mix Firmness with Concessions," *New York Times* (April 11, 1966): 1.

22. Gardner, *Pay Any Price,* 277.

23. Herring, *America's Longest War,* 165–66; and Woods, *Fulbright: A Biography,* 400–401.

24. Woods, *Fulbright: A Biography,* 401–7; Karnow, *Vietnam: A History,* 486; and Young, *The Vietnam Wars,* 205–6.

25. Gardner, *Pay Any Price,* 287–91.

26. Halberstam, *The Best and the Brightest,* 622–24; and DiLeo, *George Ball,* 141.

27. Woods, *Fulbright: A Biography,* 401–8.

28. According to Woods, it fell from "63 percent to 49 percent." Ibid., 410.

29. Ibid.

30. Memo, Komer to Bundy, NSF Komer Memos, vol. 2, LBJ Library.

31. Chester Cooper, Oral Interview, 7-9-79, LBJ Library; and Telcon, Ball, and McNamara, 1-8-66, Papers of George Ball, LBJ Library.

32. Halberstam, *The Best and the Brightest,* 622–24.

33. Ibid., 362. When the author encountered his files at the LBJ Library, he too registered astonishment at McNaughton's extensive collection of documents arguing for an end to the war through negotiations.

34. Ibid., 362–66.

35. "Some Paragraphs on Vietnam," 1-19-66, Papers of Paul Warnke, John McNaughton Files, LBJ Library (hereafter cited as Warnke Papers).

36. Ibid.

37. Ibid.

38. DiLeo, *George Ball,* 112–20.

39. Memo, Deutch to Lansdale, "Planning for Negotiations—Stand-Down," 2-22-66, Vietnam vol. 47, VCF. In February, Michael Deutch, an administration specialist on economic warfare assigned to General Edward Lansdale's staff, prepared a report on the problems of "standing down" in Vietnam. Deutch argued that GVN frailty could prevent it from carrying out the various governmental tasks associated

with making peace. He characterized the GVN problem as threefold: war-weariness on the part of large segments of the population, the narrow makeup of the ARVN-dominated GVN and the inability of pacification to bring about a social revolution in South Vietnam. At the same time, he argued that Saigon remained suspicious of American peace moves, fearing it would be sacrificed by the United States to extricate itself from South Vietnam. As with most of the reports produced during this period, it remains difficult to ascertain how widely this essay was distributed. But serious questions had arisen among some American officials just as the GVN entered the greatest crisis in its history. McNamara claims he assisted McNaughton with a report of the same name. Perhaps he is confused or his memory has failed him, but Deutch's conclusions matched McNamara's views on the prospects for an American victory.

40. Max Frankel, "U.S. Stresses Effort to Prevent Vietnam Bloodshed," *New York Times* (April 10, 1966): 1.

41. Felix Belair Jr., "Russell Favors a Poll in Vietnam on U.S. Presence," *New York Times* (April 26, 1966): 1.

42. U.S. Department of State, "Telephone Conversation between President Johnson and Secretary of State Rusk," March 28, 1966, *FRUS: Vietnam,* vol. 4, 1966, 304.

43. E.W. Kenworthy, "Senate Concern on Saigon Grows," *New York Times* (April 14, 1966): 1; and Gibbons, *The U.S. Government and the Vietnam War,* 303.

44. "If a Saigon Regime Asks U.S. to Leave, It Must, Stennis Says," *New York Times* (April 18, 1966): 4.

45. Gibbons, *U.S. Government and the Vietnam War,* 304.

46. Ibid., 304–5.

47. David Broder, "Congressmen Find Public Disturbed," *New York Times* (April 18, 1966): 1.

48. "99-Day GI Toll above 1965 Total," *New York Times* (April 16, 1966): 1.

49. "GI Dead Exceed Saigon in Week," *New York Times* (April 15, 1966): 1.

50. Memo, Rusk to the President, 4-2-66, Vietnam vol. 50, VCF.

51. Gibbons, *U.S. Government and the Vietnam War,* 278–79; and McNamara, *In Retrospect,* 261.

52. Memo, Valenti to the President, 4-4-66, Vietnam vol. 50, VCF.

53. "Observations about Vietnam," 4-4-66, Warnke Papers.

54. "Notes of Meeting," April 4, 1966, *FRUS: Vietnam,* vol. 4, 1966, 323–25.

55. "Draft Scenario Prepared in the Department of Defense," April 5, 1966, *FRUS: Vietnam,* vol. 4, 1966, 327–28.

56. Gibbons, *U.S. Government and the Vietnam War,* 286–89.

57. Ibid., 289.

58. Memo, "Planning for Viet-Nam Contingencies," 4-11-66, Warnke Papers. Unger was not alone in raising this point. According to William Bundy, when Ky attacked Danang in mid-May, he and Lodge were in the communications room when the cable arrived alerting U.S. officials to the fighting in the city. Sensing that Ky might fail, Bundy told Lodge that the U.S. role in Vietnam might be over. Lodge responded by saying, "[I]n that case we will just take over."

59. Memo, Carver to McNaughton, "Consequences of a Buddhist Political Victory in South Vietnam," 4-12-66, Warnke Papers.

60. Memo, "Politics in Vietnam: A Worst Outcome," 4-16-66, Warnke Papers.

61. Memo, Rostow to the President, 4-5-66, Vietnam vol. 50, VCF.

62. William Bundy, Oral History, Tape 3, 5-29-69, pp. 34–35, LBJ Library.

63. "Memorandum from the President's Special Assistant [Rostow] to President Johnson," April 18, 1966, *FRUS: Vietnam,* vol. 4, 1966, 355–57.

64. "Memorandum from the President's Special Assistant [Rostow] to President Johnson," April 21, 1966, *FRUS: Vietnam,* vol. 4, 1966, 357–60.

65. Memo, "How We Should Move," 4-16-66, Warnke Papers.

66. Memo, "Option A," 4–66, Warnke Papers.

67. "Course B-O," 4–66, Warnke Papers.

68. "Course B," 4-21-66, Warnke Papers.

69. "Course C, Cutting Our Losses," Warnke Papers.

70. Logevall, *Choosing War,* 376.

71. Memo, "Basic Choices in Vietnam," 4-16-66, Warnke Papers.

72. "Memorandum from Secretary of State Rusk to President Johnson," April 24, 1966, *FRUS: Vietnam,* vol. 4, 1966, 360–61; and Memo, "Agenda for Foreign Policy Discussion with the President Tuesday: April 19, 1966," 4-19-66, Rostow File, Meetings with the President, NSF LBJ Library.

73. Memo, "Agenda for Foreign Policy Discussion with the President Tuesday: April 19, 1966," 4-19-66; and, Gibbons, *U.S. Government and the Vietnam War,* 298.

74. Quoted in Herring, *America's Longest War,* 157–58; and Gibbons, *U.S. Government and the Vietnam War,* 300.

75. Karnow, *Vietnam: A History,* 485; and DiLeo, *George Ball,* 141.

76. Logevall, *Choosing War,* 390–91.

77. Karnow, *Vietnam: A History,* 485; and DiLeo, *George Ball,* 141.

78. Gardner, *Pay Any Price,* 98.

79. Ibid., 5–98.

80. Ibid., xv.

81. Quoted in Gardner, *Pay Any Price,* 139.

82. Ibid., 161.

83. Ibid, 167.

84. Quoted in H.R. McMaster, *Dereliction of Duty,* 255.

85. Gardner, *Pay Any Price,* 117.

86. Logevall, *Choosing War,* 375–413.

87. "Summary Notes of the 557th Meeting of the National Security Council," May 10, 1966, *FRUS: Vietnam,* vol. 4, 1966, 381–83.

88. McNamara, *In Retrospect,* 261.

89. William Bundy, Oral History, Tape 3, 5-29-69, pp. 34–35, LBJ Library.

90. Walt Rostow, Oral Interview, 3-21-69, Tape 1 of 3, Oral History Collection, LBJ Library.

91. DiLeo, *George Ball,* 93, 100.

92. Max Frankel, "Johnson Bids U.S. Remain Steadfast on Vietnam Issue," *New York Times* (April 23, 1966): 1.

93. Telcon, McNamara and Ball, 5-4-66, Papers of George Ball, LBJ Library.

94. "Memorandum of Conversation between Secretary of Defense McNamara and the Ambassador at Large [Harriman]," May 14, 1966, *FRUS: Vietnam,* vol. 4, 1966, 385.

95. Gibbons, *U.S. Government and the Vietnam War,* 328.

96. Embtel 4800 (Saigon), Porter to Rusk, "Tri Quang," 5-20-66, Vietnam vol. 53, VCF. On May 20, Porter informed Rusk, "[O]ur representatives in Danang are making every effort to persuade the Vietnamese military authorities not to attack any pagodas."

97. "Two Wars in Vietnam," *New York Times* (May 22, 1966), IV: 1; and Topmiller, "Buddhist Crisis of 1963," 47.

98. Richard Eder, "Washington Is Concerned and Surprised by Ky Step," *New York Times* (May 16, 1966): 1; and Memo, Rostow to the President, undated, Vietnam vol. 53, VCF.

99. R.W. Apple Jr., "Ky Denounces Thich Tri Quang, Top Buddhist Leader, as a Red," *New York Times* (May 22, 1966): 6.

100. "Ky Sees No Danger of Civil War: Calls Danang Move Essential to Prevent Secession," *Saigon Post* (May 19, 1966): 1.

101. Oka, "Buddhism as a Political Force," 12.

102. Charles Mohr, "Ky Says Adding Civilians to Junta Is a Good Idea," *New York Times* (May 25, 1966): 1; and State 3626, Rusk to Lodge, 5-25-66, Vietnam vol. 54, VCF.

103. State 3536, Rusk to Porter, 5-19-66, Vietnam vol. 53, VCF.

104. Memo, Memorandum of Conversation, 5-20-66, Vietnam vol. 53, VCF.

105. Max Frankel, "Gloom Prevails in Washington over New Civil Strife in Vietnam," *New York Times* (May 17, 1966): 2.

106. Alfred E. Clark, "Javits Links Aid to Vietnam Unity," *New York Times* (May 20, 1966): 3.

107. Max Frankel, "Johnson Appeals for Unity in War; Ky's Forces Gain," *New York Times* (May 22, 1966): 1.

108. Letter, Senator Mike Mansfield to the President, 6-29-66, Senator Mansfield, NSF LBJ Library; and Gibbons, *U.S. Government and the Vietnam War,* 334–48. Gibbons lists the senators at each meeting in a footnote on page 348.

109. "Memorandum from the President's Special Assistant [Rostow] to President Johnson," May 10, 1966, *FRUS: Vietnam,* vol. 4, 1966, 378.

110. "Telegram from the Department of State to the Embassy in Vietnam," May 15, 1966, *FRUS: Vietnam,* vol. 4, 1966, 387.

111. Gibbons, *U.S. Government and the Vietnam War,* 334–40.

112. Ibid.

113. Sidey, "The Poll Pains of a Living, Breathing Contradiction," *Life* 60 (June 24, 1966): 38.

114. Gibbons, *U.S. Government and the Vietnam War,* 334–40.

115. "Editorial Note on Phone Conversation of June 2, 1966," *FRUS: Vietnam,* vol. 4, 1966, 410–11.

116. John D. Pomfret, "Johnson Asks U.S. to Unite behind His Vietnam Policy," *New York Times* (May 18, 1966): 1, and Max Frankel, "Johnson Appeals for Unity in War; Ky's Forces Gain," *New York Times* (May 22, 1966): 1.

117. Bundy, Oral History, 35, and Gibbons, *U.S. Government and the Vietnam War,* 315–17.

118. See "Summary Memorandum," 5-21-66, "The Security Council," 5-20-66, "Points," 5-21-66; "Concentrating on the North Vietnam Problem," 5-20-66, "Making Negotiation More Attractive to the DRV," 5–66; and "Changing the Choice of the DRV," 5-17-66, Warnke Papers.

119. Memo, Rostow to the President, "Analysis of Senator Mansfield's Comments on Vietnam Policy Alternatives," 6-16-66, Mansfield File, NSF LBJ Library.

120. Memo, Rostow to the President, 5-27-66, Vietnam vol. 54, VCF.

121. Gardner, *Pay Any Price,* 307; Herring, *America's Longest War,* 152; and Gibbons, *U.S. Government and the Vietnam War,* 353.

122. The author would like to attribute this remark, but it came from an anonymous reviewer of an earlier draft of this chapter.

123. While McNaughton's files contain a wealth of information on administration attitudes toward the war, in many cases it is difficult to ascertain exactly who read the papers collected by McNaughton or how widely they were distributed. If McNaughton had not collected them, we might not even be aware of their existence, particularly the handwritten notes of conversations he had with other officials. Except for William Gibbons, historians have generally ignored these documents, which provide important clues to the administration's thinking during this period.

124. Herring, *America's Longest War,* 185.

125. Logevall, *Choosing War,* 376–77.

126. Letter, Robert S. McNamara to author, 12-5-97.

127. William Bundy, phone messages and conversations with author, 1-9-98, 1-14-98 and 3-13-98. Bundy says that the emergence of a non-Communist government in Indonesia fundamentally changed the strategic equation in Southeast Asia and should have alerted U.S. officials to the possibility of a negotiated settlement in Vietnam. Bundy admits that he "feels guilty about not raising more objections" to the war in 1966.

128. Logevall, *Choosing War,* 377.

129. Turner, *Echoes of Combat.*

130. Logevall, *Choosing War,* 389.

131. Gardner, *Pay Any Price,* 149.

5. Resolution

Epigraph: Thich Nhat Hanh, *Call Me by My True Names,* 27.

1. Hassler, *Saigon U.S.A.,* 100–101; and King, "Thich Nhat Hanh and the Unified Buddhist Church of Vietnam," in Queen and King, eds., *Engaged Buddhism,* 333.

2. Charles Mohr, "Ky Forces Fight Dissident Units, Occupy Danang," *New York Times* (May 15, 1966): 1.

3. FitzGerald, *Fire in the Lake,* 385.

4. Karnow, *Vietnam: A History,* 447–50.

5. In July 1996 and March 1997, the author visited Hue to conduct interviews for this work. One evening in March, he sat by the Perfume River in Hue as the sun set and marveled at the beauty and timeless serenity of Hue, the most lovely of all Vietnamese cities. The differences between Hue and Ho Chi Minh City seemed almost indescribable.

6. Charles Mohr, "Buddhists Appeal for Johnson's Aid to Overrule Ky," *New York Times* (May 17, 1966): 1.

7. Schecter, *New Face of Buddha,* 228; Embtel 4610 (Saigon), Porter to Rusk, 5-15-66, Vietnam vol. 53, VCF; and Embtel 4768 (Saigon), Corcoran to Bullington, 5-19-66, Vietnam vol. 53, VCF.

8. Embtel 4774 (Saigon), Porter to Rusk, 5-20-66, and Embtel 4625 (Saigon), Porter to Bullington, 5-16-66, Vietnam vol. 53, VCF; and Kahin, *Intervention,* 431.

9. Embtel 4855 (Saigon), Bullington to Rusk, 5-22-66, Vietnam vol. 54, VCF.

10. Charles Mohr, "Buddhists Appeal for Johnson's Aid to Overrule Ky," *New York Times* (May 17, 1966): 1.

11. "Buddhist Monk Defies Saigon in Plea Here for Vietnam Peace," *New York Times* (May 17, 1966): 4.

12. Max Frankel, "Rusk Says Breach in South Vietnam Stirs U.S. Disquiet," *New York Times* (May 18, 1966): 1.

13. Neil Sheehan, "Danang Monks Threaten Suicide If Attacked," *New York Times* (May 17, 1966): 3.

14. Neil Sheehan, "Ky Forces Hold Danang; Buddhists Fear Civil War; U.S. Appeals for Accord," *New York Times* (May 16, 1966): 1.

15. "Ky's Troops Use Tanks in Danang against Rebels," *New York Times* (May 20, 1966): 1; and Cable, CIA to White House Situation Room, "Progress of Struggle Forces in Danang; Anti-American Statements," 5-19-66, Vietnam vol. 53, VCF.

16. Embtel 4827 (Saigon), Lodge to Rusk, 5-21-66, and Embtel 4821 (Saigon), Lodge to Rusk, 5-21-66, Vietnam vol. 53, VCF.

17. Neil Sheehan, "Airbase Is Shelled," *New York Times* (May 21, 1966): 1; and "Dissidents' Area in Danang Shrinks," *New York Times* (May 22, 1966): 1.

18. Sheehan, "Airbase Is Shelled," 1.

19. "Ky's Troops Seize a Danang Pagoda; 2 Buddhists Slain," *New York Times* (May 21, 1966): 1; Sheehan, "Airbase Is Shelled," 1; and "Dissidents' Area in Danang Shrinks," 1.

20. Schecter, *New Face of Buddha,* 231; and "Dissidents Yield to Ky in Danang, Surrender Arms," *New York Times* (May 23, 166): 1.

21. CIA Report, "The Situation in South Vietnam," 5-25-66, Vietnam vol. 54, VCF.

22. Embtel 5124 (Saigon), Lodge to Rusk, 5-30-66, Vietnam vol. 53, VCF.

23. Embtel 5473 (Saigon), Lodge to Rostow, 6-11-66, Vietnam vol. 55, VCF.

24. Report, CIA Intelligence Memorandum, "The Vulnerability of Non-Com-

munist Groups in South Vietnam to Viet Cong Political Subversion," 5-27-66, Vietnam vol. 54, VCF.

25. Richard Eder, "Washington Is Concerned and Surprised by Ky Step," *New York Times* (May 16, 1966): 1.

26. Embtel 5307 (Saigon), Lodge to Rusk, 6-6-66, Vietnam vol. 55, VCF.

27. Embtel 5527 (Saigon), Lodge to Rusk, 6-14-66, Vietnam vol. 55, VCF.

28. "Division Moved to Saigon Area," *New York Times* (May 17, 1966): 3; and "Cops Raid, Close Buddhist Center," *Saigon Post* (May 16, 1966): 1.

29. Charles Mohr, "Political Clash in Vietnam Sharpens," *New York Times* (May 22, 1966): 3; "Buddhists Start Sit-down in Saigon," *New York Times* (May 21, 1966): 2; and "Buddhist Pose Mass Hunger Strike: Bonzes, Nuns to Lead Protest," *Saigon Post* (May 21, 1966): 1.

30. Embtel 4887 (Saigon), Lodge to Rusk, 5-23-66, Vietnam vol. 54, VCF.

31. Schecter, *New Face of Buddha,* 231–32; and R.W. Apple Jr., "Buddhist Mob Burns U.S. Vehicle after Slaying of Soldier," *New York Times* (May 23, 1966): 1.

32. "Ky Troops Let Buddhists Leave Pagoda in Saigon," *New York Times* (May 24, 1966): 1; and Charles Mohr, "Foes of Ky March," *New York Times* (May 24, 1966): 1.

33. Neil Sheehan, "Tear Gas Blocks Saigon Marches by Buddhists," *New York Times* (May 26, 1966): 1; and "Cops Blunt Buddhist Splinter Mob Tactic: Tear Gas Used; More Troops Called In," *Saigon Post* (May 26, 1966): 1.

34. "Demonstrators Fail to Mass Up: Cops Check Motley Groups," *Saigon Post* (May 28, 1966): 1.

35. R.W. Apple Jr., "Nun's Fiery Death in Hue Sets Off Clash in Saigon," *New York Times* (May 29, 1966): 1.

36. Kahin interview, September 1996; Stevenson interview, May 2001; Thi interview, April 1997. Kahin told the author that it was generally accepted in Saigon and the American embassy that Loan had ordered the attempted assassination of Thich Thien Minh. Thi confirmed it during his interview with the author. Richard Stevenson disagrees, claiming that Loan was a true patriot and not the thug characterized by many members of the American press.

37. Charles Mohr, "Ky Junta Agrees to Take Civilians into Leadership," *New York Times* (June 2, 1966): 1; and "NLC to Include Civilian Members," *Saigon Post* (June 2, 1966): 1.

38. "Buddhist Mass Up for Suicides Funeral," *Saigon Post* (June 3, 1966): 1.

39. Embtel 5215 (Saigon), Lodge to Rusk, 6-2-66, Vietnam vol. 55, VCF.

40. CIA Report, "The Situation in South Vietnam," 6-8-66 and 6-15-66, Vietnam vol. 55, VCF.

41. "Tam Chau Asks Moderation," *New York Times* (May 25, 1966): 6; and "Tam Chau Says Buddhists Not Opposing Gov't," *Saigon Post* (May 25, 1966): 1.

42. Neil Sheehan, "Moderates under Pressure," *New York Times* (May 29, 1966): 3.

43. "Buddhist Moderate Assets Leadership: Soft Anti-Government Line Prevails As Chau Nixes Violence, Self-Burnings," *Saigon Post* (May 31, 1966): 1.

44. Embtel 5195 (Saigon), Lodge to Rusk, 6-1-66, Vietnam vol. 55, VCF.

45. "Nun Dies by Fire as Sixth Suicide in Anti-Ky Drive," *New York Times*

(June 3, 1966): 1; and Neil Sheehan, "Buddhists Ease Effort," *New York Times* (June, 3, 1966): 1.

46. Neil Sheehan, "Buddhists Seek to Heal Split in Church," *New York Times* (June 5, 1966): 3.

47. Schecter, *New Face of Buddha,* 239.

48. The author made numerous attempts to interview Thich Tam Chau for this work, but he refused to answer letters, take phone calls, or respond to faxes. When the author asked his assistant about the split in the UBC, he responded, "Oh you know about that," and insisted that to gain an interview, the author had to submit the questions in advance. The next day the author faxed a list of questions, which have gone unanswered.

49. Schecter, *New Face of Buddha,* 241–42.

50. Embtel 4739 (Saigon), Porter to Rusk, "Situation in Hue," 5-19-66, Vietnam vol. 53, VCF.

51. Sheehan, "Ky Forces Hold Danang," 1.

52. See chapter three.

53. Cable, CIA to White House Situation Room, 5-17-66, Vietnam vol. 53, VCF.

54. Embtel 4688 (Saigon), Corcoran to Rusk, 5-17-66, Vietnam vol. 53, VCF.

55. FitzGerald, *Fire in the Lake,* 386; R.W. Apple Jr., "Buddhist Students Wreck American Center in Hue," *New York Times* (May 27, 1966): 1; and "Buddhists Burn Hue JUSPAO: LBJ Sends Note to Thich Tri Quang," *Saigon Post* (May 27, 1966): 1.

56. FitzGerald, *Fire in the Lake,* 386.

57. Embtel 5033 (Saigon), Lodge to Rusk, 5-27-66, Vietnam vol. 54, VCF.

58. Embtel 4999 (Saigon), Lodge to Rusk, 5-26-66, Vietnam vol. 54, VCF.

59. R.W. Apple Jr., "Dissident Vietnamese Army Unit Moved from Hue," *New York Times* (May 31, 1966): 13.

60. Memo, For the President, 6-1-66, Vietnam vol. 55, VCF; Schecter, *New Face of Buddha,* 232–33; "Student Mob in Hue Burns American Consular Office," *New York Times* (June 1, 1966): 1; and R.W. Apple Jr., "Students End Broadcasts," *New York Times* (June 1, 1966): 1.

61. R.W. Apple Jr., "Ky Orders Hue Mayor to Quell Dissident Forces," *New York Times* (June 2, 1966): 2.

62. R.W. Apple Jr., "Troops Enter Hue but Their Aims Are in Doubt," *New York Times* (June 3, 1966): 2; and "Hue Falls to Gov't Troops: Move Swift," *Saigon Post* (June 3, 1966): 1.

63. Schecter, *New Face of Buddha,* 250. Thich Tri Quang's hunger strike lasted until September, when he was ordered to begin taking food by the patriarch of the UBC, Thich Thien Khiet.

64. Queen and King, eds., *Engaged Buddhism,* 335; and Schecter, *New Face of Buddha,* 240.

65. Kahin, *Intervention,* 430.

66. Memo, For the President, 6-9-66, Vietnam vol. 55, VCF.

67. Embtel 5346 (Saigon), Lodge to Rusk, 6-7-66, Vietnam vol. 55, VCF.

68. General Westmoreland Historical Briefing, 6-12-66, Westmoreland Papers, LBJ Library.

69. Schecter, *New Face of Buddha,* 241.

70. "No Contact with (Thich) Tri Quang without Authorization," *Saigon Daily News* (June 30, 1966): 1.

71. Clarke, *United States Army in Vietnam,* 143, and FitzGerald, *Fire in the Lake,* 387–88.

72. Simmons, *The Marines in Vietnam: 1954–73,* 64.

73. Thich Nhat Hanh, "Please Call Me by My True Names," in Eppsteiner, ed., *Path of Compassion,* 38; Thich Thien Chieu interview, March 1997.

74. Queen and King, eds., *Engaged Buddhism,* 336.

75. Mole, *Vietnamese Buddhism,* A-4.

76. Gruber and Kersten, *Original Jesus,* 62.

77. Douglas Pike, Oral History, June 4, 1981, LBJ Library, 26.

78. Topmiller, "Buddhist Crisis of 1963," 37–40.

79. Thich Thien-An, *Buddhism and Zen,* 172–91; and David Halberstam, "Diem Asks Peace in Religious Crisis," *New York Times* (June 12, 1963), 7.

80. Memo, Komer to Moyers, "Vietnam Press Guidelines," 6-2-66, Name Files, Robert Komer Files, NSF LBJ Library.

81. Memo, Memo for the President, "South Vietnam," 5-29-66, Vietnam vol. 54, VCF.

82. Embtel 5124 (Saigon), Lodge to Rusk, 5-30-66, Vietnam vol. 53, VCF.

83. "South Viet Nam: The Light That Failed," 39; and "Fiery Rebellion," 48–49.

84. John D. Pomfret, "Johnson Deplores Buddhist Suicides," *New York Times* (May 31, 1966): 1; and "Johnson Says Buddhist Suicides Unnecessary," *Saigon Post* (June 1, 1966): 1.

85. Embtel 5195 (Saigon), Lodge to Rusk, 6-1-66, Vietnam vol. 55, VCF.

86. Schecter, *New Face of Buddha,* 233–34; and Oka, "Buddhism as a Political Force," 13.

87. Schecter, *New Face of Buddha,* 237–38.

88. FitzGerald, *Fire in the Lake,* 386; Charles Mohr, "4 Buddhists Die As Suicides Rise in Anti-Ky Drive," *New York Times* (May 30, 1966): 1; and "Buddhist Protest Being Intensified: Suicide Toll at 5," *New York Times* (May 31, 1966): 1.

89. R.W. Apple Jr., "Buddhist Warns of Vote Boycott Unless Ky Quits," *New York Times* (June 4, 1966): 1; and "2 More Fiery Suicides," *New York Times* (June 4, 1966): 3.

90. Queen and King, eds., *Engaged Buddhism,* 332.

91. Hassler, *Saigon U.S.A.,* 13; and Thi interview, April 1997.

92. *The Third Solution,* 3, 11, Kahin Files.

93. Hassler, *Saigon U.S.A.,* 16.

94. Elliot, *Sacred Willow,* 324.

95. Hassler, *Saigon U.S.A.,* 117–18; Vo Van Ai, e-mails to author, 5-23-96, 5-31-96.

96. Queen and King, eds., *Engaged Buddhism,* 323–24.

97. Ibid., 326.

98. For a more complete account of the work of the SYSS, see Chan Khong, *Learning True Love.*

99. Queen and King, eds., *Engaged Buddhism,* 323–24.

100. "The Third Solution," 1.

101. Hassler, *Saigon U.S.A.,* 115.

102. Ibid., 12.

103. Kahin Files, "Thich Nhat Hanh Interview with George McT. Kahin," (December 2, 1967): 1; and *The Third Solution,* 2.

104. *The Third Solution,* 5; Hassler, *Saigon U.S.A.,* 158; "Seminar with [Thich] Nhat Hanh" (September 21, 1967): 3; and Kahin Files. No one who visits Vietnam today can deny the retribution visited on former government officials and soldiers of South Vietnam by the victorious Communists after 1975. In numerous conversations during trips to Vietnam in 1996, 1997, 1999, and 2000, the author learned that almost all of them spent considerable time in reeducation camps after the war and then were denied employment until the implementation of Doi Moi. Many have been able to take advantage of the liberalization of the economy by catering to Western tourists and visitors, because most can speak English. Nevertheless, nothing can compensate for the years when they were denied the ability to work and to rebuild their lives. Their lives destroyed, most exist now for their children. One must wonder if the NLF would have been so cruel if it had been able to enter a coalition government in the early years of the war before American firepower, the Tet Offensive, and the Phoenix program delivered power to the DRV.

105. "Thich Nhat Hanh interview with Kahin," 3.

106. Hassler, *Saigon U.S.A.,* 15. Hassler claims that the book was published in "eight other languages and nine other countries" and sold an astounding 100,000 copies in South Vietnam.

107. *The Third Solution,* 1.

108. Queen and King, eds., *Engaged Buddhism,* 324–25.

109. R.W. Apple Jr., "Ousted General Confers with Ky on Ending Crisis," *New York Times* (May 28, 1966): 1; and "Ky, Thi Confer in U.S. Danang Base," *Saigon Post* (May 28, 1966): 1.

110. Rose Kushner, "The Exile of Gen. Thi: 'Only 48, and I Am Fini'" (July 22, 1973), and "Exiled Gen. Thi Returns to Saigon—& Gets Bounced" (July 25, 1972), Indochina Archive.

111. Kahin, *Intervention,* 429–30.

112. Cable, MAC 4409, Westmoreland to Walt, 5-31-66, Westmoreland Papers.

113. Lt. General John R. Chaisson, Oral History Transcript, USMC Archive.

Conclusion

Epigraph: Daniel Berrigan in Wirmark, *The Buddhists in Vietnam,* 4.

1. The first time a Vietnamese told the author that the war had occurred so that the United States could test new weapons and tactics, he was taken aback. In time, the author learned that many Vietnamese hold cynical opinions about American

goals in South Vietnam and that few see the American intervention as an act of benevolence (Da Le, interview by the author, March 1994).

2. FitzGerald, *Fire in the Lake,* 387.

3. Schecter, *New Face of Buddha,* 213.

4. "Thich Nhat Hanh Interview with Kahin," 2, Kahin Files.

5. Karnow, *Vietnam: A History,* 449.

6. Kahin, *Intervention,* 432.

7. When Washington complained that members of the Struggle Movement had been disqualified from running for office by the GVN, Lodge told Bundy that he "was happy when the writ of the GVN was restored in I Corps. To feel otherwise seems somewhat similar to our being disappointed in the U.S. because there is not a large number of active, card carrying Communists running for the House and Senate" (Embtel 1947 [Saigon], Lodge to William Bundy, 7-26-66, Vietnam vol. 56, VCF).

8. Queen and King, eds., *Engaged Buddhism,* 334; and Hassler, *Saigon U.S.A.,* 42.

9. Kahin, *Intervention,* 430; and Karnow, *Vietnam: A History,* 450.

10. Kamm, *Dragon Ascending,* 113.

11. CIA Report, "The Situation in South Vietnam," 7-18-66, Vietnam vol. 56, VCF.

12. Hassler, *Saigon U.S.A.,* 26.

13. R.W. Apple, Jr., "Buddhist Warns of Vote Boycott: Unless Ky Quits," *New York Times* (June 4, 1966): 1.

14. *The Third Solution,* 6, Kahin Files.

15. *The Third Solution,* 13; and Karnow, *Vietnam: A History,* 450–51.

16. Kahin, *Intervention,* 431.

17. Clarke, *U.S. Army in Vietnam,* 143.

18. FitzGerald, *Fire in the Lake,* 390.

19. Kahin, interview by the author, Ithaca, N.Y., September 1996. Kahin's insistence on the need to listen to what the Vietnamese, rather than the Americans, were saying was an important element in some later accounts of the war, including this one.

20. Forest, *Unified Buddhist Church of Vietnam,* 8.

21. Tran Van Dinh, "Ky vs. Buddhists—Round 2," *The New Republic* (May 13, 1967): 15–16.

22. Tran Van Dinh, "Thich Don Hau," 1171.

23. Forest, *Unified Buddhist Church of Vietnam,* 8–13.

24. Ibid.; Kahin letter to congressmen, Kahin Files; "South Vietnam: Victory to the Buddhists," *Time* (September 14, 1970): 22; and Forest, "Only the Rice Loves You."

25. Denny, "Human Rights in Vietnam," 30–31.

26. Queen and King, eds., *Engaged Buddhism,* 355.

27. Kamm, *Dragon Ascending,* 198.

Bibliography

PRIMARY SOURCES

"An Interview with the Buddhists Vo Van Ai and Thich Nhat Hanh." *War/Peace Report* 9 (June–July, 1969): 13ff.

Homer, Jack A., ed. *Religion for Peace: Proceedings of the Kyoto Conference on Religion and Peace.* New Delhi. 1973.

INDOCHINA ARCHIVE, UNIVERSITY OF CALIFORNIA, BERKELEY

"Buddhism and the Buddhist Programming of the Asia Foundation in Asia." *The Asia Foundation.* San Francisco, 1968.

"COSVN Resolution 2: Late 1963 or Early 1964."

"COSVN Resolution on Mission in the South: January 1965."

"Le Duan Letter to the Saigon Party Committee—Issued between Mid-1966 and Mid-1967."

"The Processes of Revolution and the General Uprisings." *Vietnam Documents and Research Notes.* October, 1968.

"A Short History of Buddhism in Vietnam" (July 1963).

Biography File.

KAHIN, GEORGE McT., VIETNAMESE BUDDHISM FILES

American Friends Service Committee. "Statement by Vo Van Ai." January 9, 1969: 1–4.

"Appeal Made by the National Assembly of the Unified Buddhist Church on November 1, 1972, Concerning the War." December 15, 1972: 1–17.

"CIA Report." February 25, 1965: 1.

"General Nguyen Khanh's Talk." December 6, 1973: 1–26.

"*Hoa Binh* Interview with General Ton That Dinh." May 12, 1978: 1–13.

"Excerpt from *Le Tu Hung: Bon Tuong Da-lat* (The Four Dalat Generals)." 1971: 1–6.

Bibliography

"Interview Notes and Memorandum: 1966–67 Visit to South Vietnam." March 20, 1967: 1–20.
"Interview with General Nguyen Khanh." December 6, 1973: 1–12.
"Interview with General Thi." October 5, 1966: 1–3.
"Interview with Thich Nhat Hanh." December 2, 1967: 1–4.
"Interview with Thich Tri Quang." January 19, 1970: 1–2.
"Letter to R.H. Nolte from Takashi Oka: Thich Quang Lien's Peace Movement." April 30, 1965: 1–8.
Takashi Oka. "Letter to R.H. Nolte: Buddhism as a Political Force: Danang and After." May 29, 1967: 1–16.
"Letter from Paul Kattenburg to George Kahin." April 8, 1980: 1.
"Letter from William Westmoreland to General Thi." March 11, 1965: 1.
"Letter to Congressmen." Undated: 1.
"Notes from *Hoa Binh.*" September 13, 1976: 1.
"Options in Vietnam: An Occasional Paper by the Center for the Study of Democratic Institutions." *The Third Solution.* December 15, 1967: 1–13.
"Seminar with [Thich] Nhat Hanh." December 21, 1967: 1–7.
Thich Nhat Hanh. "Kinh Gui Dong Bao Viet Nam Tai Hai Ngoai" (Open Letter from the Overseas Vietnamese Buddhist Association)." February 2, 1967: 1–11.
"Thich Tri Quang: Communiqué." November 10, 1968: 1.
"Trial Transcript and *Hoa Binh* Commentary." November 15, 1976: 1–32.

OTHER PRIMARY SOURCES

Department of State. *Foreign Relations of the United States. Vietnam.* 1963, 1964, and 1966. G.P.O.: Washington, D.C., 1998.
New York Times 1964–1966.
Saigon Daily News 1964–1966.
Saigon Post 1964–1966.
"Thich Nhat Hanh: Interview." *New Yorker* 42 (June 25, 1963): 21–23.
The Lyndon B. Johnson National Security Files: Vietnam, 1963–69. Frederick, Maryland, and LBJ Library.

U.S. MARINE CORPS HISTORICAL CENTER AND ARCHIVES, WASHINGTON D.C.

Operations of the III Marine Amphibious Force, Vietnam, January 1967.
III Marine Amphibious Force Command Chronology, April and May 1966.
III MAF Journal and File, 1966.
John R. Chaisson, Personal Papers.
Letter "Lewis Walt to Edwin Simmons." May 13, 1978.

Bibliography

Oral History Collection.
Simmons, Edwin. *The Marines in Vietnam, 1954–73: An Anthology and Annotated Bibliography.* Washington, 1985.

LYNDON BAINES JOHNSON PRESIDENTIAL LIBRARY

Name File.
Oral History Collection.
Vietnam Country File, National Security Files.

ARTICLES

Abbott, Arthur S. "World Buddhism Under Pressure." *World Affairs* 129:2 (1966): 101–108.
"Again, the Buddhists in South Vietnam." *Time* 83 (June 5, 1964): 27–28.
"Again Thich Tri Quang." *America* 110 (June 6, 1964): 784.
"Anarchy and Agony." *Time* 84 (September 4, 1964): 33–34.
Benchert, Heinz. "Sangha, State and Society, Nation: Persistence of Traditions in Post Traditional Societies." *Daedalus* 102:1 (1973): 85–96.
Bennett, John T. "Political Implication of Economic Change: South Vietnam." *Asian Survey* 7:8 (August 1967): 581–91.
Borin, V.L. "Who Killed Diem and Why." *National Review* 16 (June 2, 1964): 441–46.
"Buddha on the Barricades." *Time* 84 (December 11, 1964): 38–42.
"Buddhists vs the Generals." *Senior Scholastic* 88 (April 22, 1966): 11–12.
Cadden, Robert. "Government by Coup: The Militarization of Political Power in South Vietnam, 1960–65." *Vietnam Journal* 1 (1981): 4–8.
Carver, George A. "The Real Revolution in South Vietnam." *Foreign Affairs* 43 (1965): 387–408.
Center for the Study of Democratic Institutions. "A Discussion with the Venerable Thich Nhat Hanh." *Options in Vietnam* (December 15, 1967): 1–13.
Cleary, J.C. "Buddhism and Popular Religion in Medieval Vietnam." *Journal of the American Academy of Religion* 14:1: 93–118.
Clos, M. "Karma of Vietnam's Buddhists." *New York Times Magazine* (August 1964): 28–29.
Denny, Steven. "Human Rights in Vietnam." *Mindfulness Bell* (Summer 1994): 30–31.
"Dictatorial Regime: Khanh Promoted to President: Buddhists Again Threaten Trouble." *Time* 84 (August 28, 1964): 26–27.
"Dissatisfied Buddhists: South Vietnamese Buddhists." *Newsweek* 64 (September 7, 1964): 34.

Bibliography

Divine, Robert. "Vietnam Reconsidered." *Diplomatic History* (Winter 1988): 79–93.

Donnell, J.C., and C.A. Joiner. "South Vietnam: Struggle for Politics and the Bigger War." *Asian Survey* 7 (January 1967): 53–68.

Edwards, Adrian. "Vietnam War Could Have Been Avoided—McNamara." *Reuters* (June 23, 1997): 1–3.

"Exploding Power of the Buddhists: Instability in Vietnam." *Life* 57 (December 11, 1964): 34–41.

Fall, Bernard B. "The History and Culture of Vietnam." *Naval War College Review* 23:6 (February 1971): 48–54.

———. "The Political-Religious Sects of Viet-Nam." *Pacific Affairs* 28 (September 1955): 235–52.

———. "Vietnam's Chinese Problem." *Far Eastern Survey* 27:5 (May 1953): 65–72.

"Fiery Rebellion: Buddhists' Self Immolations and Activities to Bring down Government." *Newsweek* 67 (June 13, 1967): 48–49.

"Fighting the Reds and the Bonzes." *Time* 84 (December 18, 1964): 32.

"Fire under Diem." *Economist* (July 13, 1963): 133–34.

"Four Buddhist Leaders Freed in Vietnam." *IFOR Report* (February 1979): 1.

Freedman, Lawrence. "Vietnam and the Disillusioned Strategist." *International Affairs* 72:1 (1996): 133–51.

"Fruits of Dictatorship." ed. *Far Eastern Economic Review* 45 (September 3, 1964): 419.

Fulham, Parke. "Vietnamese Sand Castle." *Far Eastern Economic Review* 46 (October 1, 1964): 13.

Haines, David W. "Reflections of Kinship and Society under Vietnam's Le Dynasty." *Journal of Southeast Asian Studies* 15:2 (1984): 307–14.

Haseman, John B. "The Hoa Hao: A Half-Century of Conflict." *Asian Affairs* 3:6 (1976): 373–83.

Herring, George C. "'Peoples Quite Apart': Americans, South Vietnamese, and the War in Vietnam." *Diplomatic History* 14 (Winter 1990): 1–23.

Higgins, M. "Saigon Summary." *America* 110 (January 4, 1964): 18–21.

———. "Ugly Americans of Vietnam: With Editorial Comment." *America* 111 (October 3, 1964): 367, 376–82.

"The History and Culture of Vietnam." *Naval War College Review* 23:6 (February 1971): 48–54.

Hope, Marjorie. "Reluctant Way: Self-Immolation in Vietnam." *Antioch Review* 27 (Summer 1967): 149–63.

———. "Vietnam Perspectives: The Buddhist Way, Guns, Butter, or Chinh Nghia?" *War/Peace Report* 6 (August–September 1966): 14–16.

Howe, Irving. "The Buddhist Revolt in Vietnam." *Dissent* 13 (May–June, 1966): 227–29.

"Hunger and Desperation: South Vietnam's Top Three Monks Begin a Forty-eight Hour Fast in Their Campaign to Bring Down Premier Tran Van Huong." *Time* 84 (December 25, 1964): 21.

Huyen, Sanh Thong. "Literature and the Vietnamese." *Vietnam Forum* 9 (1987): 37–48.

Jamieson, Neil L. "Toward a Paradigm for Paradox: Observations on the Study of Social Organization in Southeast Asia." *Journal of Southeast Asian Studies* 15:2 (1984): 320–29.

"Job on Diem: Buddhist Campaign on the Issue of Religion." *America* 110 (May 30, 1964): 758.

Joiner, Charles A. "South Vietnam's Buddhist Crisis: Organization for Charity, Dissidence, and Unity." *Asian Survey* 4 (July 1964): 915–28.

Jones, P.M.H. "The Holy Alliance." *Far Eastern Economic Review* 48 (April 1, 1965): 48–49.

"Just Who Are the Buddhists?" *United States News* 60 (May 30, 1966): 29–30.

Kahin, George McT. "Political Polarization in South Vietnam: U.S. Policy in the Post-Diem Period." *Pacific Affairs* 52:4 (Winter 1979–80): 647–73.

"Ky's Crackdown." *Newsweek* 68 (July 4, 1966): 28.

Langguth, J. "Buddhist Way in Vietnam." *New York Times Magazine* (October 11, 1964): 29.

"Light That Failed: Self-Immolation in Vietnam." *Time* (June 10, 1966): 39.

Luu Quoc. "The Buddhists' and Students' Politics of Peace and Sovereignty in South Vietnam, 1964–1968." *Cornell Journal of Social Relations* 6 (Spring 1971): 98–114.

"Manipulators: Buddhism as a Political Force in Vietnam." *Newsweek* 65 (February 8, 1965): 37.

Markbreiter, Tuyet Nguyet. "Interview with (Thich) Tri Quang." *Far Eastern Economic Review* 47 (March 12, 1965): 436–37.

Marr, David. "Political Attitudes of Young Urban Intellectuals in South Vietnam." *Asian Survey* 6 (1966): 249–63.

Martin, R.P. "Last Days for South Vietnam? Close Look at Latest Crisis." *United States News* 58 (February 8, 1965): 36–37.

Maruyama, Shizuo. "America's Logic and Vietnam's Logic." *Japan Quarterly* 22:3 (1975): 205–13.

Minh, Chi. "A Survey of Vietnamese Buddhism: Past and Present." *Buddhist Institute for Higher Studies* (undated).

Morgan, K.W. "Buddhists in Saigon." *Christian Century* 83 (January 26, 1966): 107–10.

———. "The Buddhists: The Problem and the Promise." *Asia* 4 (Winter 1966): 503–18.

Nakhamura, Hajime. "The Buddhist Protest." *Japan Quarterly* 13 (October–December, 1966): 439–43.

Neilan, Edward. "A Long Hot Summer." *Far Eastern Economic Review* 45 (August 20, 1964): 301–2.

Bibliography

Nivolon, François. "Declining Chances." *Far Eastern Economic Review* 45 (September 10, 1964): 471.

———. "Emergency Powers." *Far Eastern Economic Review* 45 (August 27, 1964): 365.

"Our Friends, the Buddhists: Impending Purge of Catholic Generals from South Vietnamese Armed Forces." *America* 112 (April 24, 1965): 597.

"Out of the Frying Pan: Buddhist Demonstrations in Vietnam." *Newsweek* 65 (February 1, 1965): 34.

"Pilot with a Mission." *Time* 87 (February 18, 1966): 26–31.

"Question in Saigon." *America* 111 (September 19, 1964): 286–87.

"Real Trouble in Vietnam." *United States News* 57 (December 14, 1964): 46.

Reisinger, Josef. "Vietnam's Schizophrenia." *Far Eastern Economic Review* 46 (October 29, 1964): 265–67.

"Reprise from the Pagodas." *Time* 83 (December 4, 1964): 38.

Roberts, Adam. "Buddhism and Politics in South Vietnam." *World Today* (London) 21 (June 1965): 240–50.

———. "The Buddhists, the War and the Vietcong." *World Today* (London) 22 (May 1966): 214–22.

Sacks, Milton I. "Restructuring Government in South Vietnam." *Asian Survey* 7:8 (August 1967): 515–26.

Scigliano, Robert. "Vietnam: Politics and Religion." *Asian Survey* 4 (January 1964): 666–73.

Shaplen, Robert. "Letter from Saigon." *New Yorker* 40 (September 19, 1964): 179–86.

———. "Letter from South Vietnam." *New Yorker* 42 (June 4, 1966): 142–44.

"South Viet Nam, The Light That Failed." *Time* (June 10, 1966): 39.

Stuart-Fox, Martin, and Rod Bucknell. "Politicization of the Buddhist Sangha in Laos." *Journal of Southeast Asian Studies* 14:1 (1983): 60–80.

Taylor, Keith W. "The 'Twelve Lords' in Tenth-Century Vietnam." *Journal of Southeast Asian Studies* 14:1 (1983): 46–62.

"Tear Gas and Burning Books: Anti-American Outburst in South Vietnam." *Time* 85 (January 29, 1965): 25.

Thich, Nhat Hanh. "On the War by a Buddhist Monk: A Buddhist Poet in Vietnam." *New York Review of Books* (June 9, 1966): 4–5.

"Thich Tri Quang: Buddhist Mystery Man." *Senior Scholastic* 88 (May 6, 1966): 8.

"Too Little, Too Late." *Far Eastern Economic Review* 45 (September 24, 1964): 543.

Tran, Van Dinh. "Ky vs Buddhists: Round 2." *New Republic* 156 (May 13, 1967): 15–19.

———. "Thich Don Hau: Profile of a Buddhist Leader." *Christian Century* 85 (September 18, 1968): 1171–72.

Bibliography

Troelstrup, G.L. "Why Vietnam's Buddhists Act the Way They Do: Report from the Troubled Center." *United States News* 60 (May 2, 1966): 58–59.

"Vietnam: The Broadening War." *Asian Survey* 6:1 (January 1966): 49–58.

"Vietnam: The Suppression of the Unified Buddhist Church." *Human Rights Watch Asia* 7:4 (March 1995): 1–16.

"Vietnam's Buddhists Emerge as Key Power: Vital Third Force to Determine War's Course and Future United States Presence." *Business Week* (April 23, 1966): 38–40.

Warner, Dennis. "The Divided Buddhists of South Vietnam." *Reporter* 34 (June 16, 1966): 22–24.

———. "How Much Power Does [Thich] Tri Quang Want?" *Reporter* 34 (May 5, 1966): 11–14.

———. "Vietnam's Militant Buddhists." *Reporter* 31 (December 3, 1964): 29–31.

Watts, Jonathan. "Vietnamese Buddhism: Syncretic and Political Worlds." *Seeds of Peace* 2:1 (January–April 1995).

Whitmore, John K. "Chiao-Chih and Neo-Confucianism: The Ming Attempt to Transform Vietnam." *Ming Studies* 3 (Spring 1977): 51–92.

———. "Social Organization and Confucian Thought in Vietnam." *Journal of Southeast Asian Studies* 15:2 (1984): 296–306.

Wolfstone, Daniel, ed. "Buddhist Democracy." *Far Eastern Economic Review* 46 (October 22, 1964): 167.

Woodside, Alexander B. "Medieval Vietnam and Cambodia: A Comparative Comment." *Journal of Southeast Asian Studies* 15:2 (1984): 315–19.

———. "Some Southern Vietnamese Writers Look at the War." *Bulletin of Concerned Asian Scholars* 2 (October 1969): 53–58.

BOOKS

Asprey, Robert B. *War in the Shadows: The Guerrilla in History,* vol. 1 and 2. New York, 1975.

Ball, George. *The Past Has Another Pattern: Memoirs.* New York, 1982.

Bao, Ninh. *The Sorrow of War.* Hanoi, 1993.

Batchelor, Stephen. *The Awakening of the West.* Berkeley, 1994.

Bellah, Robert N., ed. *Religion and Progress in Modern Asia.* New York, 1965.

Benz, E. *Buddhism or Communism: Which Holds the Future of Asia?* New York, 1965.

Bergerud, Eric M. *The Dynamics of Defeat: The Vietnam War in Hau Nghia Province.* Boulder, 1991.

Beschloss, Michael R. *Taking Charge: The Johnson White House Tapes, 1963–1964.* New York, 1997.

Blair, Anne E. *Lodge in Vietnam: A Patriot Abroad.* New Haven, 1995.

Brigham, Robert K. *Guerilla Diplomacy.* Ithaca, 1999.

Bibliography

Buddhist Chaplain Directorate. *The Buddhist Chaplain Branch of the Republic of Vietnam Armed Forces.* Saigon, 1968.

Bui, Diem. *In the Jaws of History.* Boston, 1987.

Bureau of Naval Personnel, Chaplains Division. *The Religions of South Vietnam in Faith and Fact.* Washington, 1967.

Bushnell, Timothy P. et al., eds. *State Organized Terror: The Case of Violent Internal Repression.* Boulder, 1991.

Caputo, Philip. *A Rumor of War.* New York, 1977.

Chan Khong. *Learning True Love: How I Learned and Practiced Social Change in Vietnam.* Berkeley, 1993.

Chanoff, David, and Doan Van Toai. *Portrait of the Enemy: The Other Side of the War in Vietnam.* London, 1986.

Clarke, Jeffrey J. *United States Army in Vietnam, Advice and Support: The Final Years, 1965–1973.* Washington, 1988.

Colby, William. *Lost Victory: A Firsthand Account of America's Sixteen-Year Involvement in Vietnam.* Chicago, 1989.

Cooper, Chester. *The Lost Crusade: America in Vietnam.* New York, 1970.

Creel, Herrlee G. *Chinese Thought from Confucius to Mao Tsê-tung.* Chicago, 1953.

Critchfield, Richard. *The Long Charade: Political Subversion in the Vietnam War.* New York, 1968.

de Silva, K.M., et al., ed. *Ethnic Conflict in Buddhist Societies: Sri Lanka, Thailand, and Burma.* London, 1988.

DiLeo, David L. *George Ball, Vietnam, and the Rethinking of Containment.* Chapel Hill, 1991.

Duiker, William J. *Vietnam: Nation in Revolution.* Boulder, 1983.

Duncanson, Dennis J. *Government and Revolution in Vietnam.* New York, 1968.

Duong Van Mai Elliot. *The Sacred Willow: Four Generations in the Life of a Vietnamese Family.* New York, 1999.

Eppsteiner, Fred, ed. *The Path of Compassion: Writing on Socially Engaged Buddhism.* Berkeley, 1985.

Fall, Bernard. *The Two Vietnams: A Political and Military Analysis.* New York, 1967.

FitzGerald, Frances. *Fire in the Lake: The Vietnamese and the Americans in Vietnam.* New York, 1972.

Forest, James H. *Only the Rice Loves You.* Nyack, N.Y., 1972.

———. *The Unified Buddhist Church of Vietnam: Fifteen Years for Reconciliation.* Alkmaar, The Netherlands, 1978.

Freeman, James M. *Hearts of Sorrow: Vietnamese-American Lives.* Stanford, 1989.

Gardner, Lloyd C. *Pay Any Price: Lyndon Johnson and the Wars for Vietnam.* Chicago, 1995.

Bibliography

Gelb, Leslie H., and Richard K. Betts. *The Irony of Vietnam: The System Worked.* Washington, 1979.

Gheddo, Piero. *The Cross and the Bo-tree: Catholics and Buddhists in Vietnam.* Translated by Charles Underhill Quinn. New York, 1970.

Gibbons, William C. *The U.S. Government and the Vietnam War: Executive and Legislative Roles and Relationships.* Washington, 1994.

Gruber, Elmar, and Holger Kersten. *The Original Jesus. The Buddhist Sources of Christianity.* Munich, 1995.

Halberstam, David. *The Best and the Brightest.* New York, 1969.

Hassler, Alfred. *Saigon, U.S.A.* New York, 1970.

Herring, George C. *America's Longest War: The United States and Vietnam, 1950–75.* New York, 1979.

———. *LBJ and Vietnam: A Different Kind of War.* Austin, 1994.

Hess, Gary R. *Vietnam and the United States: Origins and Legacy of War.* Boston, 1990.

Hesselgrave, David J, ed. *Dynamic Religious Movements: Case Studies of Rapidly Growing Religious Movements around the World.* Grand Rapids, 1978.

Hickey, Gerald Cannon. *Free in the Forest: Ethnohistory of the Vietnamese Highlands, 1954–1976.* New Haven, 1982.

Hope, Marjorie, and James Young. *The Struggle for Humanity: Agents of Nonviolent Change in a Violent World.* New York, 1977.

Hue-Tam, Ho Tai. *Millenarianism and Peasant Politics in Vietnam.* Cambridge, Mass., 1983.

Jamieson, Neil L. *Understanding Vietnam.* Berkeley, 1993.

Johnson, Lyndon Baines. *The Vantage Point: Perspectives on the Presidency, 1963–1969.* New York, 1971.

Kahin, George McT. *Intervention: How America Became Involved in Vietnam.* New York, 1986.

Kaiser, David. *American Tragedy: Kennedy, Johnson, and the Origins of the Vietnam War.* Cambridge, Mass., 2000.

Kamm, Henry. *Dragon Ascending: Vietnam and the Vietnamese.* New York, 1996.

Karnow, Stanley. *Vietnam: A History.* New York, 1983.

Kattenburg, Paul M. *The Vietnam Trauma in American Foreign Policy, 1945–75.* New Brunswick, N.J., 1980.

Keys, Charles F., Laurel Kendall, and Helen Hardacre, eds. *Asian Visions of Authority: Religion and the Modern States of East and Southeast Asia.* Honolulu, 1994.

Khmer Buddhist Research Center. *Buddhism and the Future of Cambodia.* Rithisen, 1986.

Kolko, Gabriel. *Anatomy of a War: Vietnam, the United States, and the Modern Historical Experience.* New York, 1985.

Bibliography

Kraft, Kenneth, ed. *Inner Peace, World Peace: Essays on Buddhism and Non-violence.* New York, 1992.

Krulak, Victor H. *First to Fight: An Inside View of the U.S. Marine Corps.* Annapolis, 1984.

Lewy, Guenter. *America in Vietnam.* Oxford, 1980.

Ling, Trevor. *Buddha, Marx and God: Some Aspects of Religion in the Modern World.* New York, 1966.

Lodge, Henry Cabot. *The Storm Has Many Eyes: A Personal Narrative.* New York, 1973.

Logevall, Fredrik. *Choosing War: The Last Chance for Peace and the Escalation of War in Vietnam.* Berkeley, 1999.

Lomperis, Timothy J. *From People's War to People's Rule: Insurgency, Intervention and the Lessons of Vietnam.* Chapel Hill, 1996.

Luce, Don, and John Sommer. *Vietnam: The Unheard Voices.* Ithaca, 1969.

Marr, David G. *Vietnam 1945: The Quest for Power.* Berkeley, 1995.

Matthews, Bruce, and Judith Nagata, eds. *Religion, Values, and Development in Southeast Asia.* Singapore, 1986.

McMaster, H.R. *Dereliction of Duty: Lyndon Johnson, Robert McNamara, the Joint Chiefs of Staff and the Lies That Led to Vietnam.* New York, 1997.

McNamara, Robert S. *In Retrospect: The Tragedy and Lessons of Vietnam.* New York, 1995.

Minh Chi, Ha Van Tan, and Nguyen Tai Thu. *Buddhism in Vietnam.* Hanoi, 1993.

Mole, Robert L. *Vietnamese Buddhism.* Washington, 1967.

Nayan, Chanda. *Brother Enemy: The War after the War.* New York, 1986.

Nash, Manning, ed. *Anthropological Studies in Theravada Buddhism.* New Haven, 1966.

Nguyen Cao Ky. *How We Lost the Vietnam War.* New York, 1984.

Nguyen Tai Thu, ed. *History of Buddhism in Vietnam.* Hanoi, 1992.

The Pentagon Papers. The Senator Gravel edition. 5 vols. Boston, 1971–72.

Prados, John. *The Hidden History of the Vietnam War.* Chicago, 1995.

Queen, Christopher S., and Sallie B. King, eds. *Engaged Buddhism: Buddhist Liberation Movements in Asia.* New York, 1996.

Race, Jeffrey. *War Comes to Long An.* Berkeley, 1972.

Rusk, Dean. *As I Saw It.* New York, 1990.

Schecter, Jerrold. *The New Face of Buddha: Buddhism and Political Power in Southeast Asia.* New York, 1967.

Scigliano, Robert G. *South Vietnam: Nation under Stress.* Boston, 1964.

Shaplen, Robert. *The Lost Revolution.* New York, 1966.

Sharp, Gene. *The Politics of Nonviolent Action.* Boston, 1973.

Short, Anthony. *The Origins of the Vietnam War.* London, 1989.

Shulimson, Jack. *U.S. Marines in Vietnam: An Expanding War, 1966.* Washington, 1982.

Bibliography

Smith, R.B. *An International History of the Vietnam War: Revolution versus Containment, 1955–61.* New York, 1983.

Suzuki, D.T. *An Introduction to Zen Buddhism.* New York, 1964.

Swearer, Donald K. *Buddhism and Society in Southeast Asia.* New York, 1981.

———. *Me and Mine: Selected Essays of Bhikkhu Buddhadasa.* New York, 1989.

Ta, Van Tai. *The Vietnamese Tradition of Human Rights.* Berkeley, 1988.

Taylor, John M. *General Maxwell Taylor: The Sword and the Pen.* New York, 1989.

Taylor, Maxwell. *Swords and Plowshares.* New York, 1972.

Thich, Man Giac. *The Branch That Gleams in the Dark: An Introduction to Vietnamese Buddhism.* Los Angeles, 1985.

Thich Minh Chau. *Nhung Loi Duc Phat Day ve Hoa Binh va Gia Tri Con Nguio (Some teachings of Lord Buddha on peace and human dignity).* Ho Chi Minh City, 1995.

Thich, Nhat Hanh. *Call Me by My True Names: The Collected Poems of Thich Nhat Hanh.* Berkeley, 1993.

———. *Dialogue: The Key to Vietnam Peace.* Paris, 1968.

———. *Dialogue: Thich Nhat Hanh, et al. addressing Martin Luther King, et al.* Saigon, 1965.

———. *The Heart of Understanding: Commentaries on the Prajnapalamita Heart Sutra.* Berkeley, 1988.

———. *Love in Action: The Non-violent Struggle for Peace in Vietnam.* N.d., n.p.

———. *Vietnam: Lotus in a Sea of Fire.* New York, 1972.

———. *Zen Keys.* Translated by Albert and Jean Low. Garden City, N.Y., 1974.

Thich, Quang Lien. *A Short Introduction of Buddhism in Vietnam.* Saigon, 1968.

Thich, Tam Quang. *Phat Giao Duo Mat Cac Nha Tri Thuc (Buddhism in the eyes of intellectuals).* Ho Chi Minh City, 1996.

Thich, Tam Thien. *Thong Diep Niem Tin (Messages of faith).* Ho Chi Minh City, 1986.

Thich, Thien-An. *Buddhism and Zen in Vietnam in Relation to the Development of Buddhism in Asia.* Rutland, Vt., 1975.

Topmiller, Robert. "The Buddhist Crisis of 1964." *Selected Papers in Asian Studies,* New Series #58 (Fall 1997) Western Conference of the Association for Asian Studies: 1–49.

———. "Confrontation in Danang: III MAF and the Buddhist Struggle Movement in South Vietnam, 1966." *The Journal of American–East Asian Relations* (Spring 2000): 207–34.

———. "1966—A Missed Opportunity for Peace in Vietnam." *Peace & Change* (January 2002): 59–96.

———. "Thich Quang Do." *Su That 2001 (Evidence of the truth 2001).* Fremont, Calif., 2001.

Bibliography

———. "Tu Do Ton Giao Tai Viet Nam?" (Religious freedom in Vietnam?) *Que Me* (Homeland) (Winter 1997): 75–80.

———. "Vietnamese Buddhism in the 1990s." *Cross Currents* (June 2000): 232–39.

Tran, Hong Lien. *Phat Giao Nam Bo.* Ho Chi Minh City, 1996.

Tran, Van Don. *Our Endless War: Inside Vietnam.* San Rafael, Calif., 1978.

Truong, Nhu Tang. *A Viet Cong Memoir.* New York, 1985.

Turley, William S. *The Second Indochina War.* Boulder, 1986.

Turner, Fred. *Echoes of Combat: The Vietnam War in American Memory.* New York, 1996.

Vietnam Buddhist Sangha. *Vietnam Buddhism and Its Activities for Peace.* Ho Chi Minh City, 1990.

Walt, Lewis W. *Strange War, Strange Strategy: A General's Report on Vietnam.* New York, 1970.

Warner, Dennis. *The Last Confucian.* New York, 1963.

Westmoreland, William C. *A Soldier Reports.* New York, 1976.

Williams, Lea A. *Southeast Asia: A History.* New York, 1976.

Williams, Paul. *Mahayana Buddhism.* London, 1989.

Winters, Francis X. *The Year of the Hare: America in Vietnam, January 25, 1963–February 15, 1964.* Athens, Ga., 1997.

Wirmark, Bo. *The Buddhists in Vietnam: An Alternative View of the War.* Uppsala, 1973.

Wolters, O.W. *Two Essays on Dai-Viet in the Fourteenth Century.* Boston, 1988.

Woods, Randall Bennett. *Fulbright: A Biography.* New York, 1995.

Woodside, Alexander B. *Community and Revolution in Modern Vietnam.* Boston, 1976.

Wu, John C.H. *The Golden Age of Zen.* New York, 1996.

Wyatt, Clarence. *Paper Soldiers: The American Press and the Vietnam War.* New York, 1993.

Wyatt, Donald K., and Alexander Woodside, eds. *Moral Order and the Question of Change: Essays on Southeast Asian Thought.* New Haven, 1982.

Yang Sam. *Khmer Buddhism and Politics from 1954 to 1984.* Newington, Conn., 1987.

Young, Marilyn B. *The Vietnam Wars, 1945–1990.* New York, 1991.

OTHER SOURCES

Chester Cooper, letter to Robert Topmiller, 11-12-97.

Le Van Hoa. "Correlates of the Political Radical-Conservative Attitudes among Buddhist Clergyman Leaders in South Vietnam." Ph.D. diss., University of Kentucky, 1973.

Robert McNamara, letter to Robert Topmiller, 12-5-97.

Bibliography

Phone message and conversation, William Bundy and Robert Topmiller, 1-9-98
and 1-14-98.
Topmiller, Robert. "The 1963 Buddhist Crisis in South Vietnam." Master's the-
sis, Central Washington University, 1994.
Huynh Kim Nga, e-mail messages to Robert Topmiller, 2000.
"My Life as a Nun," e-mail messages to author from Thich Nu Minh Tam,
April–July, 2001
Nguyen Huynh Mai, e-mail messages to Robert Topmiller, 2000–2001.
Vo Van Ai, e-mail messages to Robert Topmiller, 1996.

INTERVIEWS

Spring 1994

Da Le
Thich Nguyen An
Thich Minh Tuyen
Thich Quang Tan
I Jut Bounto
Thinh Antone
Buicong An
Fr. Joachim Hien
Hum Dac Bui (letter)

July 1996

General Nguyen Khanh
Professor Douglas Pike
Thich Minh Chieu
Thich Nguyen An
Ban Hoang

August 1996

Thich Quang Lien
Thich Tri Quang
Thich Nguyen Tang
Professor Mac Duong
Professor Tran Hong Lien
Professor Minh Chi
Thich Minh Chau
Thich Ngo Dinh
Thich Phuoc Nhon
Thich Tam Thien
Thich Thanh Kiem

Bibliography

September 1996

> Nguyen Nam
> Dr. George McT. Kahin

December 1996

> Colonel Tran Huu Phuc

January 1997

> General Edwin Simmons

March 1997

> Eka Suvanna
> Phala Suvanna
> Nguyen Huu Nghiep
> Fr. Josephus Le Van Phuc
> Thich Dui Tri
> Thich Duc Niem
> Thich Thien Minh
> Thich Dinh Quang
> Thich Giac Vien
> Thich Thien Chieu
> Sr. Tran Thi Anh
> Truong Van Loc
> La Thanh Ty
> Tin Hap
> Kieu Huu Tu
> Huynh Thuong
> Tran Hong Chi
> Mr. Hai
> Chau Cam Sang

April 1997

> General Nguyen Chanh Thi

April 1999

> Thich Quang Do

December 2000

> Sau Ven
> Pham Cong Tam
> Lee Ngoc Minh

Bibliography

Dan Thi Lan Anh
Minh Chi
Phan Bich Hop
Do Thai Dong
Tran Huu Tai
Tran Huu Duyen
Vu The Phuc
Nguyen Chi Trung
Mr. Hieu
Ni Su Nhu Hai
Thich Nu Nhu Hong
Nguyen Thi Bich
Pham Anh Hong

May 2001

Richard Stevenson

Index

Index

Index

International Red Cross, 124

Jackson, Henry, 114
Javits, Jacob, 101, 114
Johnson, Lyndon B.: approval
  ratings, 98, 115, 116; bombing of
  North Vietnam, 97, 117; Buddhist
  Crisis of 1966 and, 95, 96, 97,
  102, 111; Buddhist self-immolations and, 135, 136, 149; call for
  national unity, 116; Cold War
  ideology and, 109, 120, 144;
  escalation of U.S. forces in
  Vietnam, 117; Ky's second attack
  on Danang and, 87; reaction
  against Buddhist movement, 96;
  Senate response to Ky's attack on
  Danang and, 114; Thich Tri
  Quang and, 123; Vietnam War
  policies, 97, 98, 99, 100, 102–3,
  105, 106, 108–12, 116, 117–19,
  120, 144; Lewis Walt and, 73, 74

Kahin, George, 34, 43, 46, 95, 119,
  120, 146, 149, 164(n68),
  182(n36), 186(n19)
Kaiser, David, 28
karma, 10
Karnow, Stanley, 34, 94, 109, 122,
  146, 148
Kennan, George, 98
Kennedy, John F., 3, 99
King, Martin Luther, Jr., 138
King, Sallie, 147
Komer, Robert, 104
Kuomintang, 63

Lansdale, Edward, 174(n73)
La Thanh Ty, 64, 170(n62)
Le Nguyen Khang, 127
Le Van Phuc, Fr. Josephus, 164(n68),
  169(nn51* 61)
Ling, Trevor, 12
Lodge, Henry Cabot, Jr., 61, 63, 84,
  100, 110, 186(n7); anti-American
  incident in Hue and, 75; Buddhist

communications with, 55;
  Buddhist Crisis of 1963 and, 3–4;
  Buddhist Crisis of 1966 and, 31,
  95, 96, 97; Buddhist disturbances
  in Hue and, 131, 132; Catholic
  demonstrations against, 62; Ky's
  second attack on Danang and, 67,
  87, 91, 177(n58); on military
  reverses in Vietnam, 65–66;
  neutralization and, 126; Nguyen
  Cao Ky and, 41–43, 52, 79, 91,
  95, 113, 126, 131, 132; Nguyen
  Chanh Thi and, 34, 35–36,
  161(n25); return to South Vietnam, 125–26; Dean Rusk and, 95,
  97; support for proposed constituent assembly, 40–41; Thich Tri
  Quang and, 121, 123, 125; views
  of Buddhists and the Buddhist
  movement, 41, 51, 96, 97, 125,
  135
Logevall, Fredrik, 108, 109, 110,
  119, 120
Lotus Blossom party, 150

Mahayana Buddhism, 7, 10
Mansfield, Mike, 101, 114
May Day demonstrations, 62
McNamara, Robert S., 27, 103, 116,
  138, 177(n39); attitude toward
  Buddhist movement, 96; Ky's
  second attack on Danang and, 87;
  peace talk proposal and, 112;
  Vietnam War policy and, 98–99,
  106, 108, 111, 119; views of
  Thich Tri Quang, 23, 102
McNaughton, John, 99–100, 103,
  104–5, 106–7, 116–17, 180(n123)
Mekong Delta, 15
M-41 tanks, 174(n73)
Mien Trung, 44
Military and Civilian Struggle
  Committee, 38
Military Assistance Command,
  Vietnam (MACV): conflicts and
  controversies with Third Marine

Index

Index

Index

U.S. Army. *See* Military Assistance Command, Vietnam
U.S. Congress: response to Buddhist Crisis of 1966, 100–102; Senate war hearings, 97–98
U.S. Department of Defense, 103
U.S. House of Representatives, 101–2
U.S. Joint Chiefs of Staff, 103, 110
U.S. Marines. *See* Third Marine Amphibious Force
U.S. Navy, 80
U.S. Senate: response to Buddhist Crisis of 1966, 100–102; response to Ky's second attack on Danang, 114; war hearings, 97–98
U Thant, 124

Valenti, Jack, 100, 102–3, 111
Vance, Cyrus, 104
Van Hanh University, 137
Vanh Hanh Institute, 165(n88)
Vien Hoa Dao, 7, 46, 49; Catholic opposition to, 60–61; cessation of antigovernment agitation, 56; erosion of popular support for, 65; failure of in 1966, 68–69, 143; ideological divide within, 144, 167(n30); Ky's attack on, 126, 127–28, 129, 140; Ky's negotiations with, 54; Lotus Blossom party and, 150; near victory over Nguyen Cao Ky, 68; nonaligned Buddhist sects and, 62; popular legitimacy of, 57; rise of radical wing in, 54–55; self-immolation of Nhat Chi Mai and, 149; Thich Tam Chau and, 54–55, 128–29, 140; U.S. reaction against, 96–97. *See also* Buddhist movement
Viet Minh, 59
Vietnam: Lotus in a Sea of Fire (Thich Nhat Hanh), 138, 139
Vietnamese Air Force (VNAF), 54, 77, 78, 79, 82, 124
Vietnamese Kuomintang, 63

Vietnam Quoc Dan Dang (VNQDD), 63
Vietnam War: Buddhist views of, 144–45; casualties, 102; consequences of the Buddhist Crisis of 1966 and, 143; decline in military effectiveness of the South Vietnamese army, 65–66; escalation of U.S. forces in, 117; historiography, 153(n1); impact on Vietnamese society, 10; Tet Offensive, 59, 90, 149; U.S. introduction of military forces, 29. *See also* American war policy; Military Assistance Command, Vietnam; Third Marine Amphibious Force
VNAF. *See* Vietnamese Air Force
VNQDD. *See* Vietnam Quoc Dan Dang
Vo Van Ai, 34, 46, 50–51, 137, 155(n20), 163(n57)
Vu Van Thai, 113

Walt, Lewis, 36–37; Combined Action Platoon program and, 72–73; command of Third Marine Amphibious Force, 72; conflicts and controversies with Westmoreland, 72–74, 75, 89; conflict with Struggle Force in I Corps, 76–78; Lyndon Johnson and, 73, 74; Ky's second attack on Danang and, 79–80, 81, 82, 86–88; Nguyen Chanh Thi and, 74, 89; Thich Tri Quang and, 121; Ton That Dinh and, 86, 89; Westmoreland's response to the Struggle Movement and, 84, 85
War Crimes Museum (Ho Chi Minh City), 164(n68)
Westmoreland, William, 76, 172(n34); advocacy of search-and-destroy strategy, 72, 73; Buddhist disturbances in Hue and, 132; CINCPAC and, 73; com-

213